PENGUIN REFERENCE BOOKS

R4

A DICTIONARY OF MUSIC

D0734960

A
DICTIONARY
OF
MUSIC

BY

ROBERT ILLING

PENGUIN BOOKS

HARMONDSWORTH · MIDDLESEX

Penguin Books Ltd, Harmondsworth, Middlesex
u.s.a.: Penguin Books Inc., 3300 Clipper Mill Road, Baltimore 11, Md
[*Educational Representative*
D. C. Heath & Co., 285 Columbus Avenue, Boston 16, Mass]
australia: Penguin Books Pty Ltd, 200 Normanby Road,
Melbourne, S.C.5, Victoria
agent in canada: Riverside Books Ltd, 47 Green Street,
Saint Lambert, Montreal, P.Q.

—

Made and printed in Great Britain by
C. Nicholls and Company, Ltd

—

Compiled specially for Penguin Books
First published 1950
Reprinted 1951

ML100
I43

FOREWORD

A few comments may help the general reader to place the various kinds of information in this modest compendium of musical knowledge in their true perspective.

Perhaps the most difficult task of all in compiling such a book as this is that of deciding which musicians shall be included, and how much information shall be given about each. Evidently composers deserve more space than executants, historians, theorists and critics, for it is the composers who most advance the art of music. Skilled performers are of course necessary, not only to the listener, but also, indeed, to the composer. Yet their service to music is confined, by its nature, to their own generation, and their fame is soon forgotten. So it is also with historians, theorists and critics. Though their contribution to music is useful, it is transient. In this book, therefore, composers are given most space. And since no generation can form a really balanced judgement concerning the artists of its own day, this dictionary does not pass judgement on musicians still alive. The most important living composers born before 1900 are mentioned here, but to discriminate between the large number of more modern composers would be invidious, and no reference has been made to them.

Many Italian terms have gained a measure of international usage, and to a limited extent Italian has become the technical language of music. Yet foreign words are often used unnecessarily, and sometimes with a more precise meaning than is proper to them. 'Lied', for instance, is simply the German word for song. Some use 'Lieder', in English, meaning 'German song of the period of Schubert and Schumann'.

But apart from a very few words such as this, the growing custom among composers of using their own language exclusively means that we are now likely to find not only Italian and German directions in a musical score, but also French, Spanish and even Russian. Their meaning should be sought in a language dictionary rather than in a book about music and musicians. But as Italian still retains a prominent place in musical terminology, the standard Italian words will be found in this book, and a table is also given of the names, in French, German and Italian, of the instruments mentioned in orchestral scores, and another of the terms and symbols used in musical notation.

*

I wish to thank all those who have given me assistance, especially my friend and one time teacher, Ernest Avery, for his many useful criticisms and suggestions, and my wife for her help in the preparation of the manuscript. I also wish to thank Professor E. J. Dent for suggesting that I should be asked to undertake the most instructive task of preparing this book.

Exmouth   ROBERT ILLING
June 1950

Tables

Diagrams

Sources of Musical Examples

Abbreviations

b.	born	Gr.	Greek
d.	died	It.	Italian
f.	flourished	Lat.	Latin
c.	(circa) about	Sp.	Spanish
Fr.	French	W.	Welsh
Ger.	German		

A

A (It.), at, by, for, **in, to**, with, in the style of. *Al, All'* or *Alla*, at the by the (and so on).

A Battuta (It.), to the beat. Similar in sense to 'a tempo'.

Abbreviations of two kinds are used in music, those of terms used as part of musical notation, terms of expression, and so on, and abbreviations in the notation itself.

Of the first kind the most important are:

p for piano	*f* for forte
pp for pianissimo	*ff* for fortissimo
D.C. for Da Capo	*V.S.* for Volti Subito
D.S. for Dal Segno	

P. or *Ped.* for Pedal (meaning the sustaining pedal on a pianoforte) or Pedals (meaning the pedal keyboard on an organ)

sf for sforzando

fp for forte piano (meaning a sudden change from forte to piano)

m.d. and *m.s.* (It.)
m.d. and *m.g.* (Fr.) } the equivalent of the English *r.h.* and *l.h.* for right hand and left hand respectively

8ve for octave

The meanings of other abbreviations of this kind such as *cresc.* for crescendo are sufficiently obvious.

Of the second kind, two types may be distinguished, abbreviations of the full notation used only sometimes, more especially in manuscripts to save clerical labour and space, and the signs representing ornaments which are only exceptionally written in full. Of the first type:

and similarly for the subdivision of any note into shorter ones

(f) the signs meaning repeat may also be considered as abbreviations of this type.

The second type, the signs representing the few ornaments which have survived into modern usage, are more appropriately considered as part of modern musical notation. The various notations of the glissando, particularly the harp glissando, may also be considered as abbreviations of this type.

Abel, Karl Friedrich (b. Cöthen 1725, d. London 1787), was a viola da gamba player and a composer. He was associated with J. S. Bach in Leipzig and J. C. Bach in London.

Absolute Music, music which does not depend for its full appreciation on any association with a story or mood or other fact of life. As opposed to programme music, absolute music depends entirely on its own structure for its comprehension.

Absolute Pitch, the pitch of a note defined in scientific terms. In music, the notes represent the relative pitch of the sounds to be produced. The actual pitch of each note at a particular performance will depend upon an arbitrary choice in fixing some one note to which the remainder are then related. Now that a standard of pitch of A equal to 440 vibrations a second has been generally adopted, the notes do, in fact, also represent the actual pitch of the notes; but this has not always been the case. Transposition does not affect the relative pitch of the notes within a composition, though changing the absolute pitch of all of them.

The ability to remember pitch with considerable accuracy (to within less than half a semitone) is possessed by some musicians and non-musicians. This ability is commonly known as having absolute pitch.

Abyngdon, Henry (b. c. 1418, d. 1497), was the first master of the children of the Chapel Royal, and first Mus. B. of Cambridge.

A Cappella (It.), in the church style. Indicates a composition for voices unaccompanied or without an independent accompaniment. Also an indication of style equivalent to 'alla breve'.

A Capriccio (It.), at will. Similar in sense to the first use of 'ad libitum'.

Accelerando (It.), accelerating. Indicates a gradual quickening of the speed.

Accent, the importance given to a note by its relation to others, particularly as regards duration, pitch, volume and its position in the time system. The accents resulting from these four considerations are called agogic accent, tonic accent, dynamic accent and metrical accent respectively. The last is implicit rather than expressed.

Acciaccatura (It.), crushed. The acciaccatura is a melodic ornament in which the grace note is sounded with the main note and instantly released. Confusion exists between the short appoggiatura and the acciaccatura, the latter name being more often used for the former ornament than for itself.

Accidental, a sign indicating a chromatic alteration of an individual note. Accidentals are properly so called only when they occur during the course of the music, and not when they form part of the key signature. The signs now used are:

♭ the flat   ♭♭ the double flat
♯ the sharp   ✕ the double sharp
♮ the natural

An accidental refers only to the note itself and each following repetition of the same note at the same pitch in the same bar. Any doubt as to the correct chromatic form of a note is avoided by the addition of accidentals (not strictly essential) in brackets. After being altered chromatically, the diatonic form of the note may be restored by the appropriate accidental.

Accompaniment, any part or parts of a musical composition which, either for a portion or for all of it, play a subsidiary part. An accompaniment may be either independent or merely a straightforward reproduction of the principal part or parts. In the course of an extended orchestral composition, at one time the strings may be accompanying the wood wind which are engaged in playing the more important role, at another the reverse may be the case. In a song, the voice may be accompanied by a keyboard or group of instruments which play a subsidiary part throughout.

From an early time instruments were used to support the voice. The development of the principal melody in the accompaniment or the introduction of some distinctive melodic or rhythmic feature enhanced the importance of the accompaniment, and led to the difference in importance between the solo and accompanying part becoming less and less. The accompaniments of vocal music may vary from parts of negligible importance to parts which are as essential to the whole as the voice part itself.

Accordion, a portable free reed keyed instrument invented by Damian in Vienna in 1829.

Act, a complete section of an opera or ballet. This term is used in the same sense as in spoken drama. In England it was formerly used in oratorio as well, and in old concert programmes where 'part' is now preferred.

Action, the mechanism of a musical instrument, particularly that part of it through which the hands or feet of the performer control the sounding of the wires, reeds or pipes of the instrument.

Acoustic Bass, an organ stop on the Pedal Organ consisting of a 16-foot stop sounding with its fifth. The differential tone resulting from the two notes a fifth apart gives the effect of a 32-foot stop.

Acoustics, the science of hearing. In its broadest sense, acoustics may be taken to include the whole physical basis of sound, its nature, production, propagation and reception. The nature of hearing itself is, however, as much a matter of psychology as of physics.

Sound is originated by a vibrating body; it is transmitted through the atmosphere or other material (not, as in the case of electro-magnetic phenomena such as light and heat, through the ether); and it is received by the ear as a physical phenomenon which the brain interprets as sound.

The most favourable design for the construction of musical instruments has been arrived at in most cases almost entirely by experiment. Only recently has scientific calculation played any prominent part in guiding the design of new or modified instruments. Likewise the suitability of different conditions for the performance of music has until recent years been almost entirely a matter of chance or experiment rather than calculation. However, many of the interesting phenomena resulting from the manner in which sound is propagated have been appreciated for a long time. The function of the ear itself is of considerable interest; but the ear does not normally require the same experi-

mental attention as musical instruments and buildings in which
music is to be performed.

The mathematics of the attributes of notes (their pitch, volume
and quality), and their combination in melody and harmony
has, in the past, been the greatest source of interest, theoretical
and experimental, to those concerned with the science of music.

(Further information on acoustics will be found in the articles
on sound, the harmonic series, interval, and so on.)

Acute, a term used with reference to the pitch of a note in the same
sense as high.

Adagio (It.), at ease. Used as an indication of speed in the sense of
slow, but not as slow as 'largo', and also as the name of a movement.

Adam, Adolphe Charles (b. Paris 1803, d. there 1856), was a composer
of opera and popular music. A vocal Christmas piece by him,
Minuit, Chrétiens, became a great favourite.

Adam de la Hale (b. *c.* 1230, d. Naples before 1288) was a prominent
trouvère and one of the most important of the early composers
of polyphonic music. He is chiefly famous for the *Jeu de Robin
et Marion*.

Adaptation, a term commonly used in a similar sense to 'arrangement'. It would be convenient to limit adaptation to faithful
reproductions of the composer's original work for some other
medium.

Additional Accompaniments, accompaniments added to the original
parts in a score. The practice began during the 19th century of
revising the scores of 17th- and 18th-century composers. The two
reasons given for these additions are that the original scores
were left incomplete by the composers, and that the modern
conditions of performance demand a revision of the score in
order to convey the intentions of the composer to the modern
audience. The first reason given is now generally considered as
incorrect, and there is now a growing preference for the performance of compositions, as near as scholarship can ensure,
in the manner intended by the composer.

Adler, Guido (b. Eibenschutz 1855, d. Vienna 1941), was a distinguished writer on music. His *Handbuch der Musikgeschichte*
(published under his editorship in 1924) is one of the most
important contributions to musical literature of recent years.
It deals exhaustively with music from the earliest until recent
times.

Ad Libitum (Lat.), at will. Indicates that style, speed and expression are at the discretion of the performer. Also indicates that a part may be omitted.

Aeolian Harp, a stringed instrument allowed to sound by the natural wind blowing against strings stretched over a sounding board. The music of the Aeolian harp, being produced by the chance blowing of the wind unguided by man, has been referred to as 'nature's music'.

Affettuoso (It.), affectionate. Used as an indication of style in the sense of 'with feeling', usually with terms such as 'allegro' and 'andante'. By itself, affettuoso implies a rather slow pace.

Affrettando (It.), hastening.

Afranio (early 16th century), was a canon of Ferrara. He is unjustifiably credited with the invention of the bassoon which bears little or no resemblance to his instrument the phagotus.

Agitato (It.), agitated or restless.

Agogic Accent, the importance given to the longer of two successive notes.

Agrément (Fr.), ornament. The French term is commonly used on account of the important part played during the 18th century by French musicians in standardizing the numerous ornaments used in keyboard music.

Agricola, Alexander (d. Valladolid *c.* 1506), was an important composer of the school of Okeghem.

Air, commonly used in the same sense as tune. In the 16th century the English air or ayre, and the French air de cour, were the counterpart of the Italian aria. After the development of opera in the 17th century, aria came to mean a formal operatic song. However, as an instrumental movement the air or aria remained, usually a simple song-like composition in contrast to the dance-like compositions which formed the majority of the movements of the suite. Purcell, unlike Bach and Handel, did not include airs in his suites, though airs are to be found amongst the remainder of his harpsichord music, and as instrumental items, generally of a song-like character, in his dramatic music.

Alalá, a typical folk song of North-West Spain.

Albéniz, Isaac (b. Camprodón 1860, d. Cambó les Bains 1909), showed outstanding musical ability from an early age. He studied in Madrid and later in Brussels, and before he was twenty accompanied Rubinstein on a concert tour of Europe and America. Albéniz achieved success both as a pianist and composer. His later compositions for the pianoforte are a brilliant display of the qualities of Spanish folk music.

Albeniz, Pedro (b. Logroño 1795, d. Madrid 1855), was the son of a musician and followed music as his profession from his youth. He is credited with introducing the modern style of pianoforte playing into Spain.

Alberti, Domenico (b. Venice *c.* 1710, d. Rome 1740), gained a reputation as a singer and harpsichord player. He is remembered by the accompaniment formula of which he made excessive use, commonly known as the 'Alberti bass'. The left hand part in the example given in the article on transposition (from a pianoforte sonata by Mozart) is a typical instance of the use of this figure.

Albrechtsberger, Johann Georg (b. Klosterneuburg 1736, d. Vienna 1809), had a distinguished career as a teacher and organist. He is now remembered as a teacher of Beethoven.

Alcock, John (b. London 1715, d. Lichfield 1806), gained distinction as an organist and composer. He handed to Dr Greene the music he had prepared for *Cathedral Music*.

Alcock, Walter Galpin (b. Edenbridge 1861, d. Salisbury 1947), became organist of Salisbury Cathedral in 1916. He held the Mus.D. of Durham, was an M.V.O., and was knighted in 1933.

Aldrich, Henry (b. Westminster 1647, d. Oxford 1710), was a musician of considerable ability besides being an able scholar in, amongst other subjects, theology and architecture. He became Dean of Christ Church, and his collection of music in Christ Church Library is of great importance. He was Vice-Chancellor of Oxford University from 1692 to 1695. A number of his sacred and secular compositions are still sung, and, though not of great musical value, are by no means without merit.

Alfonso el Sabio (b. Toledo 1221, d. Seville 1284), Alphonso X, King of Castille and Leon, is remembered in musical history for his collection of *Cantigas*, popular sacred songs fitted to melodies of his day.

Alla Breve (It.). The origin of this term is disputed. It indicates that the minim rather than the crotchet is the unit of time.

Allargando (It.), becoming broader. Indicates an increase in the dignity of style by a slackening of pace with the same or greater volume.

Alla Tedesca (It.), in the German style, generally implying Landler or Waltz tempo.

Alla Zoppa (It.), limping.

Allegretto (It.). Diminutive of 'allegro'. Used as an indication of speed, slower than allegro and faster than andante, and also as the name of a movement.

Allegri, Gregorio (b. Rome 1582, d. there 1652), was famous as a composer of Latin church music. His *Miserere* for nine voices, sung each year during Holy Week in the Sistine Chapel, was kept for a time as the exclusive property of that chapel. It is very short, and Mozart's writing it down at the age of fourteen from hearing it was not a particularly exceptional achievement. It was much admired, especially during the Romantic period.

Allegro (It.), cheerful. Used as an indication of speed in the sense of lively or quick, and also as the name of a movement.

Allemande (Fr.), German. This dance form is usually the first movement in a suite unless preceded by a prelude. The dance of this name was obsolete by the time the movement was introduced into the suite, and the form of the allemande in the suite does not appear to be that of the dance. In the suite, the allemande is in four-four time and usually begins with a short quaver.

French Suite No. 4
BACH

A highly figured melody and a simple accompaniment are common characteristics of the allemande. The movement consists of two parts, each repeated.

A different dance of the same name, still danced by the peasants in certain parts of Germany and Switzerland, is in triple time.

Allen, Sir Hugh Percy (b. Reading 1869, d. Oxford 1946), achieved distinction as an organist, teacher, and conductor of Choral Societies. He became Director of the Royal College of Music and Professor of Music at Oxford, both in 1918.

Allison, Richard (f. 1592–1602), was an English musician. His published madrigals are included in *The English Madrigal School*. He helped to harmonize the tunes for the Psalter of 1592, published by Thomas East, and prepared on his own a Psalter, published in 1599.

Almain or *Almand*, and other variants, English forms of 'Allemande'. Elizabethan composers used the name for numerous separate pieces, and the Almand occurs in Purcell's Harpsichord Suites.

Alphabet. The musical alphabet employs the letters A, B, C, D, E, F and G, in that order, for the successively higher degrees of the scale, repeating the series as often as necessary as the scale is extended up or down. The interval between any note and the next of the same name is one octave. The intervals between B and C and between E and F are each a semitone; the intervals between other adjacent notes and between a G and the A of the next octave are each a tone. These notes correspond to the white notes of the keyboard. The black notes, dividing the intervals of a tone into two semitones, have no independent names and are called sharps or flats of the white (natural) notes next to them.

In Germany, B flat is called simply B, and B as we know it is called H, so making possible the succession of notes on which Bach himself, as well as other composers, wrote fugues.

Al Rovescio (It.), in reverse. This term is applied to a composition which may be played backwards — that is, the entire harmonic and melodic sequence is effectively reversible. Examples of this structure are rare; a double chant by Dr Crotch, and a minuet from a sonata by Haydn embody this device.

Alternativo (It.), commonly used in 17th- and 18th-century compositions, particularly in the suite, in precisely the same sense as trio is used with minuet or scherzo.

Alto, the vocal part sung by women or boys with a low range, or by men singing falsetto. The normal compass of alto parts is about an octave and a half upwards from the G below middle C.

Alto Clef, the C clef placed on the middle line to show that that line corresponds with middle C.

middle C

Amati, Andrea (b. *c.* 1520, d. *c.* 1580), was the first known and most important member of the well-known family of violin makers of Cremona. In one step he appears to have jumped from the design of the viol to that of the violin, and his instruments are but little different in the essentials of their design from the perfect models of Stradivari. A number of violins (in one or two sizes) and a few violas and violoncellos by Andrea are known. Most important of his descendants, who invariably followed his designs with but slight modifications, were *Antonio* (b. 1550, d. 1638) and *Gerolamo* (b. 1551, d. 1635), both sons of Andrea, *Nicolo* (b. 1596, d. 1684), son of Gerolamo, and *Gerolamo* (b. 1649, d. 1740) son of Nicolo.

Ambros, August Wilhelm (b. Vysoké Mytò 1816, d. Vienna 1876), was by birth a Czech. His *Geschichte der Musik* gives him claim to be considered as one of the most important German authorities on the history of music.

Ambrose, Saint (b. Treves 340, d. Milan 397), was Bishop of Milan from 374. He is credited with the introduction of Antiphonal Psalmody and Hymnody into worship. The hymns sung at the Hours are commonly known as Ambrosiani, and the liturgical and musical usages of Milan established about his time are referred to as Ambrosian.

American Organ, a keyboard free reed instrument similar to the harmonium. The American organ differs from the harmonium in that the wind is drawn through the reeds by suction, and in the structure of the reeds and of the cavities containing them, with the result that it has a more organ-like tone. The principle of the American organ was discovered by a workman in the factory of Alexandre, the leading harmonium maker of Paris. The workman took the invention to America. The first instruments of this kind were called Melodeons; improved models under the name of American organ were introduced by Mason and Hamlin of Boston in 1860. Varieties of the instrument appeared later under different names.

Andamento (It.), a fugue subject of a relatively elaborate kind, commonly consisting of two distinct sections.

Andante (It.), going. Used as an indication of speed in the sense of 'rather slow' or 'at a moderate pace', and also as the name of a movement. Used by older composers to indicate strict time after a recitative. Handel uses 'andante allegro', which means 'going along cheerfully', and is not a contradiction in terms.

Andantino (It.), diminutive of 'andante'. Used as an indication of speed. Properly, andantino means slower than andante but it is often used in the opposite sense (quicker than andante).

André, Johann (b. Offenbach 1741, d. there 1799), was the head of a musical family. He founded a publishing house which was later associated with Mozart.

Anerio, Felice (b. *c.* 1560, d. Rome 1614), and his brother, *Giovanni Francesco* (b. Rome *c.* 1567, d. *c.* 1620), were both composers of church music. The printed publications of Felice also include a number of sets of madrigals.

Anglaise (Fr.), English. Various dance movements have been given this title, presumably implying that their character is supposedly English. There is an Anglaise in Bach's third French suite.

Anglican Chant, the form of chant now in use in the English church. The Anglican chant began to evolve from the Gregorian chant

shortly after the introduction of the English Prayer Book. In
the first instance the Anglican chant was simply a harmonized
form of the Gregorian chant, the latter being placed in the
tenor.

The Imperial Tune
(CLIFFORD 1664)

The tenor is an adaptation of
the 8th tone, 4th ending

It was but a short step to the composition of original chants on
the same pattern. It has been commonly supposed that double
chants (simply, two-fold forms of the single chant) were first
introduced sometime during the early 18th century, the time of
the first collections of chants. However, the music given in
Crowley's Psalter of 1549 is near enough to what would now be
called a double chant.

During the 18th and 19th centuries the number of chants
composed was very great, and there was a marked tendency for
them to become first unduly florid and later chromatic.

At first the method of pointing must have been somewhat
haphazard. The earliest printed attempt at pointing appears to
have been that of a Robert James (organist of Ely Cathedral)
in 1837. Since then, numerous pointed versions of the psalms
have appeared, in some of which the natural prose rhythms were
grossly distorted. The method of singing psalms to Anglican
chants became stereotyped and degenerate. Rather than the
chant being a flexible formula to be fitted to the words, the
Anglican chant became a short part song to which the words
were fitted.

During the present century many attempts, led by Robert
Bridges, have been made to reconcile a sensible delivery of the
words with the traditional Anglican chant form.

Anima (It.), spirit. *Animato* (It.), spiritedly. Animato now often
implies an increase in speed.

Answer, the repetition of a theme by a second vocal or instrumental
part following a statement of the theme. The term is particularly
used in fugue.

Anthem, a sacred vocal composition authorized to be sung at Matins
and Evensong in the Church of England. The name is derived
from antiphon, but the anthem corresponds to the motet in the

Roman Catholic liturgy, though the Reformers transferred it from the Mass to Morning and Evening Prayer. After the Reformation it developed as an exclusively English form.

Anticipation, a melodic device in which a part moves to a note of the next chord before the accent on which the chord is properly sounded.

Pianoforte Sonata No.20, Op.49, No.2
Second Movement
BEETHOVEN

Antiphon, a verse of a psalm or other traditional passage, sung in the Mass or Offices, particularly as an introduction to and refrain throughout a psalm sung antiphonally. In the Mass the psalms (which were merely incidental) gradually disappeared, leaving the antiphon, which has survived in the Introit, Communion and Offertory. In those services in which the psalms played an important part, the psalm remained, while the antiphon was reduced to a short phrase sung only at the beginning and end of each psalm.

Antiphonal Psalmody, the method of psalm singing officially used in the Roman church to-day. It grew up alongside Responsorial Psalmody, which it gradually surpassed in popularity. In Antiphonal Psalmody the psalms are sung by two choirs singing alternately. They are intoned, generally to the Gregorian tones, in conjunction with antiphons.

Antiphoner, generally the Latin Service Book containing the music sung at the Hours. Since, however, antiphons were used in both the Mass and the services of the Hours, the name was originally applied to the book containing the music for either of them.

A Piacere (It.), at pleasure. Indicates that the speed is at the discretion of the performer.

Appassionata (It.), impassioned.

Appoggiatura (It.), supported. The appoggiatura is a melodic ornament in which the principal note is delayed by a grace note introduced before it. The grace note may be long or short, the short appoggiatura being distinguished by a dash through its tail (the old Italian way of writing, not printing, a normal semiquaver). In both cases the grace note falls with the beat, not before it.

For the long appoggiatura the duration of the grace note may be taken from the written value of the grace note, the principal note receiving what is left over. For the short appoggiatura the duration of the grace note is as short as possible, and the accent falls on the principal note. However, from time to time composers have intended various interpretations of the appoggiatura.

Arabesque, a term adopted from decorative art. Schumann used it once as the title of a composition, and it has been occasionally used by later composers, including Debussy.

Arbeau, Thoinot (b. Dijon 1519, d. Langres 1595), was a priest whose pseudonym is an anagram of his real name Jehan Tabourot. His book *Orchesographie*, 1589 (translated into English and republished by C. W. Beaumont in 1925) is the earliest extant treatise on dancing, and is a particularly valuable source of French dance tunes and the manner of executing the dances.

Arcadelt, Jacob (b. *c.* 1514, d. *c.* 1575), was one of the most important of the Netherland musicians who taught in Italy during the 16th century. He was a madrigal composer as well as a writer of church music. The *Ave Maria* by which he is commonly remembered, transcribed by Liszt, is spurious.

Archlute, the English form of the Italian arciliuto, also known as a theorbo. The archlute was a large lute with extra bass strings and a long neck.

Arco (It.), bow. Indicates to string players that the bow is to be used again after a passage played 'pizzicato'.

Arensky, Antonio Stepanovich (b. Novgorod 1861, d. Finland 1906), was the son of musical parents. He studied with Rimsky-Korsakov, and was on the staff of the Moscow Conservatorium. His operas met with considerable success. His songs, pianoforte music and chamber music are perhaps the best known in England of his compositions.

Aria (It.), air or song. This term is generally used for the extended songs in operas and oratorios, and also for song-like instrumental movements. A second section followed by a Da Capo was sometimes a feature of the arias in the older operas and oratorios. During the period of Handel, arias were classified according to their style — cantabile, portamento, parlante and so on — no two of the same variety being allowed to follow each other.

Arietta (It.), the diminutive of 'aria'.

Arioso (It.), song-like. This term is used for a vocal movement half-way between recitative and aria, more or less declamatory, but always sung in strict time.

Ariosti, Attilio (b. *c.* 1660), was a Dominican Friar, remembered for his association with Handel and Bononcini in London particularly as one of the three Directors of the Royal Academy of Music which had its first season of opera in 1720. He was a performer on the viola d'amore and a composer of cantatas and operas. He left England in 1728 and the facts of the rest of his life are not known.

Arkwright, Godfrey Edward Pellew (b. Norwich 1864, d. Highclere 1944), was editor of the *Old English Edition,* an important collection of old English music, and of the edition of Purcell's church music published by the Purcell Society.

Arne, Thomas Augustine (b. London 1710, d. there 1778), was the son of an upholsterer. He was educated at Eton and was intended for the legal profession. His desire for a musical career was at first opposed by his father. From 1733 he gained success with operas and other dramatic works. He is chiefly remembered by *Rule Britannia* from Thomson and Mallet's Masque *Alfred,* and by his settings of the songs for Shakespeare's *As You Like It.* Besides his works for the stage he left numerous catches, canons, glees and a quantity of instrumental music.

His son, *Michael* (b. 1740, d. London 1786), composed a number of dramatic works and numerous songs.

Arnold, Samuel (b. London, 1740, d. there 1802), is remembered for his edition of the works of Handel and his collection of *Cathedral Music.* The former was full of inaccuracies and the latter contained mainly compositions by inferior composers of his own day. He composed a considerable number of dramatic works.

Arpeggio (It.), harp-like. Indicates that the notes of a chord are to be played successively instead of simultaneously.

Arrangement, the presentation of a composition in other than its original form. Adaptation and transcription are used in similar senses. Arrangement may be said to begin in the 16th century with the innumerable lute and keyboard versions of madrigals. Bach, Beethoven, and Mendelssohn, among others, have left masterly examples of their own compositions in more than one form; in some cases the second or arranged version is more simple and in others fuller in texture than the original. Keyboard versions of orchestral music, such as are found in vocal scores, have been produced as a matter of expediency for rehearsal purposes and the use of the singers. They are, unfortunately, more often than not of little artistic merit. Some excellent reductions of orchestral accompaniments do, however, exist. Arrangements have been made to enlarge the repertory of certain instruments, such as the viola, which in the past have had little music of their own.

The arrangements of music of all kinds for the pianoforte are legion. The purpose and value of these is a matter of dispute. It is hardly necessary to enlarge the literature of the pianoforte. The original forms may, in most cases, be readily heard. Generally speaking, a comparison of arrangements with their originals shows the poverty of imagination and of scholarship amongst arrangers.

Ars Antiqua (Lat.), old art, and *Ars Nova* (Lat.), new art. These names were given during the early 14th century to the old and new styles of music. The new style was free from the domination of triple time and of the rhythmic modes which had been a feature of the old style. Duple time was secular, triple sacred. The ars nova was mainly a secularization of music, and the beginning of a cultivated, artistic, and highly sophisticated technique of secular music.

Assai (It.), very. Used to qualify indications of speed.

Aston, Hugh (f. early 16th century), was an English musician. No personal details are known with certainty. Sacred music by him is included in *Tudor Church Music*.

Astorga, Emanuele Gioacchino Cesare Rincón, Baron d' (b. Augusta 1680, d. Madrid or Lisbon, *c.* 1756), had a reputation for his knowledge in various sciences and arts. He is remembered for his *Stabat Mater*, and as a composer of chamber cantatas.

A Tempo (It.), in time. Indicates a return to the original speed after a brief change.

Atonal, not having tonality. This term has been used to describe modern systems of harmony not conforming to the traditional key system, evolved during the 17th century, which dominated harmony until towards the end of the 19th century. Schönberg has objected strongly to this use of atonal, particularly in connection with 'twelve note music'.

Attacca (It.), begin. Indicates at the end of a movement that the next movement is to follow without a pause.

Attacco (It.), a fugue subject of a relatively short kind, or merely a point of imitation.

Attaingnant, Pierre (f. 1528 to 1549 in Paris), was one of the earliest and most important of music printers.

Attey, John (d. Ross *c.* 1640), was an English musician. His published songs are included in *The English School of Lutinest Songwriters*.

Attwood, Thomas (b. London 1765, d. there 1838), was a chorister in the Chapel Royal. He studied under Mozart in Vienna, and was later organist of St Paul's Cathedral. In his earlier days he was successful in composing for the stage. Some of his church music is deservedly remembered.

Aubade (Fr.), morning music. This name is the counterpart of nocturne or serenade.

Auber, Daniel François Esprit (b. Caen 1782, d. Paris 1871), was an opera composer, particularly of comic opera. His opera *Masaniello*, 1828, became associated with the revolutionary movements of the period, and rioting in Brussels broke out after a performance of it in 1830.

Augmentation, the proportionate increase of the note values of a theme.

(a) Subject as in the exposition
(b) Subject by augmentation

This term is the antithesis of 'diminution'. Both terms are particularly used in canon and fugue.

Augmented Interval, an interval a semitone more than one which is perfect or major.

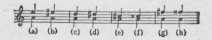

(a) perfect fifth   (e) major third
(b) augmented fifth   (f) augmented third
(c) perfect fourth   (g) major sixth
(d) augmented fourth   (h) augmented sixth

These augmented intervals are incorporated in several of the more important chords. The augmented triad in root position incorporates the augmented fifth, and the diminished triad in its inversions incorporates the augmented fourth.

(a)   (b)   (c)
(a) Augmented triad in root position
(b) and (c) Diminished triad, (b) first
inversion and (c) second inversion

Several chords of the sixth also incorporate augmented intervals.

Aulos (Gr.), flute or reed.

Authentic Modes, those ecclesiastical modes which lie between their final and its octave. The plagal modes have the same finals as the authentic modes to which they correspond, but their dominants and ranges are different.

Auxiliary Note, a melodic device in which a part moves from a note of the harmony to the note one degree above or below and back again.

Pianoforte Sonata No.3, K.281
Second Movement
MOZART

Ave Maria (Lat.), Hail Mary. This well known prayer used in the Roman Catholic Church has often been set to music. It consists in part of the salutations of the Archangel Gabriel and of Elizabeth. It took its present form in the 15th century.

Avison, Charles (b. Newcastle-upon-Tyne *c.* 1710, d. there 1770), is remembered for his critical essays, particularly *An Essay on musical expression,* published in 1752.

Ayre, the old English spelling of air. This title is the name by which Dowland and his contemporaries generally called their compositions for a voice accompanied usually by the lute. Many volumes of these songs have been transcribed by Fellowes and published as a series under the title of *The English School of Lutenist Song-writers.*

B

Bach, Johann Sebastian (b. Eisenach 1685, d. Leipzig 1750), the most famous member of a numerous family with an unsurpassed record for practising music as the family profession. The ancestry of John Sebastian can be traced to Veit Bach, though the family was settled in Thuringia certainly from the 16th century.

J. S. Bach's Ancestry

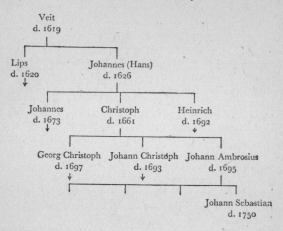

Until Johann Sebastian, the branch descended from Christoph appears to have been the least distinguished. Johann Sebastian married twice; his first wife, a cousin, Maria Barbara, had seven children, his second, Anna Magdalena, thirteen. Of these, three sons of Maria, Wilhelm Friedemann, Carl Philipp Emmanuel and Johann Gottfried Bernhard, and two sons of Anna, Johann Christoph and Johann Christian, reached eminence in their profession. Johann Sebastian's grandson, *Wilhelm Friedrich Ernst* (b. 1759, d. 1845), was an accomplished musician and held appointments to the courts of Friedrich William II and Friedrich William III in Berlin. All but a few of the Bachs identified as descended from Veit during seven generations practised music as their profession.

Johann Sebastian's parents died before he was ten; he was brought up by his elder brother Johann Christoph, organist at Ohrdruf and pupil of Pachelbel. His first post, obtained in 1700, was in the choir of St. Michael's Church, Lüneburg; he failed on account of his youth to obtain a post of organist two years later, but obtained employment at Weimar in 1703 in the chamber orchestra of the Duke. He left Weimar after a few months for his first appointment as organist at Arnstadt, and four years later he became organist at Mühlhausen, a position not to his liking, from which he resigned after a year. His next appointment in 1708 was to the ducal musical establishment at Weimar, where he became a member of the select body of string players and acted as court organist. During this period much of his organ music was written. Later, in 1714, he was appointed Konzertmeister. He left Weimar in 1717 for the post of Kapellmeister to the princely court at Cöthen, staying there till 1723; to this period most of his secular instrumental music belongs. In 1723 he became Cantor of the St Thomas School in Leipzig and remained there till his death; during this period the great bulk of his church music was written. During his life Bach was distinguished as a player. His ability to extemporize was greatly admired, enough to warrant an invitation to Potsdam by Frederick of Prussia (to whom he later sent the *Musical Offering* in tribute, a series of fugues and canons on a subject set by Frederick).

Most of the amazing quantity of music Bach wrote was written as part of his routine duties. Two settings of the Passion, one each according to St John and St Matthew, stand at the head of his sacred works, together with the *Christmas Oratorio* and those which have survived (nearly two-thirds of the total) of the five complete annual cycles of fifty-nine cantatas. Nearly all these works were written at Leipzig. The *B minor Mass* was partly written for his application for the post of Court Composer at Dresden and finished after his appointment. These, with six motets, of which *Jesu, meine Freude* is perhaps the best, and a small quantity of Latin church music, written after the *B minor Mass*, constitute his sacred compositions.

Though no other composer can be placed beside him as a writer for the organ, his organ music forms but a small part of all he wrote; the preludes, fantasias, toccatas and fugues are generally better known than the choral preludes. The *Trio Sonatas* and the *Passacaglia and Fugue* were written for a two manual cymbalo with pedals rather than for an organ.

The *Brandenburg Concertos*, the concertos for clavier and those for violin are perhaps the best known of his concerted instrumental music. His sonatas and suites (with and without accompaniment) for violin, for flute and for violoncello are notable contributions to the repertory of these instruments. Of his clavier music, the forty-eight preludes and fugues forming the *Well Tempered Clavier* (two complete sets of twenty-four, one in each major and minor key) form a complete essay on fugal writing and, at the time, assisted in establishing the system of tuning the scale as twelve equal semitones, so making music in every key possible.

The *Forty-eight* with the *French Suites*, *English Suites* and *Partitas* are the best known of his clavier music.

The outstanding characteristic of Bach's compositions is his use of fugue as a style of composition rather than a form. Few of his compositions, whatever their title, fail to make use of fugue. Perhaps his most remarkable fugal essay, incomplete, is the *Art of Fugue*, which displays, in its systematic treatment of one subject, very nearly, if not quite, all the possibilities of fugue, and illustrates his complete mastery of its art.

Very few of Bach's compositions were published during his lifetime, and for nearly a hundred years after his death his grandeur was forgotten. Forkel's biography of Bach, published in 1802, and Mendelssohn's performance of the *Matthew Passion* began the revival. The complete Bach-Gesellschaft edition was begun in 1851.

Carl Philipp Emmanuel (b. Weimar 1714, d. Hamburg 1788), was, as a composer, the most remarkable of John Sebastian's sons. He stands at the beginning of a new musical era. He is generally recognised as the representative predecessor of Haydn and Mozart in the early experiments in style and form associated with the development of the sonata and symphony.

John Christian (b. Leipzig 1735, d. London 1782), was the youngest of John Sebastian's sons. He settled in London, became an important figure in London musical life, and became generally known as the 'English Bach'. Mozart as a child of eight met him in London, and was to some extent influenced by him.

Back, of a stringed instrument. The underneath or behind part of the instrument as distinct from the belly. The back serves various functions: in particular, in the violin, the back vibrates sympathetically with the belly, reinforcing the vibrations of the air between the two and so assisting the production of a powerful tone.

Bagatelle (Fr.), a trifle. A short light piece of music generally for the pianoforte.

Bagpipe, a wind instrument of considerable antiquity, and known by this name in England since the Middle Ages. The bagpipe commonly associated with the Highlands of Scotland consists of a blow pipe, a leather airtight bag and four reed pipes. The bag is filled with air through the blow pipe and kept at pressure under the arm. Three of the pipes, called drones, are single reeds and fixed in pitch. The fourth pipe, called the chaunter, is a double reed variable in pitch by finger holes in the pipe. The tuning of the drones and the approximate scale of the chaunter are:

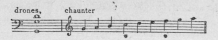

The notes marked * are distinctly sharper than as represented by the notation. The Irish pipes as commonly used are pitched lower than the Highland pipes and have but two drones, corresponding to the two upper drones of the Highland pipes.

Bairstow, Edward Cuthbert (b. Huddersfield 1874, d. York 1946), achieved distinction as an organist, teacher, and conductor of choral societies. He was organist of York Minster and Professor of Music in the University of Durham.

Balakirev, Mily Alexeinich (b. Nijny-Novgorod 1837, d. St Petersburg 1910), was a composer and teacher, and the prime mover in the formation of the Russian school of nationalist music. He learnt music from his mother, and profited from spending part of his early life at the house of the nobleman Oulibishev, an enthusiastic patron of music. At eighteen, Balakirev moved to St Petersburg. His enthusiasm impressed Glinka and from 1861 onwards, Balakirev became the leader of a musical movement in which Cui, Moussorgsky, Rimsky-Korsakov and Borodin, among others, joined. In 1862, with the help of Lomakin, a choral conductor, and Stassov, a critic, he established in St Petersburg the Free School of Music. His compositions are few, a small number of orchestral overtures and symphonic poems, a few collections of songs and some pianoforte music.

Balalaika, a variety of guitar popular in Russia. It has a triangular shaped body and is made in various sizes.

Balfe, Michael William (b. Dublin 1808, d. Hertfordshire 1870), was a successful composer of opera. He is remembered by a number of his ballads and his opera *The Bohemian Girl.*

Ballad, a term etymologically associated with dancing. It has varied in meaning from time to time and tended to lose its association with the dance. Old English ballads are narrative verse and are commonly set to dance tunes. Later, ballad has been used loosely for both vocal and instrumental compositions. The narrative songs of Schubert and Brahms, the pianoforte 'ballades' of Chopin, and the modern English use of ballad to describe a song with little claim to musical worth show the variety of uses of this title.

Ballad Opera, a form of musical dramatic production peculiar to England. Its characteristic features were its spoken dialogue and the settings of the songs to existing tunes. The first craze for ballad opera was started by *The Beggars' Opera;* it lasted scarcely ten years. A second craze which began in 1762 lasted an even shorter time.

Ballet, the sophisticated performance of dancing and music as opposed to the personal social enjoyment of dancing. No absolute division between the two exists in the history of dancing, though from time to time, as now, ballet has become an independent art form. The Roman pantomime, for instance, was derived from the Greek tragedy by the omission of the chorus and of the dialogue between the actors who danced their parts while a singer chanted the story. Ballet played a part in the mimes and plays of the Middle Ages.

The history of modern Ballet has been considered to have begun with *Le Ballet Comique de la Reine,* produced in Versailles in 1581. The favour ballet gained at the court of Louis XIV stimulated the interest of the most talented; Lully and Rameau incorporated and developed the ballet in opera. During the 18th century the fetters of extravagant dress and stiff ceremony which impeded freedom were gradually broken. The 19th century brought romanticism and realism to the ballet, and the strength and dexterity of the dancers played an increasingly prominent part. However, by the end of the century a certain lifelessness and formalism tended to discredit ballet. A remarkable revival came from Russia and led to the present popularity of the art. One of the most important features of the revival was the raising of the standard of the music. Arrangements of the music of eminent composers were adopted, as is the case for example in *Les Sylphides* (to music by Chopin), and composers were encouraged to write music specially for ballet, resulting in such works as Stravinsky's *Petrouchka.*

Ballet, a madrigal. Ballets are commonly light in character and frequently have a 'Fa-la' refrain.

Band, any combination of instruments for the performance of music. This name had come into use in England and France by the middle of the 17th century. Various kinds of bands are known by names describing either their purpose, as military band and dance band, or the instruments of which they are composed, as brass band and percussion band. No simple classification of bands is possible; it is convenient to consider together those bands which may be called a wind band, for whatever purpose they may be used, and the band now commonly called an orchestra whether used in the theatre or concert hall. It would be impracticable, even if possible, to distinguish between the very great variety of bands used for entertainment outside the theatre and concert hall.

Bandora, another form of the name 'pandore'.

Bandurria, a Spanish instrument similar to the English cither. It was known in the 16th century, and is still common in the south of Spain.

Banjo, an instrument of the guitar variety, having from five to nine strings with a belly of parchment stretched over a hoop, but no back. Various suggestions as to the origin of the name of the banjo have been made. Arab traders may have introduced a guitar-like instrument to the West African Negroes who then applied their name for such an instrument, bania, to the instrument they found and adopted as their own in America.

Bantock, Sir Granville (b. London 1868, d. there 1946), was the son of a distinguished London surgeon. He succeeded Elgar as Professor of Music at Birmingham University in 1908, resigning in 1933. He was knighted in 1930. His compositions include a number of large scale choral and instrumental works. His setting of *Omar Khayyám* and his *Hebridean Symphony* reflect his interest in oriental thought and the spirit of the Gael.

Bar, the line across the stave, though the name now is commonly used in the sense of the period from one such line to the next, and the line itself known as the bar-line. Bars now correspond to the metrical accent and are placed, therefore, at regular intervals. Originally, however, bars were placed at irregular intervals, mainly as an aid to the eye.

Barbieri, Francisco Asenjo (b. Madrid 1823, d. there 1894), was a composer who contributed to a distinctive kind of Spanish operetta.

Barcarolle (Fr.), a boat-song. Barcarolles, written in imitation of the songs of the Venetian gondoliers, have as their essential characteristic alternating strong and weak beats in six-eight time.

Bardi, Giovanni, Count of Vernio (b. Florence 1534, d. Rome 1612), was associated with the rise of opera. The earliest performances of entertainment in the nature of opera took place in his house.

Baritone, a male voice having a range between that of tenor and bass.

Baritone, a brass wind instrument of the saxhorn family.

Barnard, John (f. 1641), was a minor canon of St Paul's Cathedral during the reign of Charles I. He published a collection of cathedral music in 1641.

Barrel Organ, a mechanically operated organ. Barrel organs were first made towards the end of the 18th century and were commonly used in churches during the early 19th century. They superseded the church bands and were themselves superseded by the harmonium. These organs were capable of playing a number of the tunes popular at the time, and usually had a few stops to give variety in volume and quality.

The name barrel organ is now inappropriately used for what are better called street pianos. Even this name, however, is hardly apt, as these instruments cannot produce the gradation of tone which gave the pianoforte its name. The street piano superseded the street variety of the barrel organ proper; hence, no doubt, the transference of the name from the one to the other.

Bartlett, John (f. 1606-10), was an English musician. His published songs are included in *The English School of Lutenist Songwriters*.

Bartók, Bela (b. Nagyszentmiklós 1881, d. New York 1945), achieved distinction as a composer. He studied at the Budapest Academy and was later appointed to its staff. He was associated with Kodály in researches into Hungarian folk music, a study which profoundly affected his own composition. His compositions include a quantity of orchestral and chamber music and many arrangements of folk-songs.

Baryton, a bass viol with sympathetic strings passing under the fingerboard. Barytons were found almost exclusively in Germany, though the invention is attributed to English makers of the late 17th century.

Bass, the vocal part sung by men with a low range. The normal compass of bass parts is about an octave and a half upwards to middle C. Bass voices are sometimes distinguished as basso profundo, the lower, basso cantante, the higher, and contra basso, the exceptionally low Russian basses with a range extending to two and a half octaves below middle C.

Bass-bar, a fitting inside the body of instruments of the violin family, consisting of a thin strip glued to the inside of the belly longitudinally from the feet of the bridge. It helps to spread the vibrations from the feet of the bridge over the belly.

Bass-Baritone, a name conveniently used to describe those bass voices with the resources of both bass and baritone, having developed neither the lower nor the higher register at the expense of the other.

Bass Clarinet, the low single reed woodwind instrument of the orchestra, very similar to the ordinary clarinet. It is built one octave below the B flat clarinet and is treated as a transposing instrument sounding a ninth lower than written, its part being written on the treble clef. In Germany, but seldom elsewhere, bass clarinets in A are also used. Also in Germany, bass clarinet parts are written on the bass clef, transposing down a tone or minor third in the same way as the ordinary clarinet.

Bass Clef, the F clef placed on the fourth line to show that that line corresponds with the F below middle C.

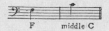

F   middle C

Basse Danse (Fr.), a stately dance for two persons, popular in France during the 14th, 15th and early 16th centuries. The basse danse was characterised by the gliding movement of the feet, and was commonly in triple time.

Basset Horn, a single reed woodwind instrument differing but little from the ordinary clarinet. It is built in F, has a prolonged bore, and has additional keys which enable it to reach the F an octave and a fifth below middle C.

Bassoon, the low double reed woodwind instrument of the orchestra. Like the oboe, to which it is closely related, the bassoon has a conical bore and overblows the octave. It is sounded from a double reed mouthpiece, and its pitch is varied by the pitch holes in the tube. The natural scale of the bassoon is G, a twelfth below that of the oboe; the lower limit to its compass is, however, the B flat just over two octaves below middle C. Its effective compass is about three octaves, but may be readily increased to the E flat a fourth higher. Music for the bassoon is written on the bass clef or tenor clef as is convenient.

The distinctive characteristic of the bassoon is the doubling of its tube; in principle it does not differ from the oboe. This distinctive characteristic seems to have been associated, sometime during the 16th century, with the pommers of the family from which both the bassoon and oboe evolved.

Bassoon, a reed organ stop of 16-foot pitch usually on the Pedal Organ. Its quality resembles that of the orchestral bassoon.

Bateson, Thomas (b. c. 1570, d. Dublin 1630), was an English musician. His published madrigals are included in *The English Madrigal School.*

Batten, Adrian (d. London 1637), was organist at St Paul's Cathedral. He was a prolific composer of church music, most of which remains in manuscript. The *Batten Organ Book,* a book in his handwriting, is a valuable collection of church music (mainly 16th century) condensed into an organ score.

Battery. an ornament used in harpsichord music.

Battishill, Jonathan (b. London 1738, d. Islington 1801), was a composer mainly of church music and various kinds of music for the theatre.

Bax, Sir Arnold Edward Trevor (b. London 1883), still living.

Beat, the accents, greater and lesser, which arise from the orderly grouping of notes by their time values. The beat is, therefore, a feature of time.

Beats, the alternations in intensity which occur when two notes of slightly different pitch are sounded together. The frequency of the beats is simply the difference between the frequencies of the notes themselves.

Beethoven, Ludwig van (b. Bonn 1770, d. Vienna 1827), was the son of a musician in the court band of the Elector of Cologne. Inevitably Beethoven was reared in a musical atmosphere, learning first from his father and later from the court organist. His progress was such that in 1784 Neefe, who had become court organist three years earlier, could leave him as his regular deputy with confidence. Beethoven visited Vienna in 1787 and had a few lessons from Mozart. Like Brahms, but unlike many other composers of the first rank, Beethoven's youth was unremarkable, though both Mozart and Haydn had been impressed by his ability.

In 1792 Beethoven moved to Vienna, settling there for the rest of his life. He studied energetically under Haydn and Albrechtsberger, among others; a large number of his exercises are still in existence. He made his reputation first as a performer at the musical gatherings of Viennese nobility, as Mozart had done before him; but in contrast with Mozart, who was good mannered and modest, craving favours, Beethoven was rude and arrogant, granting them. Beethoven's reputation as a composer became established, and the remainder of his life is mainly a chronicle of the production of his compositions. From 1798 onwards he suffered from increasing deafness, and for the last five years of his life his hearing was negligible.

The new and forcible style which distinguishes Beethoven from Haydn and Mozart was derived technically from Cherubini and the other French Revolution composers (Beethoven played in many French operas when in the orchestra at Bonn), and emotionally from the new spirit of liberalism and enlightenment characteristic of the age generally.

His prime contributions to the musical repertory are in those musical forms associated with the growth of the sonata, the outline of which had been established by C. P. E. Bach, Mozart and Haydn. His treatment of the piano established it as an instrument quite distinct in range of expression and sustaining quality from its predecessors, and his use of the orchestra went far from the modesty in treatment with which Mozart and Haydn had expressed their more numerous but lighter essays. Thirty-two piano sonatas, ten violin sonatas, five violoncello sonatas and ten trios for violin, violoncello and piano; sixteen string quartets, nine symphonies, five piano concertos and one violin concerto are a remarkable contribution to these forms. The majority of his compositions are dedicated to his acquaintances among the nobility and known by their names. Such are the three *Rasoumowsky* string quartets and the *Waldstein* piano sonata. He named his third and sixth symphonies *Eroica* and *Pastoral,* and though the *Kreutzer* violin sonata and the *Pathetique* piano sonata were so named by himself, he did not give the fanciful title *Moonlight* to what is perhaps the most popular of his piano sonatas.

The opera *Fidelio* is a particularly good example of Beethoven's methods of working; it was revised a number of times and was in turn supplied with four overtures known as *Leonora No. II* and *Leonora No. III* (a revision of No. II) and later with *Leonora No. I* and *Fidelio*. Besides these four, the overtures *Egmont, Prometheus* and *Coriolanus* are well known.

His *Missa Solennis* is his only work in the field of sacred music which can be considered of first rank. He did not write sympathetically for the voice, and his many songs are little known.

Bell, the spreading mouth of most wind instruments, particularly those of the brass family. A wide bell, as in the French horn, damps the higher overtones and so mellows the quality of the notes produced by the instrument.

Bell, a musical instrument of great antiquity, known throughout the world. The oldest bells discovered are plates of metal bent into shape. The process of bell casting was known in the Middle Ages, and the oldest dated bells are of this period. The best bell metal is a bronze of thirteen parts of copper to four of tin. The shape and proportions of bells are the result of experience and intricate calculations.

Apart from the numerous utilitarian uses of bells, the carillon has long been traditional on the continent of Europe, and change ringing has a small but enthusiastic following in England. Bells have occasionally been introduced into the orchestra. Handel uses a large set of bells in *Saul*, Bach uses two bells in his Cantata No. 53 *Schlage doch*, Wagner's use of bells in *Parsifal* is notable, and bell effects have been particularly popular with Russian composers.

Bellini, Vincenzo (b. Catania 1801, d. Puteaux 1835), was the son of an organist. He studied at the Naples conservatory and gained success as an opera composer while still a student. Amongst his operas are *Il Pirata, I Puritani, Norma* and, perhaps most successful of all, *Sonnambula*.

Bellows, the source of wind supply in keyboard wind instruments, particularly the organ, from the primitive blacksmith's bellows of the earliest organs to the elaborate electrically blown bellows of a large modern organ.

Belly, the upper or front part of the sound box of stringed instruments across which the strings are stretched. The belly of a pianoforte is commonly known as the sound-board.

Ben (It.), well.

Benedict, Sir Julius (b. Stuttgart 1804, d. London 1885), was an intimate pupil of Weber, and a particularly energetic and successful champion of music. He was a prolific composer, but is now remembered only for his opera *The Lily of Killarney*.

Benjamin, Arthur (b. Sydney 1893), still living.

Bennet, John (f. 1599-1614), was an English musician. His published madrigals are included in *The English Madrigal School*, and he contributed to *The Triumphes of Oriana*.

Bennett, William Sterndale (b. Sheffield 1816, d. London 1875), was in his day a distinguished composer and teacher. He was Principal of the Royal Academy of Music and Professor of Music at Cambridge University. As a composer he is now remembered only by a few sacred compositions.

Berceuse, a cradle song. This title is used for both vocal and instrumental compositions of a lullaby character.

Berg, Alban (b. Vienna 1885, d. there 1935), was one of Schonberg's most important pupils. Berg's opera *Wozzeck*, 1922, his seventh numbered work, placed him beyond question among the most important figures in the development of such modern idioms as 'twelve note music'. His *Lyric Suite*, 1927, for string quartet, is considered one of the most outstanding modern examples of chamber music.

Berlioz, Hector (b. La Côte St André 1803, d. Paris 1869), was the son of a doctor. In spite of Hector's preference for music, his father insisted on an education for the medical profession. In 1822 Berlioz entered the Medical School of Paris, but left after a short while to devote himself entirely to music. He entered the Paris Conservatoire the following year, and after seven years of struggle won the Prix de Rome. He married in 1833. Though the next seven years were full of difficulties, towards the end of them his reputation as a composer and as a conductor became established and his livelihood assured. The next twenty years are a record of successful tours and of the production of his compositions. During the last six years of his life his health was failing and he wrote nothing.

Berlioz is the most representative composer of the French Romantic Movement. He is important as a master of orchestration rather than simply as a composer. In his symphonic compositions *Harold in Italy*, *Romeo and Juliet*, and *Symphonie Fantastique* he shows a remarkable power of effect. His most important stage work and his last composition is *Les Troyens*, a grand opera in two parts. The demands in size of orchestra and scale of performance prohibit the frequent performance of his compositions. His entire writings number only some fifty compositions, nearly all large-scale instrumental or choral works.

Berners, Gerald Hugh Tyrwhitt-Wilson (b. Bridgnorth 1883, d. Faringdon 1950), was the fourteenth Lord Berners in the English Peerage. He was educated at Eton and served in the diplomatic service from 1909 to 1920. Writing, painting and composing were all prominent among his many varied interests. He had a taste for the bizarre and an ironic wit; both are reflected in his works. Important among his compositions are several works for the stage, including the choral ballet *A Wedding Bouquet*, written for Sadler's Wells and produced in 1937, for which he designed the scenery and costumes as well as composing the music.

Best, William Thomas (b. Carlisle 1826, d. Liverpool 1897), was a brilliant and successful organist. He was appointed organist of St George's Hall, Liverpool, in 1855. His arrangements for the organ of good music of all kinds were a feature of his recitals.

Binary Form, form in which balance is obtained by a second phrase (or section) answering the first.

The terms 'binary form' and 'ternary form' have played a prominent part in the explanations of the evolution of form which have been given by some theorists. One reputable author defines 'binary form' as equivalent to 'sonata form' and 'ternary form' as equivalent to 'rondo form'. Grove's Dictionary avoids defining either of them. About fifty years ago 'binary form' was the usual term for 'first movement form' or 'sonata form', but Hadow decided that 'sonata form' was ternary (exposition, development, recapitulation), though it was binary in the sense of being based on two subjects.

A great many tunes, particularly of the folk song and hymn tune variety, consist of four phrases. In most cases there is a sense of rest half way, often coinciding with a modulation to the dominant. Where the sense of balance is clearly between the first half and the second half of the tune, the form may be described as binary. But four phrases may be balanced in a number of ways. In this piece for harpsichord by Purcell:

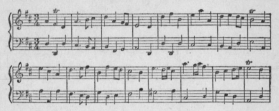

the third phrase is a transposed and modified version of the first phrase; the second and fourth phrases are quite different from each other. 'Binary form' inadequately describes the form of this tune. The balance between the first half and the second half of this tune is simply incidental to the similarities and contrasts which give balance to the four phrases.

Neither the majority of simple melodies nor those extended movements which were the precursors of the mature 'first movement form' can reasonably and adequately be described as being in either binary or ternary form.

Bind or *Tie,* a curved line joining two notes of the same pitch, indicating that only the first note is to be struck and that its duration is to be extended to the end of the second. The bind is necessary when a note is to sound across a bar, or when its duration can be represented only by a combination of the standard notes.

Bishop, Sir Henry Rowley (b. London 1786, d. there 1855), achieved success as a composer and arranger of music for the stage, and is remembered for *Home Sweet Home,* a song from one of his operas.

He edited many important works, including Handel's Messiah. He became Professor of Music at Oxford in 1848.

Bizet, Georges (*Alexandre César Léopold*) (b. Paris 1838, d. near there 1875), was a successful pupil of the Paris Conservatoire. He won the Prix de Rome in 1857, and his ability as a pianist was remarkable. Though he gained a certain success with a number of his dramatic compositions, he is remembered almost entirely by his masterpiece the opera *Carmen* and the two orchestral suites arranged from the incidental music to the play *L'Arlésienne*.

Bliss, Sir Arthur (b. London 1891), still living.

Blitheman, William (d. 1591), was organist of the Chapel Royal, and had an important influence on his pupil Bull.

Bloch, Ernest (b. Geneva 1880), still living.

Blockx, Jan (b. Antwerp 1851, d. there 1912), was a distinguished Belgian composer who gained an early local popularity with his many Flemish songs. A number of cantatas and operas are among his principal compositions.

Blow, John (b. Nottinghamshire 1648 or 49, d. Westminster 1708), became one of the children of the Chapel Royal when it was re-established in 1660. Details of the earlier part of his life are uncertain. Blow was appointed organist of Westminster Abbey in 1668, and subsequently held appointments at the Chapel Royal and St Paul's Cathedral. He relinquished his appointment at Westminster Abbey in 1679 in favour of Purcell, and was re-appointed in 1695 on Purcell's death. The precise details of these various changes and appointments are uncertain. Blow had considerable merit as a composer, particularly of church music. A great number of anthems and some services by him are extant, mostly in manuscript. He has been overshadowed by his pupil Purcell.

Boccherini, Luigi (b. Lucca 1743, d. Madrid 1805), was an able and industrious composer. Though his chamber music has considerable merit, it does not compare with that of his contemporary Haydn, and little of it is now commonly heard.

Boehm, Theobald (b. Munich 1793, d. 1881), was an eminent flute player. He introduced a number of improvements in the mechanism of the flute, in particular a system of fingering which has now been generally adopted. The system makes the fingering of different keys more or less equal in difficulty, and many duplicate fingerings make possible passages otherwise impracticable. The Boehm system of fingering has been applied to the Oboe, and was adapted to the Clarinet by Klosé.

Boëllmann, Léon (b. Ensisheim 1862, d. Paris 1897), was an organist and composer. His small quantity of compositions for the organ has proved a useful contribution to the organ repertory.

Boethius, Anicius Manlius Torquatus Severinus (b. Rome c.475, d. Pavia 525), was one of the most brilliant scholars of his day. He wrote five books on music.

Boieldieu, François Adrien (b. Rouen 1775, d. Jarcy 1834), achieved success as an opera composer.

Boito, Arrigo (b. Padua 1842, d. Milan 1918), was a composer and poet. The first of his two operas, *Mefistofele,* which caused a scandal on its first appearance, is now accepted as a sort of classic, though it has never been really popular. His librettos *Otello* and *Falstaff,* which were written for Verdi, are considered amongst the best of their kind.

Bolero, a Spanish dance. The rhythm of the bolero has been successively modified:

(i)

(ii)

and, as the rhythm of the castanets used by the dancers was introduced into the music

(iii)

or (iv)

The rhythm

(v)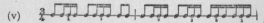

is that used in the well-known bolero for orchestra by Ravel.

Bombardon, either of the two lower members of the tuba group of brass valve wind instruments.

Bononcini, Giovanni Battista (b. Modena 1672, d. after 1748), was the most important member of a family of musicians who flourished during the 17th and 18th centuries. He was associated with Handel and Ariosti as one of the three directors of the Royal Academy of Music which had its first season of opera in 1720. Twenty-two operas are ascribed to him, and as an opera composer, rival to Handel, he met with considerable success; he also left a number of choral works, mostly sacred. After 1732 he left London, and little is known about the rest of his life.

Borodin, Alexander Porphyrievich (b. St Petersburg 1833, d. there 1887), was the illegitimate son of a prince of Imeretia. He studied medicine, becoming assistant professor of chemistry at the Academy of Medicine in St Petersburg in 1862. Throughout his life he remained first a scientist, but devoted his leisure to writing music. He became a distinguished member of the Russian musical circle which included Balakirev and Rimsky-Korsakov. Among Borodin's very few compositions are two symphonies, the symphonic sketch *In the Steppes of Central Asia*, and the opera *Prince Igor*.

Bouffons, another name for the 'matassins'.

Boughton, Rutland (b. Aylesbury 1878), still living.

Bourdon, a stopped wooden organstop of 16-foot pitch whether on the manuals or pedals.

Bourgeois, Lois (b. Paris *c.* 1510, d. after 1561), played a prominent part in the evolution of the Genevan Psalter. Little is known of the facts of his life. He was invited to Geneva in 1541, when Calvin returned there from Strasbourg, and left it in 1557. During the time he was in Geneva, Bourgeois was responsible for the music of the successively enlarged editions of the Psalter which, however, did not reach completion until 1562. He adapted tunes from the Strassburg Psalter, prepared by Calvin after he was expelled from Geneva in 1538, and added new ones.

Bourrée (Fr.), a dance form often found in a suite. The bourrée is in two sections, each repeated, and is written in two-two time beginning on the fourth crotchet in the bar:

English Suite No. 1
BACH

Often a second bourrée follows the first, after which the first bourrée is repeated.

Bow, the implement with which the strings of the violin and similar instruments are made to vibrate. Originally the form of the bow was like that of the weapon from which it took its name. From the 13th to the 18th century the shape and structure of the bow evolved to the present shape, being brought to perfection by François Tourte.

Bowing, the manner in which the bow is employed by a string player, and the particular way in which a passage is to be played. Groups of notes to be played with one movement of a bow are placed under a slur; whether a slur is an indication of the bowing or phrasing must be judged from the text; a long legato phrase indicated by one slur may need a number of movements of the bow. The upward and downward motions of the bow are indicated by the signs V and ⊓ respectively. In addition, particular styles of bowing may be indicated by such terms as 'spiccato'. In the time of Bach and Handel bowing was rarely indicated by the composer. In modern music, however, the bowing is generally indicated in considerable detail.

Boyce, William (b. London 1710, d. Kensington 1779), achieved distinction as an organist and composer of sacred and secular music. He is remembered chiefly, however, for his collection *Cathedral Music*, begun by Greene who handed on the work he found himself unable to complete.

Brace, the bracket and line joining two or more staves, indicating that the music written on those staves belongs to one instrument, one group of instruments or one group of voices.

Brahms, Johannes (b. Hamburg 1833, d. Vienna 1897), was the son of an undistinguished double-bass player. Though he showed promise of becoming an able musician, Brahms' youth was in no way remarkable; he was taught the piano and wrote a good deal, but later he destroyed his early works. In 1853 Brahms met a Hungarian violinist Reményi and with him toured North Germany, finishing in Hanover; there Brahms was introduced to Joachim who was impressed by his piano playing and composition. Brahms subsequently met Liszt, and became a close friend of Schumann at Düsseldorf, continuing in close friendship with Clara Schumann after Robert's death.

Brahms' reputation grew quickly, and his mature compositions established him as a composer. His life was remarkably uneventful; he held the post of director of the court concerts and choral society to the Prince of Lippe-Detmold from 1854 to 1858, was appointed conductor of the Vienna Singakademie shortly after he took up residence there in 1862 but resigned after a year, and was conductor of the Gesellschaft der Musikfreunde from 1872 to 1875. He held no official appointment during the remainder of his life. With Vienna as his centre, he made occasional musical tours, but refused to visit England to receive a Doctorate of Music from Cambridge. He took part in the rivalries between his various contemporaries. The circumstances of his life were congenial and he lacked neither recognition nor reward during his lifetime.

The best known of Brahms' choral works is his *German Requiem*. His four symphonies appeared in pairs, the first two in 1876 and 1877 and the second two in 1883 and 1884. Two overtures, his *Academic Festival Overture*, composed in acknowledgment of the degree of Doctor of Philosophy conferred on him by Breslau University, and his *Tragic Overture*, appeared between the pairs of symphonies. His *Variations on a theme by Haydn*, an early work, was presented by Brahms in two forms, for the orchestra and for two pianos (neither form being properly an arrangement of the other).

Brahms made a number of notable contributions to chamber music, both instrumental and vocal, and was one of the few to contribute to the repertory of the vocal quartet. Of his piano music the sixteen waltzes for four hands and the two rhapsodies are well known, and his songs, of which he wrote many, are becoming better known. The eleven choral preludes, for the organ, published after his death, represent him at his best.

Branle (Fr.), a round dance in duple measure popular in France particularly during the 16th century. The branle popular in England during the 16th century may have differed from the French form, and the brawl was probably identical with it.

Brass, instruments of the trumpet, horn and related families are so called when they form part of an orchestra or wind band.

Brass Band, a band consisting solely of brass wind instruments. Brass bands usually include instruments of the cornet and saxhorn families and trombones, with the addition of side drums, bass drums and cymbals. Saxophones are often added, in which case the name brass band, though used, is not properly applicable.

The repertory of the brass band is poor, and consists mainly of arrangements. All the instruments except the bass trombone are treated as transposing instruments, and are written for in the treble clef; the octave in which the B flat or E flat corresponding to a written middle C sounds depends on the instrument.

THE BRASS

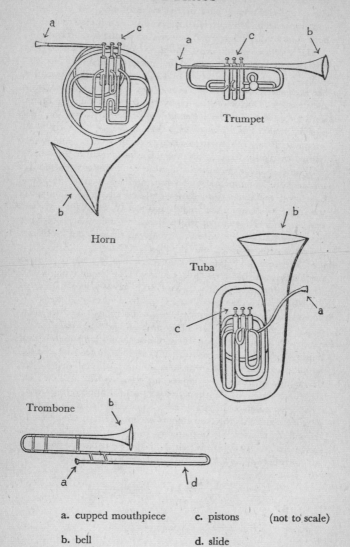

Horn

Trumpet

Tuba

Trombone

a. cupped mouthpiece   c. pistons   (not to scale)

b. bell   d. slide

    (a) E flat soprano (cornet),

    (b) B flat cornet and B flat flugelhorn,

    (c) E flat horn (alto saxhorn),

    (d) B flat baritone (tenor saxhorn), B flat trombone and euphonium.

    (e) E flat bass (E flat bass tuba or bombardon),

    (f) B flat bass (B flat bass tuba or bombardon).

The bass trombone sounds as written. Hence for some instruments their treatment in the brass band and orchestra differs.

Bravura (It.), bravery. Indicates a style of music or performance which displays brilliancy and technical power.

Breve, twice a semibreve. It is written ▯ or ▭ and its corresponding rest ▭ . It is now seldom used.

Bridge, the support over which the strings of a stringed instrument are stretched. In instruments of the violin family one foot of the bridge rests firmly on the belly over the sound post. The other foot transmits the vibrations from the strings to the belly.

Bridge, Frank (b. Brighton 1879, d. Eastbourne 1941), achieved distinction as a conductor and as a composer particularly of chamber music.

Brillante (It.), brilliant. Used as an indication of the style of a composition or its interpretation.

Brio (It.), vigour.

Bruch, Max (b. Cologne 1838, d. Friedenau 1920), had a distinguished career as a musician. He held a number of musical directorships, including that of the Liverpool Philharmonic Society for three years, and of the branch of composition in the Hochschule of Berlin, and received a number of distinctions such as the Prussian order 'Pour le mérite'. At one time his importance was considered to be as a composer of works for choir and orchestra; now, however, his best known compositions are those for violin or violoncello and orchestra.

Bruckner, Anton (b. Ansfelden 1824, d. Vienna 1896), was first a schoolmaster but devoted himself entirely to music after his appointment as organist to the Cathedral at Linz. In 1868 he moved to Vienna to become a teacher of theory and the organ at the conservatorium. His compositions include nine symphonies, the last unfinished.

Bruneau, Louis Charles Bonaventure Alfred (b. Paris 1857, d. there 1934), was a composer mainly of opera. Though not influenced by Wagner's style, he applied Wagner's principles to French opera, and in this he was closely associated with his friend Emile Zola.

Buccina, a Roman brass instrument, with a bore similar to that of the bugle, curved nearly to a circle so that the bell rested on the shoulders of the player.

Buck, Sir Percy Carter (b. West Ham 1871, d. London 1947), had a distinguished career in the field of musical education. He was Director of Music at Harrow from 1901 to 1927, became Professor of Music at London University in 1925, and was knighted in 1935.

His liberal outlook and scholarship have had a considerable influence in several directions. He played a prominent part in establishing the teachers' course at the Royal College of Music, and he was a member of the editorial committee of *Tudor Church Music.* He was President of the Royal College of Organists, and Music Advisor to the Education Committee of the L.C.C. He wrote a number of excellent text books, and contributed important articles to musical journals.

Bugle, a wind instrument of brass or copper similar to the trumpet but having a shorter and more widely conical tube. As commonly used in bugle bands and in the army for Infantry calls, it is pitched in B flat and valves are not used. The first eight notes of the harmonic series may be obtained, but only the second, third, fourth, fifth and sixth are used for the calls which are written in C, the bugle being treated as a transposing instrument. Both valves and keys have been applied to the bugle, though the natural bugle has retained its popularity in bugle bands. The valve and keyed instruments have been superseded by the valve cornet.

Bull, John (b. *c.* 1562, d. Antwerp 1628), was an English musician. He was appointed organist of Hereford Cathedral in 1582, became a member of the Chapel Royal in 1585, and acted as organist from 1591. He took the degree of B. Mus. at Oxford in 1586 and Mus. D. in 1592, having previously taken this degree at Cambridge. In 1601 Bull travelled abroad to recover his health. He left England again in 1613 and four years later was appointed organist of Antwerp Cathedral. A few of his vocal compositions have survived, but his importance is as a writer of keyboard music. Some hundred and fifty of his compositions for organ and virginal are extant, many of them in *Parthenia* and *The Fitzwilliam Virginal Book.*

Bülow, Hans Guido, Freiherr von (b. Dresden 1830, d. Cairo 1894), was one of the most eminent musicians of his day, an outstanding pianist, an able conductor, and an advocate of Brahms and Wagner. Before devoting himself entirely to music he had studied law.

His scholarship and musical understanding have made his editions of the classical pianoforte works of great value.

Burden, the common name for the refrain of a song until the 17th century. Hence songs or ballads with refrains were commonly themselves called burdens.

Burla or *Burlesca,* an instrumental composition of a playful or joking character.

Burletta, a form of musical dramatic production having some of the features of both ballad and comic opera. Originally an Italian form, burletta reached England through France, and had a popularity for some seventy years at the end of the 18th and beginning of the 19th centuries.

Burney, Charles (b. Shrewsbury 1726, d. Chelsea 1814), was a musical historian who made an outstanding contribution to musical research. The material he collected from books and from a tour of Italy, France and Germany, to learn of the state of music in those countries, is contained in his *General History of Music,* which appeared in four volumes between 1776 and 1789. At that time Burney's *History* was considered superior to Hawkins' *History* which appeared in 1776. However, time has shown that they have comparable merits and faults.

Busoni, Ferruccio Benvenuto (b. Empoli 1866, d. Berlin 1924), was the son of musical parents. He established a reputation as a pianist, and later as a composer. His compositions include a few operas (the last, *Doktor Faust,* unfinished but completed by a pupil, is considered his best work), a number of orchestral compositions, some chamber music and songs, and a considerable quantity of pianoforte music.

Butterworth, George Sainton Kaye (b. London 1885, killed in action on the Somme 1916), showed great promise as a student of folk music and composer of songs.

Buxtehude, Dietrich (b. Helsingborg 1637, d. Lübeck 1707), was an organist and composer. His father was organist at Helsingör, Denmark, for over thirty years. In 1668 Buxtehude became organist at Lübeck. He influenced Bach, who journeyed 200 miles on foot to make his acquaintance.

Byrd, William (b. 1542 or 3, d. 1623), was the outstanding English representative of the polyphonic period, and ranks as a composer beside Palestrina, Lassus and Victoria. London and Lincolnshire have been suggested as Byrd's birthplace but nothing is known with certainty of the early part of his life. He became organist of Lincoln Cathedral in 1563, and about 1574 left Lincoln to become with Tallis joint organist of the Chapel Royal. In 1575 Byrd and Tallis were granted a licence for printing music which amounted to a monopoly; this licence passed to Byrd on Tallis' death and later to Morley and East. From 1577 until 1592 or the next year Byrd lived at Harlington in Middlesex; he then moved to Stondon in Essex, which remained his home until his death. During a considerable part of his life he was involved in lawsuits over property and the like, and he was not untouched by the troubles of the Church. He held his Royal Appointment until his death, though virtually in retirement during the last years.

In spite of the time occupied in lawsuits, duties at the Chapel Royal and pupils, the quantity of Byrd's compositions is remarkable. He contributed with unsurpassed success to all the forms of his day, in many cases standing unquestionably above his contemporaries. Byrd contributed to both the Latin and the English Liturgy. Three masses (one each for three, four and five voices), three volumes of *Cantiones Sacrae* (the first jointly with Tallis) and two volumes of *Gradualia* were published during his lifetime; a considerable number of motets have survived in manuscript. Two complete services are among his music for the English rite. Three volumes published during his lifetime contain the greater part of his vocal music in the form of anthems and madrigals. The bulk of his songs, sacred and secular, survive in manuscript. A large quantity of virginal music by Byrd survives, some in *Parthenia* and a great deal more in the various collections of Virginal music, such as *The Fitzwilliam Virginal Book*; and a considerable quantity of string music also survives in manuscript. Byrd shows himself to be a master of contrapuntal technique. He uses his ingenuity in the construction of strict canon with restraint – examples are rare. The remarkable versatility of Byrd, greater than that of Palestrina, is one of the features of his genius.

C

Cabezón, Antonio de (b. near Burgos 1510, d. Madrid 1566), was a famous organist, and one of the first composers for keyboard instruments. He was blind, apparently from birth.

Caccini, Giulio (b. Rome c. 1545, d. Florence 1618), was a singer and composer. In 1578 he moved to Florence where he was closely associated with the rise of opera.

Cachucha (Sp.), a dance the music of which resembles that of the bolero. Originally the tune was sung to a guitar accompaniment.

Cadence or *Close,* now used indiscriminately for resting places during the course of and at the end of a composition. Hence cadences are the musical equivalent of punctuation in literature. During the polyphonic period the harmonies resulting from a polyphonic treatment of melodies in the various modes gave rise to cadences which could be recognised as belonging to particular modes. With the rise of the major and minor key system, certain progressions of chords became recognised as conventional endings of greater or lesser finality.

The types of cadences recognised were (a) perfect cadence or full close, in two forms authentic and plagal; (b) imperfect cadence or half close; (c) interrupted cadence.

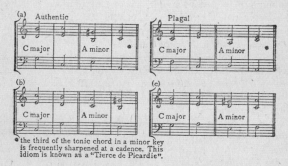

* the third of the tonic chord in a minor key is frequently sharpened at a cadence. This idiom is known as a "Tierce de Picardie".

In more modern music, in which the harmonic conventions of the 18th and 19th century have been discarded, almost any succession of chords may be used with cadential effect.

Cadenza (It.), cadence. This term was first used for a passage introduced by singers immediately before the close of a song to show off their voices. Later the cadenza was introduced into instrumental music, particularly concertos, not only to display the virtuosity of the soloist but also, by coming immediately after the climax, to delay the close which would otherwise be abrupt. The cadenza commonly begins from the second inversion of the tonic chord; it delays the dominant chord with which the cadenza closes, which would normally follow the second inversion of the tonic chord immediately. In older concertos the cadenza was left to be improvised by the soloist (often the composer himself);

the custom now is for the composer himself to write the cadenza as an integral part of the composition.

Calando (It.), diminishing. Indicates a decreasing of speed and volume.

Callcott, John Wall (b. Kensington 1766, d. Bristol 1821), was a composer mainly of glees and similar vocal pieces.

Cambert, Robert (b. Paris *c.*1628, d. London 1677), has been claimed as the originator of French opera.

Campanology, the science and art of bell making and ringing.

Campian, Thomas (b. London 1567, d. there 1620), became famous as a poet and song writer, though by profession apparently a physician (he styled himself Doctor of Physic about 1602). Campian was by comparison with his contemporaries a prolific writer, and ranks high both as a poet and a composer. He published four volumes of ayres, and another volume by him was published by Rosseter; these are included in *The English School of Lutenist Songwriters.* He also wrote songs for four masques, and published a treatise on musical composition.

Canarie, a dance probably of Spanish origin, similar to the gigue. The canarie had passed out of use by the 17th century, though a few instrumental canaries were written by Purcell and Couperin. Its characteristic rhythm was ♩♫, and always began on the first beat of the bar.

Cancrizans, canon in which the imitating part has the same notes as the subject but in reverse order.

Canon, strict imitation or a composition in which strict imitation plays a predominant part.

Here the choral is imitated strictly at the fifth below, and the left hand and pedals add three free parts (parts not in canon) below the two upper parts in canon.

The imitation in a canon may be by inversion, augmentation or diminution, or by reversion, and it may be at the unison, octave, fifth or other interval. One or more parts may be imitated by the others; for example, canon 'four in two' implies that two different themes are in canon at the same time, two voices being concerned with each theme. A canon by reversion is called 'per recte et retro', backwards and forwards, or cancrizans.

Though canons have been used largely as a form of musical mental gymnastics, there are many examples of compositions of unquestionable beauty in which the devices of canon have been used either strictly or freely. Byrd and Bach in particular were masters of canon.

Cantabile (It.), in a singing style. Indicates a smooth expressive style.

Cantilena (It.), a little song. The present use of cantilena is in instrumental music to describe a phrase of vocal character. It is sometimes used instead of 'cantabile'.

Cantata (It.), sung. This term is used as a title for certain vocal compositions. The earliest form was the 'Cantata da Camera'. It began as a musical setting in recitative, for solo voice accompanied by one instrument, of a short drama, in verse, to be sung without action. The first development was the introduction of an aria, and in this form the 'Cantata da Camera' was perfected in the 17th century by such as Carissimi who adapted the form for church use, the 'Cantata da Chiesa'. The elaboration of the accompaniment from one instrument shortly followed. Extended compositions of this form were written by Alessandro Scarlatti, Pergolesi and Handel.

The 'Church Cantata', as developed particularly by Bach, is a more elaborate form than that of the 'Cantata da Camera' and 'Cantata da Chiesa', being written variously for soloists and chorus, accompanied by various groups of instruments and having a mixture of movements, choruses and chorals as well as recitatives and arias.

By cantata is now meant a sacred or secular choral composition of a dramatic character, though not intended to be acted, a sacred cantata being distinguished from an oratorio merely by being of smaller dimensions.

Canticle, a hymn, such as Magnificat and Nunc Dimittis, taken from the Bible, other than from the Book of Psalms.

Canto Fermo (It.), fixed song. The term is used for a melody adapted for contrapuntal treatment. The name is now connected mainly with exercises in counterpoint rather than composition proper. Prior to the 16th century the adoption of portions of the liturgical plainsong as a canto fermo was a common practice.

Cantor, the Latin form of the title 'Precentor'.

Cantoris, the side in a cathedral of the Cantor's stall, the distinction between Decani (the Dean's side, the south side) and the Cantoris being drawn for the purpose of antiphonal singing between the sides of the choir.

Canzona (It.), an early form of fugue. The Italian name is derived from the French 'chanson', a song, because the chansons of the 15th century were harmonized in imitations.

Canzonetta (It.), a little song of the folk song type. The name was adopted by Morley for his 'canzonets or little short songs' in the madrigal style.

Caoine, the traditional death song commonly used in Ireland until the end of the 19th century. Caoine is pronounced 'keen'.

Capriccio (It.), originally, it seems, a name given to pieces for the harpsichord in a figured style. In the 17th and 18th centuries it was used as the name for pieces in the nature of studies on a definite figure. Later it was used for compositions in a modified first movement or rondo form, and for brilliant arrangements of material borrowed from other composers. Brahms used the name alongside 'intermezzo', capriccio for faster and intermezzo for slower pieces.

Carillon, a chromatic set of bells of three to four octaves hung in a tower and played from a keyboard either by hand or feet, or by some automatic mechanism.

The idea of the carillon appears to have been anticipated by the Chinese in ancient times. The making of carillons flourished particularly in Northern France, Belgium and Holland during the 15th to 18th centuries. The name carillon was originally that of the music played. Carillon music is written in two or more parts, mostly arrangements made by carillon players to suit their own instruments.

Carissimi, Giacomo (b. Marino 1605, d. Rome 1674), was appointed to St Apollinare attached to the German College in Rome in 1628, and remained there till his death. He was a prolific composer, though most of his work has been lost, and what survives has not yet received the attention it may deserve. He is particularly important for his contribution to the development of recitative and to the cantata and oratorio generally.

Carlton, Richard (b. *c.*1558, d. *c.*1638), was an English musician. His published madrigals are included in *The English Madrigal School* and he contributed to *The Triumphes of Oriana*.

Carol, generally a song sung at Christmas in honour of the birth of

Christ, and in this specialized sense equivalent to the French Noël. It appears that in England prior to the mid 16th century carol was used in the sense of a song having a refrain, regardless of subject matter. Subsequently the name was used in a variety of senses, including simply that of a song. The name has come to mean a song, rather than a hymn, associated with a festival of the church, particularly, but not necessarily, Christmas. The origins of those songs now regarded as carols are very varied. The borrowing, adaptation and modification which has resulted in the present repertory of carols popular in England almost defies classification. English folk songs and medieval poetry, later poems of unknown origin, paraphrases of medieval and later Latin poetry, translations of Noëls and similar songs as well as acknowledged recent compositions are among the very great number of sources which contribute to the modern English carol book.

Caruso, Enrico (b. Naples 1873, d. there 1921), was the most successful operatic tenor of his day.

Cassation, used in the 18th century as the title for instrumental music suitable for use in the open air. The structure of such compositions is no different from that of a 'divertimento'.

Casella, Alfredo (b. Turin 1883, d. Rome 1947), came of a musical family. He studied at the Paris Conservatoire, where he was a pupil of Fauré, and where his rapid progress was astonishing. He identified himself with the Italian school of modern music. His compositions include two symphonies, a violin concerto and a quintet for strings and wind, besides numerous songs and pianoforte pieces.

Castanets, two small pieces of hardwood hinged with string. The castanets are held in the hand of the player, the string passing over the thumb and first finger of the player. Single clicks and trills, with a certain variety of tone as well as a considerable variety of intensity, are possible. Two pairs, one in each hand, are used. These enable a variety of rhythmic combinations, as well as smooth crescendos and diminuendos. Castanets are thought to be of Spanish origin. Their use was, and is still, a characteristic feature of Spanish dances, and in the hands of a skilled dancer the emotional effect of their use can be considerable.

Castrato, the high-pitched voice of the eunuch. The voices of eunuchs in rare instances reach a remarkable strength and quality, and until recent times the successful castrato gained great popularity. Eunuchs were employed in the churches of Rome and elsewhere, and influenced very considerably the Italian opera of the 18th century. The castration of singers was abolished by Napoleon, but it is alleged to have gone on in Italy (for church purposes) to the end of the 19th century, if not later.

Catch, originally merely a round for voices, not written in score; each singer had to begin his part at the appropriate time — therein lay the catch. Later, the arrangement of the words to give ludicrous effects became a feature of catches. During the later Stuart period catches became particularly popular, but they were unfortunately affected by the indecency of the times; consequently many examples of clever musical invention of this kind by Purcell and his contemporaries are not commonly known.

Causton, Thomas (d. 1569), was an English musician. An amount of his church music is extant.

Cavalieri, Emilo del (b. Rome *c.* 1550, d. there 1602), was a cultured Roman musical enthusiast. He was closely associated with the rise of opera in Florence.

Cavalli, Pietro Francesco (b. Crema 1602, d. Venice 1676), was associated with St Mark's, Venice, from 1617, first as a singer under Monteverdi. Cavalli was a composer particularly important in the early history of opera.

Cavendish, Michael (b. *c.* 1565, d. 1628), was an English musician. His published madrigals and songs are included in *The English Madrigal School* and *The English School of Lutenist Songwriters*. He contributed to *The Triumphes of Oriana*, and helped to harmonise the tunes for the Psalter of 1592, published by Thomas East.

Cavatina (It.), originally a short song. This term is now often used of a melodious portion of operatic scene.

Cebell, a name used by Purcell and others for a form of gavotte.

Celesta, a keyboard instrument in which the sound is produced by plates of metal suspended over wooden resonators. It was invented in 1886 by Mustel of Paris.

Celestina, a keyboard stringed instrument giving a continuous sound from the friction of an endless rosined silk band on the strings.

Cello, a commonly used contraction of violoncello.

Cembal d'Amore, a rare keyboard stringed instrument. It is considered to have been a development of the clavichord, not of the harpsichord. The strings were twice as long as in the ordinary clavichord. The tangents struck exactly in the middle of the strings, so setting both halves of the string in vibration simultaneously.

Cembalo, originally the Italian name for the dulcimer, subsequently a common abbreviation for clavicembalo, and then frequently used to designate the continuo part of a concerted composition. In old Italian, cembalo sometimes means cymbal.

Chabrier, Alexis Emmanuel (b. Ambert 1841, d. Paris 1894), achieved some success with several operas of the lighter style.

Chaconne, an instrumental form similar to the passacaglia. The chaconne was originally a dance, probably of Spanish origin; the earliest mentions and descriptions of it date from the end of the 16th and the beginning of the 17th centuries. The differences, if any, between the chaconne and passacaglia as instrumental forms are vague. Like the passacaglia, the chaconne is built on a ground bass and is in three-four time; the chaconne had an accent on the second beat of the bar. The chaconne in the fourth sonata for unaccompanied violin, and the passacaglia (followed by a fugue) for organ, both by Bach, are among the finest examples of these forms, and illustrate the characteristics of these forms mentioned here. However, the features originally peculiar to each of these forms have long been confused between them.

Chair Organ, in old organs the second organ added to the Great Organ, possibly so named because it was placed below and in front of the main organ, so forming the back of the player's seat.

Chalumeau, an obsolete beating single reed instrument of cylindrical bore, the predecessor of the clarinet. Also the name, especially in its German form of Schalmey, of an entirely different instrument, a double reed instrument of conical bore, one of the predecessors of the oboe.

Chamber Music, originally music for the chamber as distinct from music for the church and music for the theatre. During the 16th and 17th centuries at least, chamber music was under the patronage of the nobility. The publicly supported concert hall did not exist. Most of the orchestral music of the 18th century retains the domestic and intimate nature of the chamber music of the earlier centuries, and is more properly classed with it than with the large scale orchestral music of the 19th century. Music requiring few performers is now as much a matter for public performance as music requiring many. The title chamber music still distinguishes, quite naturally and conveniently, music which may (at any rate) be used domestically.

Chamber Organ, a small organ suitable for use in a house or small hall.

Change Ringing, ringing a set of bells in a continuously changing order governed by certain rules. It is an almost exclusively English art.

The possible permutations, or changes in order, in which a set of bells may be rung increases rapidly with the number of bells. With three bells, for instance, only six changes are possible:

1	2	3
2	1	3
2	3	1
3	2	1
3	1	2
1	3	2
1	2	3

and so on.

With twelve bells, the number of changes is nearly 480 million. Many changes have been given special names, such as Grandsire Triple, Bob Major and the like.

Changing Note, a melodic embellishment of the harmony. It has taken several similar forms. A typical example of this idiom is

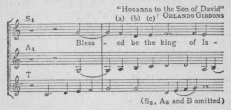

"Hosanna to the Son of David"
ORLANDO GIBBONS

Bless - ed be the king of Is -

(S₂, A₂ and B omitted)

where the passing discord (a) jumps to (b) before resolving on (c).

Chant, a term which has been used with successively more limited meaning. To chant means, in its widest sense, simply to sing, and in a narrower sense to sing the psalms, canticles and songs of the church according to the customary church rule. Psalms and canticles are now said to be chanted to the Anglican chant as distinct from being intoned to the Gregorian tones.

Chanting, in its common modern usage, is the singing of verses of prose to a short melody repeated as necessary for each verse or group of verses. Particularly, chanting refers to the singing of the psalms, canticles and similar portions of the Anglican liturgy to Anglican chants.

Charpentier, Marc-Antoine (b. Paris after 1634, d. 1704), was in his day a prominent composer of dramatic and sacred music.

Chekker, a keyboard stringed instrument popular in Burgundy, England (especially), France and Spain during the 14th, 15th and

16th centuries. There is evidence that it differed from both the clavichord and spinet, though similar to both of them, and that its action anticipated by over four centuries the invention of the pianoforte action at the beginning of the 18th century.

Cheng, an ancient Chinese small portable reed organ, introduced into France in the 18th century. It may be considered as the ancestor of the accordion, concertina and harmonium.

Cherubini, Maria Luigi Carlo Zenobio Salvatore (b. Florence 1760, d. Paris 1842), was the son of a musician at the Pergola Theatre. He was one of the most famous composers of his day, having a remarkable command of counterpoint. Beethoven held him in high regard. From 1786 onwards Paris became more or less his home. In 1822 he became Director of the Paris Conservatoire. He gained wider recognition in France, Germany and Italy than in England, and is now remembered by but a few works — some of his chamber music and his opera *The Water Carrier*, and, the greatest of all his works, *Requiem in C minor*.

Chest of Viols, a set of viols (usually two treble viols, three tenor viols, and one bass viol) matched in size, power and colour, fitted in a chest. Such sets of viols for chamber use were often made by English makers of the 16th and early 17th centuries.

Chest-Voice, a term commonly used for the lower sounds of the voice, and for higher sounds when forcefully produced in the same manner.

Child, William (b. Bristol 1606, d. Windsor 1697), was an organist and composer of church music.

Chime-Bells, a set of small hand bells arranged on a frame. Chime-bells were commonly used in churches with the organ during the Middle Ages.

Chitarrone, a large double necked lute, differing from the theobo or archlute by being smaller in body but longer in the neck.

Chladni, Ernst Florens Friedrich (b. Wittemberg 1756, d. Breslau 1827), was one of the founders of the modern study of acoustics. He is remembered particularly for his experiments showing the modes of vibration of glass and metal plates.

Choir or Quire, the part of a church where the services are celebrated east of the nave, or the singers who sit in the choir. Choir is also used with the same meaning as chorus — simply a body of singers, irrespective of the sacred or secular nature of what they sing.

Choir Organ, the third manual organ of a modern English church organ, played from the lowest keyboard. Its name is said to be derived from its employment for accompanying the choir. However, it is just as likely that Choir Organ is a corruption of Chair

Organ. Whatever may be the professed qualities of a true Choir Organ, it is sometimes in quality a small-scale replica of the main organ, but more often in effect a Solo Organ (particularly on medium-sized three manual organs).

Chopin, Frédéric François (b. Zelazowa Wola 1810, d. Paris 1849), was the son of a teacher of French. The Chopin family had been resident in Lorraine for some three generations at least. Chopin's father had come to Warsaw in 1787 as a bookkeeper, had joined the National Guard, and later become a teacher. His mother, said to be of a noble Polish family, was lady-in-waiting to Countess Skarbek, to whose son Chopin's father was tutor. Shortly after Chopin's birth the family moved to Warsaw, where his father held a number of academic appointments. Chopin was reared in an atmosphere of culture and from his youth was associated with the nobility. From about the age of twelve he received instruction in composition from the head of the Warsaw Conservatorium. He appears to have had no difficulty in beginning a career as a virtuoso pianist; in 1830 he left Warsaw, visiting Vienna, among other centres, on his way to Paris. His success as a pianist appears to have been limited to his interpretation of his own compositions. In 1832 and 1833 John Field was in Paris and undoubtedly influenced Chopin's development as a composer. Chopin's reputation as a writer for the pianoforte was steadily established; from 1835 onwards he rarely appeared in public as a pianist. In 1835 he visited Karlsbad, Dresden and Leipzig, meeting Mendelssohn and Schumann, and the next year made similar journeys. In 1837 he visited England mainly to seek medical advice; his delicate health began to decline and show unmistakable signs of pulmonary tuberculosis. Chopin did not marry. In 1835 he had been rejected by Maria, daughter of Count Wodzinski; from 1837 he was associated with the writer George Sand. The care given him by the latter undoubtedly helped him to maintain his health for a number of years, though the abrupt breaking of their association in 1847 was probably largely responsible for his rapid decline in health during his remaining two years. Chopin visited England again in 1848 to escape from the disturbance of the revolution; he returned to Paris in low spirits at the indifferent reception he received. He was buried in Paris.

Chopin's importance is solely as a composer for the solo pianoforte. His other compositions (a few songs and a little chamber music) are hardly worth notice. As a writer for the pianoforte he is pre-eminent, and established by his compositions those idioms peculiar to and characteristic of the pianoforte. His compositions include a set of twelve studies, a set of twenty-four preludes, a number of groups of waltzes, mazurkas, polonaises and nocturnes, and two concertos. His pianoforte music does not lend itself to orchestration; in fact, the accompaniment in his concertos is considered more effective when played on a second pianoforte, and his pianoforte music is invariably more effective in its original form than in any orchestrated version.

Choral or *Chorale*, commonly one of the hymn melodies of the German Evangelical Church. In providing the Evangelical Church with the material for congregational praise, Luther made use of official Latin hymns, earlier popular hymns and folk songs, translating and paraphrasing the words and adapting the tunes as well as writing new material. The choral became the inspiration and basis of the greater proportion of the sacred music and organ music of Bach.

Earlier, choral had implied those portions of the mass sung by the choir (or a few voices) such as the Introit, Tract and Kyrie. Choral is now used to imply concerted vocal as distinct from solo vocal compositions.

Chord, two or more notes sounded simultaneously. Chords are classed as concords or discords. Certain chords and groups of chords have special names:

(a) chords of two notes (these are named by the interval between the two notes),
(b) triads and their inversions,
(c) chords of the seventh and their inversions,
(d) chords of the ninth, eleventh and thirteenth and their inversions.
(e) certain chords of the sixth (most of them inversions of chords of the seventh).

These are described in the articles on concord, discord, triad, seventh and sixth.

Chorister, strictly speaking any singer in a choir. The title, however, is generally reserved for boy singers in cathedral, collegiate and church choirs.

Chorus, a body of singers, a composition written for such a body of singers or the refrain of a song in which all available singers join.

Chromatic, originally the name of a Greek scale form which was supposed to embody certain features of the later scale named after it. A melody, harmony or instrument is said to be chromatic when it employs or is able to produce the notes of the chromatic scale, and is not limited to a particular diatonic or harmonic scale. Individual notes or harmonies not natural in the normal diatonic scale are said to be chromatic in that scale.

Chromatic Scale, the succession of semitones, twelve to the octave, which is now the basis of Western music. The notation of this scale has never been, and could hardly be, consistent.

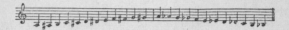

This may be considered the most convenient notation, but where chromatic chords in a particular key system are obviously derived from certain diatonic chords it is clearer to write them as chromatic alterations of the diatonic chord. In certain modern idioms where the chromatic scale rather than a diatonic scale is the starting point of the harmony or counterpoint employed, the notation appears to be inadequate, and no consistent system appears possible.

Chrysander, Friedrich (b. Lübthee 1826, d. Bergedorf 1901), is remembered for his researches on Handel, whose complete works he edited for the German Händel-Gesellschaft.

Cimarosa, Domenico (b. Naples 1749, d. Venice 1801), was the son of poor parents. He became one of the most popular Italian composers of opera of his day, and by some was considered to be a master of serious opera. His ability lay in comedy, his comic ópera *Il matrimonio segreto* (*The Secret Marriage*) being his most successful work.

Cither or *Cittern,* an instrument somewhat similar to the lute. The cither enjoyed considerable popularity in England and on the Continent during the 16th and 17th centuries. The cither should not be confused with the zither descended from it.

Clarabel Flute, an open wooden flue stop on English organs, of 8-foot pitch on the manuals. It is usually found on the Great Organ.

Clarinet, the single reed woodwind instrument of the orchestra. The clarinet has a cylindrical bore and overblows the twelfth. It is sounded from a single reed mouthpiece, and the pitch is varied by the pitch holes in the tube; its fingering is particularly complicated. Clarinets are now used in two sizes, that in B flat and that in A, both being treated as transposing instruments. The range in both cases is three octaves and a sixth.

This may be extended upwards according to the ability of the player. Normally only the bottom three octaves should be used.

The instrument is said to have been invented at Nuremberg by John Christopher Denner about 1690, though crude instruments, similar in principle, were known from ancient times. The chalumeau may be considered as the predecessor of the clarinet. The clarinet was remodelled about 1842 by Klosé, following the system of fingering evolved by Boehm for the flute.

Clarinet, a reed stop on English organs, of 8-foot pitch on the manuals. Its quality imitates that of the orchestral clarinet. It is usually found on the Choir Organ.

Clarion, a small trumpet of narrow bore.

Clarion, a reed organ stop of 4-foot pitch on the manuals.

Clarke, Jeremiah (b. *c.*1659, d. London 1707), became organist at St Paul's Cathedral in 1695, and later joint organist with Croft of the Chapel Royal. His compositions include a number of anthems and, jointly with Daniel Purcell and Leveridge, the music for two operas.

Classical, a term that is used in various senses. It is commonly used as synonymous with 'highbrow'. In this sense, it often erroneously implies that 'highbrow' music is inevitably complex and that it is above the appreciation of those who are not musical enthusiasts. The word classical is also used in the sense of that which has shown itself to be worthy over a period of time. In this sense classical is complementary to modern, and music of any period may, in time, become classical. In a third sense, classical describes the outlook and style of those composers who attempt to express ideas which are absolute. Such music must inevitably be expressed through the established forms or through forms which are in the process of being established. In this sense, classical is complementary to romantic.

Clavecin (Fr.), a harpsichord.

Clavichord, a keyboard stringed instrument, oblong in shape, placed upon a stand or legs. The clavichord evolved from the monochord, the earliest records of it dating from the beginning of the 15th century. The oldest existing clavichord is dated 1537, and is in the Metropolitan Museum, New York. The strings of the clavichord were set in vibration by brass tangents which also marked off the length of string to vibrate. Though its tone was weak, the player, by feeling the pressure of the tangent on the string, was able to control it and obtain a range of expression unrivalled by a keyboard stringed instrument until the invention of the pianoforte.

Clavicembalo (It.), a harpsichord. The Italian name means, literally, a keyed dulcimer.

Clavier (Fr.), the keyboard of any keyboard instrument; and (Ger.), any keyboard stringed instrument.

Clavicytherum (Lat.), a vertical harpsichord.

Clef, the sign placed at the beginning of each stave to indicate the absolute pitch of the notes on it. Three clefs are now in general use:

    𝄞   the G clef which indicates the G above middle C
    𝄢   the F clef which indicates the F below middle C
    𝄡   the C clef which indicates middle C itself

The first two are now commonly known as the treble clef and bass clef respectively and are invariably placed in the same position on the stave. The third is known as the soprano clef (the most rarely used), alto clef or tenor clef, according to its position on the stave.

A variation of the G clef is now often used for the tenor voice.

    𝄞 or (less satisfactory) 𝄞 𝄞

indicates that the pitch is an octave below that implied by the normal G clef.

The forms of the signs for the F clef and more particularly the C clef often vary:

    𝄢 or ℭ is used for the F clef
    𝄡, K or |H| for the C clef

All the clefs have been derived from the letters G, F and C with which they were originally identical.

Clemens non Papa (Jacques Clément) (b. before 1558) was a renowned and prolific composer. The name by which he became commonly known to distinguish him from Pope Clement VII, is proof of the high regard in which his contemporaries held him. His compositions include numerous masses and motets.

Clementi, Muzio (b. Rome 1752, d. Evesham 1832), was the son of a workman in silver who was interested in music. Clementi showed marked musical ability from an early age; he was brought to England when he was barely fourteen and continued his musical studies. Apart from two concert tours, he remained in

England till 1802, after which he visited in Russia, France, Germany and Italy before settling again in London in 1810.

Clementi is important as one of the first composers to distinguish between the harpsichord and piano. This he does in his many pianoforte sonatas for which he is justly remembered. Cramer and Field were among his many pupils. He was successful in establishing the firm of Clementi and Co., music publishers and pianoforte makers, of London.

Coates, Eric (b. Hucknall 1886), still living.

Cobbett, Walter Willson (b. Blackheath 1847, d. London 1937), was an amateur musician who rendered conspicuous service to the art of music. His *Cyclopedia of Chamber Music* is the most authoritative work on the subject.

Cobbold, William (b. Norwich 1560, d. Beccles 1639), contributed to *The Triumphes of Oriana* and helped to harmonise the tunes for the Psalter of 1592, published by Thomas East.

Coda (It.), tail. This term is used for the concluding section of a composition which, while falling outside the essential features of the particular form in which the composition is cast, often forms an important portion of the composition itself. A coda is essential to conclude a canon, and commonly occurs after the final variation of a set, at the end of a fugue, after the final recurrence of the theme of a rondo, after the da capo of a minuet and trio, and after the recapitulation of a movement in first movement form.

Codetta (It.), diminutive of 'coda'.

Coleridge-Taylor, Samuel (b. London 1875, d. Croydon 1912), was the son of a doctor. His mother was English, his father was a native of Sierra Leone. Coleridge-Taylor had a distinguished career as a student at the Royal College of Music. In 1898 he established his reputation as a composer with the first part of *Hiawatha*, the other two parts following in 1899 and 1900. Many of his later and smaller works have enjoyed a certain popularity, but *Hiawatha* remained his highest achievement.

Colla Parte (It.), with the part. Indicates that the accompaniment is to follow the speed of the solo part.

Colla Voce (It.), with the voice. Similar in sense to 'colla parte'.

Col Legno (It.), with the wood. Indicates to string players that they are to strike the strings with the wood of the bow.

Coloratura (It.), coloured. Vocal music which is highly coloured or figured with runs and ornaments.

Combination Pedals, pedals on an organ similar in use, in some respects, to composition pedals. They control the wind supply to groups or ranks of pipes independently of the stop action. A similar control is found on modern electric organs, particularly those built on the extension system. Ranks of pipes may be put out of action regardless of whether the stops controlling the registers derived from the particular rank under consideration are on or off.

Come Sopra (It.), as above.

Comic Opera, opera of a humorous character. The name is applied to a wide range of musical dramatic works, at one extreme approaching musical comedy, in which music is loosely associated with plays of a light amusing nature, at the other extreme the serious musical product of opera. In comic opera spoken dialogue is accepted as a recognised feature. The French opéra-comique, though beginning with the aim of amusement as one of its features and so including humour in its plot, was not comic opera in the sense in which this title is used in English.

Comma, the very small interval between notes ostensibly the same but calculated in different ways from a common source. Thus adding 4 fifths upwards from middle C, and then 2 octaves and a third upwards from middle C ostensibly produces the same note E. Calculating the addition of the intervals mathematically discloses a small difference between them, the common comma. A similar process with octaves on the one hand and fifths on the other produces a slightly larger difference, the Pythagorean comma.

Common Chord, a major or minor triad.

Common Time, those times which are a multiple of two but not three, such as two beats, four beats and eight beats in a bar.

Communion Service, the English counterpart of the Mass. As a musical art form, the Communion Service consists of settings of the same portions of the liturgy as those set in the Mass, with a few small modifications following the difference between the Latin and English liturgies.

Comodo (It.), convenient. Applied to speed.

Compass, the range of notes between the extreme limits which a voice or instrument is able to produce.

Compensating Valve, a variety of valve used on a brass wind instrument. Valves add a proportion to the natural length of the tube; consequently they do not add a sufficient proportion to the increased length of the tube when one of the other valves is already in use. As a result, valves in combination give notes which are too sharp; with two valves the effect is slight, but with three, serious. This deficiency has been overcome by the use of compensating valves; with these, the addition of a second valve adds an appropriately greater length of tubing than would be added by that valve used alone.

Composition Pedals, pedals placed above the pedal keyboard of an organ, serving the same purpose as pistons.

Compound Interval, an interval greater than an octave. A simple interval corresponds to each compound interval.

For many purposes, compound intervals are treated as equivalent to their corresponding simple interval.

Concertante (It.). This term distinguishes the solo from the accompanying instruments, particularly when the two do not have independent parts in tutti passages. Like 'ripieno' the complementary term, concertante belongs to old instrumental music and is found in such works as the concertos of Bach and Handel.

Concertina, a portable keyboard free reed instrument. The instrument consists of an expanding bellows between two hexagonal ends each with a keyboard. The instrument is made in various sizes, and was first designed in 1829 by Charles Wheatstone. Its resourcefulness has achieved for it a certain popularity, but it has not received any attention from serious composers.

Concerto, generally an extended instrumental composition for a solo performer accompanied by an orchestra. The name was first used at the beginning of the 17th century for motets with organ accompaniment, later with other instruments added to the organ, then for purely instrumental compositions in the church style, and towards the end of the century for similar secular compositions. The 'concerti grossi' of Torelli, Corelli, Vivaldi and Handel introduce the apposition of solo and accompanying instruments which became one of the prime features of the concerto.

Some, but by no means most, of the concertos of Bach and Handel treat one or a group of instruments in a solo fashion. In many instances the texture of the parts for the solo instruments is no different from that for the accompanying groups of instruments. The two groups merely give the opportunity for variety. The form of the concerto established by Mozart reserved this title for compositions designed largely to display the skill of the solo performer, in a form closely following that of the sonata. These features have since remained characteristic of the concerto, though, as with the sonata, many modifications and innovations have been introduced from time to time, and the title has sometimes been used in other senses.

The concertos of Mozart and Beethoven differed from their sonatas in certain features. The concertos (with very rare exceptions) had three movements, the third movement (minuet or scherzo) of the symphony for no obvious reason being left out. The first movement of the concerto was in first movement form, adapted to display the resources of a solo instrument combined with the orchestra. The second movement similarly corresponds to that in the sonata. The third and last movement was most often a rondo. The introduction of cadenzas is a special feature of concertos. In older concertos a cadenza was generally placed towards the end of the first movement, beginning on a second inversion of the tonic chord and ending with a long shake on the dominant chord. A cadenza was sometimes similarly placed towards the end of the second movement, and one or more short cadenzas in the last movement.

Beethoven introduced many innovations, the more important being the running together of the second and third movements, giving greater prominence to the orchestra and the writing himself of the cadenza to be played by the soloist.

Concertos for more than one solo instrument follow the same plan as the concerto for one solo instrument. Modern concertos, like the modern sonatas and symphonies, accept and reject precedent in their design with a considerable degree of freedom. Further, in a number of modern instances the title concerto is used in its 18th-century sense of a composition for a group of solo performers with or without accompaniment for an orchestra.

Concerto Grosso, a title belonging to the 17th and early 18th centuries. It was given to a concerto for a group of solo instruments with orchestral accompaniment as distinct from a concerto simply for a group of solo instruments.

Concord, a chord sounding satisfying by itself. The octave, fifth and fourth are classed as perfect concords. The major and minor fourths and fifths as imperfect concords. It will be noticed that the major and minor triads in root position and in their first and second inversions do not contain intervals other than those classed as concords; they are, therefore, also classed as concords.

The augmented fourth and diminished fifth are borderline between concord and discord, as are also the triads which incorporate them. The augmented triad, formed from the combination of two major thirds, is not considered as possessing the same inherently satisfying qualities as the major and minor triad, and is on the edge of the field of concordance. Clearly the division between discord and concord, being a matter of degree of dissonance, is somewhat arbitrary and a matter of usage. Modern harmonic systems hardly support the theory on which this distinction between concord and discord was made.

Conducting, directing the performance of a number of singers or instrumentalists. Conducting entails a control over the technical and artistic aspects of the performance, a clear indication of the speed and other broad features to which the individual performers must conform, and an insight into the intentions of the composer to admit a balanced artistic performance of the individual parts.

As early as the 15th century at least, it was customary for the beat to be given to the Sistine Choir. In the 18th century, the conducting was more or less divided between the first violin, who at times actually conducted with his bow, and the harpsichordist. Spohr, in 1820, was the first to conduct with a baton in London.

The end of the 19th century saw the rise of specialization in conducting, and a parallel improvement in the quality of orchestral performances. Unfortunately, conducting can be learnt only by conducting and the opportunities for learning are few and costly. Not infrequently public performances under the direction of a novice may be heard, but this does not diminish the desirability of orchestral performances being in the hands of technically and artistically able conductors.

Conductus, a form of composition used in the 12th and 13th centuries. Its distinguishing features appear to have been that the tenor was not taken from the church plainsong but was a popular song or original melody, and that words were not fitted to all the parts.

Conjunct Motion, the movement of a part by step. The complementary term is 'disjunct motion'. The example given in the article on 'contrary motion' (from an invention by Bach) is also an example of conjunct motion.

Con Moto (It.), with movement. Used to qualify indications of speed; also used as an indication of speed in the sense of 'rather fast'.

Consecutive, a term applied to adjacent occurrences of a particular interval between two parts or voices. This term is especially applied to a succession of octaves or fifths (commonly referred to as 'consecutives'). Generally speaking, the techniques of the 16th, 17th, 18th and 19th centuries avoided consecutives between parts or voices which had any semblance of independence.

The consecutives marked in (a) are typical of the kind occurring in unskilful work and should be avoided. Those marked in (b) cause no evil effect. The third example shows how consecutives are avoided by the crossing of parts. Modern techniques have made deliberate use of consecutives.

Console, the part of an organ from which it is played; that is, the keyboards, stops and accessories as distinct from the motor, bellows and pipes.

Consonance, the pleasing effect of a concord. The degree of consonance depends on the ratio of the frequencies of the notes concerned; the more simple the ratio the more consonant the interval.

octave	1 : 2	—	
fifth	2 : 3	fourth	3 : 4
major third	4 : 5	minor sixth	5 : 8
minor third	5 : 6	major sixth	3 : 5

The relation between the ratios corresponding to intervals which are inversions of each other should be noticed.

Con Sordini (It.), with mutes. Indicates to string players that mutes are to be used. Mutes for the violins seem to have been first used by Lully.

Consort, the 16th- and 17th-century name for a group of instruments playing together. A consort of like instruments such as treble, tenor and bass viols is described as whole, while one of mixed instruments, such as lute, flute and viols is described as broken.

Continuo (It.), short for basso continuo, translated thorough-bass or through-bass, a part played continuously throughout a composition, generally from a figured bass. The custom of having an accompaniment part to be played continuously throughout a composition from a bass part arose towards the end of the 16th century. During the 17th and 18th centuries, the accompaniment of a recitative was commonly left entirely to the continuo. Compositions for a few instruments depended largely on an extemporary accompaniment from the continuo to supply the harmonic background to their melodic lines; even compositions with a full texture remained incomplete without a continuo.

Towards the end of the 18th century the practice of writing a figured bass continuo was gradually discontinued, keyboard accompaniments when required being written out in full by the composer. The problem of supplying adequate continuo accompaniments for the compositions of Purcell and Bach and their contemporaries continually receives the attention of musical scholars. Many of the inartistic renderings of the figured basses supplied by editors are, not even faithful to the original text.

Strictly speaking, a figured bass and a thorough-bass are not synonymous. A thorough-bass should be continuous and be formed from the lowest part, generally of course the bass, though from an upper part wherever the bass has rests.

Contralto, a woman's voice with a low range.

Contrary Motion, the movement of parts moving in opposite directions.

Invention No. 6
BACH

Contredanse (Fr.), a term now generally accepted as being a corruption of 'Country Dance', at the same time implying (by false etymology) a dance in which the dancers were arranged in rows facing one another, as was the case with the majority of English country dances.

Cooper, John (b. c. 1570, d. 1627), was an English musician. He travelled in Italy, sometime before 1604, and subsequently called himself Coprario. His compositions include a number of pieces for strings and for the organ, and he contributed to *The Teares or Lamentacions* compiled by Leighton.

Copula, a form of descant used during the early polyphonic period in which a florid part sounded against one or more notes of the plainsong, generally at a cadence.

Cor Anglais, the medium double reed woodwind instrument of the orchestra, very similar to the oboe. It is built a fifth below the oboe, and is treated as a transposing instrument, sounding a fifth lower than written. Its history follows that of the oboe.

Corelli, Arcangelo (b. Fusignano 1653, d. Rome 1713), was a violinist and composer about whose early life little is known. Before 1685 he settled in Rome and lived under the patronage of Cardinal Ottoboni, for the most time living at the Cardinal's Palace. His importance in musical history is twofold. As a great violinist, though hardly an innovator, he established a style of playing which influenced the subsequent development of violin technique. As a composer he contributed to the advancement of both concerted and solo string music and the extended instrumental forms in his concerti grossi and sonatas.

Corkine, William (f. 1610–12), was an English musician. His published songs are included in *The English School of Lutenist Songwriters*.

Cornelius, Peter (b. Mainz 1824, d. there 1874), was a close relation of the painter Peter Cornelius. Cornelius was a notable composer and author. His songs and choral works are his most important compositions.

Cornet, a brass wind instrument with valves, similar to the trumpet. The bore of the cornet is more tapering than that of the trumpet, making the lower harmonics more readily obtainable. The cornet is usually in B flat and A, shanks for both pitches being built into the one instrument. A small E flat cornet is also used in military and wind bands. The cornet can be played with greater facility than the trumpet, but is inferior to it in brilliance and dignity, having a more vocal quality of tone.

Cornett, a wind instrument, usually of wood, played from a cupped mouthpiece of horn, ivory or wood, with finger holes. Cornetts were usually curved and of three sizes, a small treble cornett, the ordinary cornett and the great cornett. The cornett was popular from the 10th to the 18th century.

Cornyshe, William (b. c. 1465, d. 1523), was an English composer, dramatist and actor. He attended Henry VIII at the Field of the Cloth of Gold, and was important as a composer of secular music to humorous and satirical words by Skelton and others.

Cosyn, Benjamin (f. 1622-1643), was an English composer and organist. He is remembered chiefly by his collection of virginal music, *Benjamin Cosyn's Virginal Book*. He was organist of Alleyn's College in Dulwich, and subsequently of Charterhouse.

Counterpoint, the art of combining melodies or, more strictly, adding a second melody to a first. The term counterpoint and its adjective contrapuntal differ in use rather than meaning from polyphony and polyphonic, the former being used for the academic practice of composition embodying the interplay of melodies, and the latter for the compositions displaying this feature as their prime characteristic, in which the interest of the harmony is of markedly subsidiary if not negligible interest.

The term counterpoint, but not polyphony, is extended to music of any period. The first period of contrapuntal evolution culminated in Palestrina and Byrd (the end of the 'polyphonic period'); the second, building on the harmonic systems initiated by Monteverdi and other composers of the first homophonic period, culminated in Bach. And, so it would appear, the stabilization of each fresh development in the harmonic system gives scope for a new counterpoint.

For convenience the study of counterpoint may be isolated to a limited degree from that of harmony, melody, rhythm and form, and contrapuntal exercises have been highly conventionalized. Five standard species of counterpoint against a canto fermo are recognized, First, Second and Third Species being respectively one, two and four notes in the counterpoint to each note in the canto fermo, Fourth Species being a syncopated form of First Species (the counterpoint being a chain of suspensions), and Fifth Species a mixture of the features of the other species examples. These five species are, however, only a few of the methods of strict counterpoint enumerated by such as Morley.

These examples obey the rules of strict counterpoint as expounded by Kitson and others. They do no more than indicate the essential difference between the species; the rules vary from one authority to another.

The practice of counterpoint by exercises was in the first place a training for free composition. By the time of Fux, contrapuntal exercises had become a training for an otherwise obsolete church style, based on tradition rather than on a scholarly knowledge of Palestrina, Byrd and the other important composers of the polyphonic period. As the outlook on music became less modal and more squarely rhythmical, contrapuntal exercises changed their character and rules. In modern times there has been a reaction towards a scholarly analysis of 16th-century music, as for instance in Knud Jeppesen's masterly study *The Style of Palestrina and the Dissonance*. A revision of the rules for the purpose of strict exercises in the style of the 16th century would be quite feasible. However, there is a growing tendency to approach the study of counterpoint through the later contrapuntal style of Bach and Handel, and to relate the practice of strict exercises to it.

Country Dance, a dance originally associated with country folk rather than with the ballroom. The term is a generic one, applicable to a whole series of figure dances originating on the English village green. Many of them became popular at court during the Elizabethan period, and appear to have been introduced into France towards the end of the 17th century, probably to the court of Louis XIV. The music and steps of a great number of dances have been preserved in Playford's *English Dancing Master*, and in recent years the English Folk Dance Society has fostered a revival of their use.

Couperin, François (b. Paris 1668, d. there 1733), was the most distinguished member of a family of musicians who flourished from the middle of the 17th to the early 19th century. He was organist of the King's Chapel from 1693, and of St Gervais from 1685 till his death. Some of his vocal choral music was published during his lifetime. Though he is said to have been a good organist, Couperin wrote little, if any, organ music. His importance is as a composer for the clavecin, an instrument on which he is reputed to have been a first-class performer. His music for the clavecin clearly had considerable influence on the clavier music of Bach, and on its own merit takes an important place in the history of keyboard music.

Coupler, a device on the organ by which the stops drawn may be sounded in some way other than the ordinary. The couplers usually found are those coupling each manual to the pedals, so that any stop drawn on the manual sounds on the pedals (but not conversely), those coupling the manuals together, so that any stop drawn on one manual sounds on the manual to which it is coupled, and those coupling the octave and sub-octave to the unison, so that any stop drawn sounds not only at the unison but also the octave or sub-octave as the case may be. The precise effect of any coupler depends on the nature of the action of the organ, tracker, pneumatic, electric as the case may be. With some actions one coupler will work through another, for instance 'Swell to Great' plus 'Great to Pedal' will effect the sounding of the Swell Organ on the pedals. Again, with some actions, usually the more primitive, the keys of the coupled manual are depressed by the coupling action.

Two aspects of the octave and sub-octave couplers call for comment. They invariably act indiscriminately on all the stops on the manual concerned, and they are ineffective over the top and bottom octave, the sub-octave coupler over the bottom octave and the octave coupler over the top octave.

On a large organ octave and sub-octave couplers are considered superfluous as well as inartistic, and in a small organ they are more artistically replaced by a judicious use of the extension system.

Couplers are also used on the harpsichord, especially on modern ones. The device has also been applied to the pianoforte, but without much success.

Courante, a dance form often found in the suite. The dance, of French origin, was in duple time; in the suite, however, the courante changed to three-two or three-four time. It begins with a short note, has dotted rhythms as a common characteristic, has its last bar in effect in six-four or six-eight time, and consists of two sections each repeated.

Partita No. 4
BACH

and
ending

The Italian courante is a distinct form. Running passages are its typical feature, so making it more closely akin than the French courante to the etymological meaning of their title.

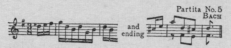

Cowen, Sir Frederic Hymen (b. Jamaica 1852, d. London 1935), achieved distinction as a conductor and composer.

Cramer, Johann Baptist (b. Mannheim 1771, d. London 1858), was the best known member of a family of German musicians. He was an eminent pianist, and influenced the development of pianoforte playing; his piano studies are excellent. In 1824 he founded the firm of Cramer, music publishers, of London.

Crescendo (It.), increasing. Indicates a gradual increase in volume from soft to loud.

Cristofori, Bartolommeo di Francesco (b. 1655, d. 1731), was a harpsichord maker who worked first in Padua and later in Florence. He is credited with the invention of the pianoforte.

Croft, William (b. Nether Ettington 1678, d. Bath 1727), became organist of Westminster Abbey in 1708. He made a number of notable contributions to English church music, among them his setting of the Burial Service. The well-known tune *St Anne,* to which *O God our help* is sung, is attributed to him.

Crotch, William (b. Norwich 1775, d. Taunton 1847), was an organist and a distinguished teacher. He became Professor of Music at Oxford, and was the first Principal of the Royal Academy of Music.

Crotchet, a quarter of a semibreve. It is written ♩, and its corresponding rest ↱ or ↯.

Crüger, Johann (b. near Guben 1598, d. 1662), was cantor of St Nicolaus, Berlin, from 1622 till his death. He is remembered as a composer of chorals.

Crwth, the old Welsh name for a bowed stringed instrument which preceded the viol.

Cue, a portion of one part indicated in another to assist the performer of the latter in making an entry after being silent for a period.

Cue-ing, the practice of marking in one part some other part, so that it may be played by the performer of the first part if a performer for the second is not available.

Cui, César Antonovitch (b. Vilna 1835, d. St. Petersburg 1918), was the son of a French officer who was unable to retreat from Moscow in 1812. Cui showed a marked aptitude for music at an early age, but was trained at the School of Military Engineering in Petersburg. He was one of the first disciples of Balakirev, and was one of the important early composers of the school of Russian national music, though he has not gained the success and popularity of many of his contemporaries. His opera *Angelo* has been regarded as his finest work, but it has not achieved popularity, and Cui is at his best in small-scale compositions.

Cummings, William Hayman (b. Sidbury 1831, d. London 1915), was a singer and organist. He became Principal of the Guildhall School of Music. He possessed a splendid library of music, which included many rare copies of early music, now in the British Museum.

Cupped Mouthpiece, a mouthpiece of the kind used with the trumpet, horn and other brass instruments. The shape of the cup greatly affects the quality and range of the notes produced from a particular instrument. The cup of the trumpet mouthpiece is hemispherical, that of the horn funnel shaped, and those of the trombone and other brass instruments intermediate between these extremes.

CUPPED MOUTHPIECES

Trumpet   Horn

(longitudinal section)

Curtall, the 16th-century English name for the bassoon.

Curwen, John (b. Heckmondwike 1816, d. Manchester 1880), was the founder of the Tonic Sol-fa method of teaching sight-singing. In 1863 he founded the firm of Curwen, music publishers, of London.

Cushion Dance, an English action dance popular during the 16th and 17th centuries.

Cymbals, two thin round metal plates held by a leather strap through the centre of each. The cymbals may be sounded in a variety of ways, by striking them together or with a drum stick.

Czerny, Karl (b. Vienna 1791, d. there 1857), was the son of a musician and became a fine pianist, a prolific composer, and a most successful teacher. His studies for the pianoforte are, perhaps deservedly, the best known of his compositions.

D

Da Capo (It.), from the beginning. Indicates a repetition from the beginning.

D'Albert, Eugene Francis Charles (b. Glasgow 1864, d. in Germany 1932), was the son of French parents. He was a pianist and a composer particularly of German opera.

Dale, Benjamin James (b. London 1885, d. there 1943), achieved distinction as a composer.

Dal Segno (It.), from the sign. Indicates a repetition from the sign 𝄋

Daman, William (d. *c.* 1590), was an English musician. He harmonized the psalm tunes in four parts with the tune in the tenor, and again with the tune in the highest part.

Damper, of a pianoforte, essentially a pad of felt, controlled by the key, which stops a string vibrating after the key is released.

Damper Pedal, the pedal on a pianoforte which raises all the dampers, regardless of whether any keys are depressed.

Dance Form, any form derived from a dance. The dance forms commonly found in music may be summarized as (a) those found in the suite, (b) the minuet, adopted as a movement of the sonata and symphony, (c) the chaconne and passacaglia, (d) the waltz and (e) the numerous national dances, old and new, which have given rise to instrumental compositions often related to them in little more than name. The essential characteristics of dance forms are their simplicity of structure, and their use of metrical figures characteristic of the individual dances. Even where there is a clear link between a dance form and the characteristics of the dance from which it has been derived, the treatment of those characteristics is invariably such as to make the instrumental form quite different in effect from the original dance, and quite unsuitable for dancing.

Dancing, the graceful and rhythmical movement of the body, usually to music. The dance has importance in music in three ways. Popular dancing, whether on the village green or in the ballroom, calls for music conforming to clearly defined patterns. Many instrumental and sometimes vocal dance forms have been derived from dances. Ballet has become an independent sophisticated art combining dancing and music.

There is no essential difference between the relatively artless dances of country folk and the cultured dances of lords and ladies. In folk art, song and dance have been inseparably interwoven. The origin of many old dances and their tunes had been forgotten long before they were recorded. Thoinot Arbeau in his *Orchésographie* of 1589, and John Playford in his *Dancing Master* of 1651, have preserved the details of numerous dances (steps, words and tunes), many of them already obsolete by the time they recorded them. Even the origin of many later dances is obscure. The differences between dances of the same name, claiming to be versions of the same dance, are often greater than the difference between dances with distinct names. Innumerable dances, mostly varying in detail and name rather than in their essential characteristics, are to be found wherever local tradition is still strong.

Danyel, John (b. c. 1565, d. 1630), was an English musician. His published songs are included in *The English School of Lutenist Songwriters*.

Daquin, Louis Claude (b. Paris 1694, d. there 1772), showed a marked musical ability from a very early age. He became an accomplished and successful organist. His first volume of pieces for the harpsichord contains the well-known *Coucou*.

Dargomijsky, Alexander Sergeivich (b. Toula 1813, d. St Petersburg 1869), was educated in St Petersburg and received musical instruction from an early age. His attention to music increased after a meeting with Glinka. He occupies an important place in the history of Russian opera, his dramatic compositions forming the main part of his small output.

Dash, the sign ▼ placed above or below a note. The dash indicates that the note is to be played markedly staccato.

David, Félicien César (b. Vaucluse 1810, d. St Germain-en-Laye 1876), was a composer who influenced the composition of dramatic works of oriental character. Such works as Verdi's *Aïda* owe much to David's innovations. His most important composition, *Le Désert*, a vocal choral work, reflected his impressions of the East.

Davies, Sir Henry Walford (b. Oswestry 1869, d. near Bristol 1941), achieved distinction as an organist, teacher and composer. He was appointed Professor of Music in the University of Wales in

1919, Gresham Professor of Music in 1924, and became Master of the King's Musick. He was knighted in 1922.

Davy, Richard (f. late 15th and early 16th centuries), was an English composer mainly of church music. A setting of the Passion by him, parts of which are extant, is one of the earliest known English examples of this form.

Davy, John (b. Dunwich 1552, d. London 1584), was one of the earliest English music typographers. His publications included a number of psalters.

Debussy, Claude Achille (b. St Germain-en-Laye 1862, d. Paris 1918), kept the circumstances of his childhood a mystery. He appears to have been the son of a china shop proprietor. Debussy entered the Paris Conservatoire in 1873; eleven years later he won the Grand Prix de Rome for his cantata *L'Enfant prodigue*. Apart from a short stay in Moscow and a longer one in Italy, he spent his life in Paris as a composer. He held no public appointments and made only rare appearances as a conductor or as a pianist. He conducted his own compositions twice in London, in 1908 and 1909.

Debussy was among the first to break away from the melodic and harmonic conventions of the 18th and 19th centuries, and has been described as the founder of modern musical impressionism. He made extensive use of chords built from the higher members of the harmonic series, and from the whole tone scale.

His piano music includes *Two Arabesques, Suite Bergamasque, Children's Corner Suite*, two sets of three *Images* and two sets of twelve *Preludes*, and the *Petite Suite* for piano duet. Among his best orchestral pieces are *L'Après-midi d'un faune* and the three orchestral *Nocturnes*. His setting of *La Damoiselle élue* and his opera *Pelléas et Mélisande* are the best known of his works for voices and orchestra. His chamber music includes a string quartet, and a number of his songs are among his best compositions.

Decani, the counterpart of 'cantoris'.

Decrescendo (It.), decreasing. Similar in sense to 'diminuendo'.

Degree, the step from one note to the next in the musical alphabet regardless of the actual interval involved. Thus, A♭♭, A♭ A, A♯ and A✕ are said to be of the same degree while A✕, B and C♭ are not.

Delibes, Clément Philibert Léo (b. St Germain du Val 1836, d. Paris 1891), began to study music in the Paris Conservatoire in 1848. He became accompanist at the Théâtre Lyrique and at the

Opéra in 1863. He began composing dramatic works from an early time. He is remembered mainly by his ballet *Coppélia*.

Delius, Frederick (b. Bradford 1862, d. Grez-sur-Loing 1934), was the son of a wealthy German merchant who refused to let his son devote himself to music. When he was twenty years old, Delius left home and spent four years in Florida cultivating oranges and studying music. He returned to Europe and studied at the Leipzig Conservatorium, where he came under the influence of Grieg. From 1890 onwards he lived mainly in France, Grieg having persuaded his father to let him follow music as his career. Delius married Jelka Rosen, an artist, in 1897, and they lived at Grez-sur-Loing till his death. During the last years of his life Delius, blind and paralyzed, dictated a number of works to Eric Fenby.

Though he made little effort himself to obtain performance of his music, by 1910 the distinctive nature of his style was widely appreciated in England and Germany. Most of his music is pictorial and he was markedly influenced by the varying circumstances of his life. The very considerable demands made on a conductor's understanding of Delius' music is the probable reason for the comparative rarity of its performance.

The operas *Koanga* and *A Village Romeo and Juliet,* and the incidental music to *Hassan* are among his principal works for the stage. *Brigg Fair, On hearing the first Cuckoo in Spring, Appalachia* and *Over the Hills and Far Away* are typical examples of his orchestral music. *Sea Drift* is representative of his best for voices and orchestra. These, with several concertos, a little chamber music and some songs, indicate the range of his compositions.

Demisemiquaver, a thirty-second of a semibreve. It is written ♪ or in groups 𝅘𝅥𝅰𝅘𝅥𝅰𝅘𝅥𝅰, and its corresponding rest 𝄿.

Dering, Richard (d. 1630), was an English musician. He was educated in Italy. A number of volumes of his sacred music were published in Antwerp and London during his lifetime. Some music for viols by him is also extant.

Descant, the name given to polyphony from its inception until at least the end of the 16th century, and used in various more or less restricted senses. More particularly, descant implied the art of adding a second part to a given part, and was commonly used as the name of the first part so added. The modern use of descant, therefore, as the name of a free part added above a given melody, such as a hymn tune, is in keeping with its origin.

Development, the changes contributing to the musical growth of subject which gradually disclose the implications and latent

possibilities of it. Also the section of a composition mainly concerned with these changes.

Diapason, a term, derived from Greek, originally meaning an
octave; later, in France, it meant a tuning fork, and then the
pitch given by the tuning fork.

Diapason, the common name for the chief flue stop on English
organs, of 8-foot pitch on the manuals and 16-foot pitch on the
pedals. Diapasons are either open or stopped. Open diapasons
on the manuals are invariably of metal, on the pedals sometimes
of wood. Stopped diapasons are normally of wood.

Diaphonia, a term used during the early polyphonic period as the
equivalent of dissonance, and also for various forms of descant.

Diatonic, originally one of the Greek scale forms, which was supposed
to embody certain features of the later scale named after it.
Apart from the accidentals which different forms of the minor
scale involve, diatonic melody or harmony in the key of the
signature will not require the use of accidentals. A modulation
need not necessarily involve melody or harmony which is not
diatonic.

Dibdin, Charles (b. Southampton 1745, d. Camden Town 1814),
composed the music for a great number of stage entertainments
for many of which he also wrote the words.

Dieren, Bernard van (b. Holland 1884, d. London 1936), was educated
for a scientific career. He settled in London in 1909, and his
earliest compositions which have been preserved date from 1912.

Differential Tones, the more important of the two kinds of resultant
tones.

Diminished Interval, an interval a semitone less than one which is
perfect or minor.

(a)   (b)   (c)   (d)   (e)   (f)   (g)   (h)

(a) perfect fifth	(e) minor third
(b) diminished fifth	(f) diminished third
(c) perfect fourth	(g) minor seventh
(d) diminished fourth	(h) diminished seventh

Three of the more common chords which incorporate diminished
intervals are:

(1)   the diminished triad and its inversions which include the
diminished fourth and fifth,

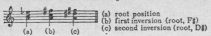

(a) root position
(b) first inversion (root, F♯)
(c) second inversion (root, D♯)

(2) the chord of the diminished seventh which may be formed from the diminished triad by adding a diminished seventh to it,

(3) the chord

It will be noticed that this chord and the chord

differ in notation but not in the notes corresponding to them on the keyboard. The difference is one of treatment.

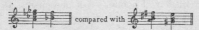

compared with

Diminuendo (It.), diminishing. Indicates a gradual lessening in volume from loud to soft.

Diminution, the proportionate decrease of the note values of a theme. This term is the antithesis of 'augmentation'.

Direct, the sign ⌇ used as a warning of the first note on the next line or page.

Direct Psalmody, the simplest method of singing the psalms, used in the Christian church from early times. It survives in only a few special uses.

Discord, a chord causing a sense of dissatisfaction to the ear and a desire for a subsequent chord on which the discord may be resolved. All chords other than those classed as concords are classed as discords. Familiarity makes discords more readily acceptable, so that chords at one time considered discordant and requiring preparation and resolution are now treated with the same freedom as those chords formerly recognized as concordant.

Disjunct Motion, the movement of a part by leap, the complementary term to 'conjunct motion'.

Pianoforte Sonata No. 5, Op. 10, No. 1
BEETHOVEN

Dissonance, the complementary term to consonance. It is the unpleasant effect, however slight, of the beats between the fundamental tones, overtones or resultant tones of two or more notes sounded together. The dissonances of many chords is so slight as to pass unnoticed. The ear readily accepts both the major and minor triads as concords, though the relatively lesser dissonance of the major triad makes it more satisfactory as a final chord than the minor triad.

Dithyramb, originally the name of an ancient Greek wild choral hymn in honour of the god of wine, Dionysus (Bacchus). It is sometimes used as the title for compositions.

Dittersdorf, Karl Ditters von (b. Vienna 1739, d. near Neuhaus 1799), was a distinguished violinist and popular composer. His output of all kinds was prolific, but he enjoyed his greatest success with his operas.

Divertimento (It.), the title with which Haydn generally headed his string quartets. Mozart used it for several instrumental compositions consisting of a number of movements. It is also used for an arrangement of a selection of items from, for instance, an opera.

Divertissement (Fr.), nominally the equivalent of 'divertimento', but used in various senses — a short ballet, a group of pieces on given themes, and so on.

Divided Stop, any stop on the organ controlled in two parts, one stop handle controlling the treble pipes, another the bass pipes.

Divisi (It.), divided. Indicates that a group of players playing in unison are to divide into two or more parts.

Do, the later name used in place of 'ut' for the first note or tonic of the scale in solmisation.

Doh, the first note or tonic of the scale in Tonic Sol-fa.

Dohnányi, Erno von (b. Presburg 1877), still living.

Dolce (It.), sweetly. An indication of style, usually, though not essentially, associated with 'piano'.

Dolmetsch, Arnold (b. Le Mans 1858, d. Haslemere 1940), became well known as a student of old musical instruments and their music. *The Interpretation of the Music of the XVII and XVIII Centuries* is his most important work.

Doloroso (It.), painful. Used in the sense of 'with poignant expression'.

Dominant, the fifth note of any scale in the modern key system. In the various modal systems the position of the dominant varied.

Dominant Seventh, the principal chord derived from the dominant triad.

(a) the dominant triad; (b), (c), (d) and (e) the chord of the dominant seventh in root position, first, second and third inversion respectively.

This chord plays a prominent part in defining key in music written in the major and minor key system. The chord of the dominant seventh followed by the tonic triad leaves no room for ambiguity in key.

Further additions of thirds (one above each other) to the chord of the dominant seventh form the chords of the dominant ninth, dominant eleventh and dominant thirteenth.

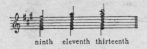

ninth   eleventh   thirteenth

The full chord of the thirteenth rarely occurs, the fifth and eleventh being usually omitted. The chords of the dominant seventh, dominant eleventh and dominant thirteenth are resolved by moving to the tonic triad or, alternatively, to the submediant triad.

(the chord of the dominant thirteenth, marked *, with the fifth and eleventh omitted, resolving on the tonic triad).

Donizetti, Gaetano (b. Bergamo 1797, d. there 1848), became famous as a composer of operas. His first opera was produced in 1818, and this was followed by the regular production of a long series. Among his more important operas are *Lucrezia Borgia* and *Lucia di Lammermoor*, and the comic operas *La Fille du Régiment* (which achieved great popularity in England), and *Don Pasquale*. His operas fed the fashion for displaying the virtuosity of the singers and fall far below the level reached by Rossini and Verdi.

Dot (placed after a note or rest), the sign increasing the duration of the note by half; whereas a semibreve equals two minims, a dotted semibreve equals three minims, and so on.

𝅝	=	2 𝅗𝅥		𝅝.	=	3 𝅗𝅥
𝅗𝅥	=	2 ♩		𝅗𝅥.	=	3 ♩
♩	=	2 ♪		♩.	=	3 ♪
♪	=	2 ♬		♪.	=	3 ♬
♬	=	2 ♬		♬.	=	3 ♬

and similarly for rests. A second dot adds half as much again as the first dot, and so on.

$$\text{𝅗𝅥. } = \text{ 𝅗𝅥 } + \text{ ♩}$$
$$\text{𝅗𝅥.. } = \text{ 𝅗𝅥 } + \text{ ♩ } + \text{ ♪}$$
$$\text{𝅗𝅥... } = \text{ 𝅗𝅥 } + \text{ ♩ } + \text{ ♪ } + \text{ ♪}$$

In older music the value of the dot was variable, the precise duration of a dotted note in a particular context being decided by taste and common sense. The double dot was introduced by Leopold Mozart in 1769 to avoid this inexactitude, and Wolfgang Mozart used a triple dot.

Dot (placed over or under a note or chord), the sign of 'staccato'.

Double (Fr.), the name commonly used until the 18th century for variations. A double, however, consisted of a decoration of the melody alone, the harmony of the original remaining unchanged.

Double, an organ stop sounding an octave lower than the normal pitch for stops of its name.

Double Bar, a double line across the stave. It is used to divide a movement into sections, usually at a pause or repeat, and to mark the end of a movement.

Double Bass, the largest member of the strings of the orchestra. Its four strings are usually tuned

Sometimes a fifth string is added sounding the lower C. The double bass sounds an octave lower than written, the octave

transposition not being shown in the part. The normal compass of the double bass is about two and a half octaves. It is far less agile than the other three members of the violin family, but played pizzicato it is particularly effective.

Double Bassoon, the bass double reed woodwind instrument of the orchestra, very similar to the ordinary bassoon. It is built one octave below the bassoon, and sounds an octave lower than written; its range is about two and a half octaves.

Double Chant, an Anglican chant of double length.

Double Concerto, a concerto for two solo instrumentalists.

Double Counterpoint, two part invertible counterpoint.

Double Diapason, a diapason organ stop of 16 foot pitch on the manuals or 32 foot pitch on the pedals.

Double Flat, the sign ♭♭ which lowers a note one tone from its natural pitch. It is contradicted by ♭ or ♮ according to whether the note is flat or not by reason of the key signature.

Double Fugue, a fugue on two subjects which are stated together in the exposition, or, more rarely, in which the second subject appearing later receives prominence in its treatment together with the first subject.

Doubles, changes rung on a peal of five bells, so called since at each permutation two pairs of bells interchange.

Double Sharp, the sign ✕ which raises a note one tone from its natural pitch. It is contradicted by ♯ or ♮ according to whether the note is sharp or not by reason of the key signature.

Double Stopping, the sounding together of two notes on an instrument of the violin family. The term is used regardless of whether either or both of the notes are produced from open strings.

Double Tonguing, a method of tonguing used on certain wind instruments for playing quick passages. The tongue moves as in saying alternately the letter T with the letter D or K. Double tonguing is particularly applicable to the flute and cornet; it is not possible on the oboe, clarinet and bassoon, which can employ only single tonguing.

Double Touch, a device sometimes found on the keyboards of organs. The keys of a manual keyboard having double touch may be depressed beyond the normal (first) touch to a second touch which brings into play stops not affected by the first touch.

Down Beat, the downward movement of a conductor's arm or stick. The down beat invariably corresponds to the first beat in the bar; hence the term down beat is often used as meaning the first beat in the bar without any reference to a conductor.

Down Bow, the movement of the bow across the strings of a member of the violin family from the player's left to his right. In the case of the violin and viola this is generally more or less downwards. A down bow is indicated by the sign ⊓ placed above a note.

Dowland, John (b. 1563, d. London 1626), was an English musician. Few details are known about his life. He visited France in 1580, in the services of the English ambassador, and became a Roman Catholic, which appears to have gone against his advancement in England. He travelled from court to court in Germany and Italy and in 1598 was appointed an instrumentalist to King Christian IV of Denmark; he failed to return from a second visit to England and was dismissed in 1606. He professed re-conversion to Protestantism and in 1616 was appointed as lutenist to King James.

Dowland was outstanding amongst English lutenist song-writers, and as a virtuoso on the lute was probably unrivalled in Europe. Five volumes of airs to the lute by him were published during his lifetime, the last, under the title of *A Pilgrim's Solace*, 84 songs in all; and another three were included in *A Musical Banquet* published by his son Robert. He contributed to *The Teares or Lamentacions* compiled by Leighton, and helped to harmonize the tunes for the Psalter of 1592 published by Thomas East. His published volumes of songs are included in *The English School of Lutenist Songwriters*, and some of his lute music has been transcribed by Peter Warlock.

Drone, any one of the lower pipes of the bagpipe which sound one continuous note. A bass 'pedal' similar in effect to the drone of a bagpipe, as is common in a musette, is often referred to as a drone bass.

Drone, a bowed monochord used by wandering minstrels in England until the beginning of the 19th century.

Drum, any percussion instrument consisting of a skin stretched over a frame. The drums now commonly used are the kettledrum, the bass drum and the side drum, and, to a lesser extent, the tenor drum.

Dubois, François Clément Théodore (b. Marne 1837, d. Paris 1924), was a brilliant pupil at the Paris Conservatoire and gained success as a composer, but his importance was mainly as a teacher at the Conservatoire, of which he was head from 1896 to 1905.

Duet, a composition for two singers or instrumentalists who share the interest of the music. The commonest uses of this term are in association with voices and with the pianoforte. A composition for two instrumentalists in the form of a sonata is commonly called sonata rather than duet.

Dufay, Guillermus (b. before 1400, d. Cambrai 1474), was a leader of the Netherland School of polyphonic composers. The established facts of his life are few. Most of his compositions are in manuscript in the Archives of the Sistine Chapel and Vatican Library.

Dukas, Paul (b. Paris 1865, d. there 1935), achieved distinction as a composer, particularly of music for the stage. His opera *Ariadne and Bluebeard* and his symphonic scherzo *The Prentice Sorcerer* are representative of his best work.

Dulcet, an organ stop similar to the dulciana but of 4-foot pitch on the manuals.

Dulciana, a small scale open metal organ stop of 8-foot pitch on the manuals.

Dulcimer, an ancient stringed instrument in which the strings were struck by hammers. It is, therefore, considered the ancestor of the pianoforte. It is the national instrument of Hungary, and is still constantly played there, and in Hungarian bands in other countries. It may occasionally still be seen played in the streets of London.

Dulcitone, a keyboard instrument similar to the celesta but having tuning forks instead of metal plates.

Dumka, used by Dvořák in his chamber music as the title of a melancholy movement.

Dump, used in 16th- and 17th-century instrumental music as the title of a melancholy piece.

Duncan, William Edmonstoune (b. Sale 1866, d. there 1920), achieved some success as a writer of popular books on music, such as *The Story of Minstrelsy* and *The Story of Carol.*

Dunhill, Thomas Frederick (b. London 1877, d. Windsor 1946), achieved distinction as a composer and writer. His light opera *Tantivy Towers* met with success, and his book *Chamber Music: a Treatise for Students* has become a standard work.

Dunstable, John (d. 1453), was an English musician. He was the foremost contributor of his time to the development of the new art of polyphony (in which England appears to have been leading); he spread the knowledge of it to the Continent, where the most valuable collections of his compositions have been found. Almost nothing is known of the details of his life; he was buried in St Stephen's, Walbrook, in London.

Duo, has been used for compositions for two intrumentalists as against duet, which was then reserved for compositions for two singers.

Dussek, Jan Ladislav (b. Časlav 1760, d. St Germain-en-Laye 1812), was a renowned pianist and one of the most important writers for the pianoforte of his day.

Dvořák, Antonín (b. Nelahozeves 1841, d. Prague 1904), was the son of a butcher and inn-keeper. Dvořák showed his musical ability from an early age. He received very considerable help from Leihmann the schoolmaster-musician, organist and band leader at Zlonice, and by his encouragement and help was able to begin study at the Organ School in Prague in 1857. On leaving the Organ School two years later, Dvořák was engaged first in a town band and after a while at the National Theatre. Though he busied himself with composition, only during his last few years at the National Theatre were any of his compositions performed; in 1873 after his first real success he resigned from the theatre to devote himself entirely to writing. In 1875, on the occasion of his winning a state grant, he met Brahms, receiving from him encouragement and friendship. From this time Dvořák's reputation as a composer grew quickly, both in his own country and abroad; he visited England in 1884 and a number of times later. He received the degree of Mus.D. from Cambridge in 1891, and in the same year joined the staff of the Prague Conservatoire; next year at the invitation of the National Conservatory of Music in New York he became its director, staying in America for three years. On his return to Prague, he resumed his duties at the conservatoire, becoming director in 1901, an appointment he held till his death. He married in 1873 a singer from the chorus of the National Opera. He had six children and his home life was happy.

Dvořák made some useful contributions to instrumental chamber music; his Biblical songs are the most successful of his compositions for solo voice. His operas have not met with more than initial success, largely because of the poor quality of their librettos. Dvořák is best known by his large scale instrumental and sacred choral compositions. The most important of his nine symphonies is the last, *From the New World,* written and first performed during his stay in America; his *Slavonic Dances* were originally written for pianoforte duet. Also among his orchestral music are a set of *Symphonic Variations* and a number of overtures and symphonic poems. Amongst his sacred choral works are a *Requiem* and a *Stabat Mater*.

Dvořák made considerable use of Czech folk music. His importance as a teacher and composer is as one of the founders of modern Czech national music.

Dynamic Accent, importance given to a note by relatively greater volume.

Dykes, The Reverend John Bacchus (b. Hull 1823, d. St Leonards 1876), composed a quantity of chuch music. He took a prominent part in the preparation of *Hymns Ancient and Modern;* many of the tunes he contributed to it became popular.

Dyson, Sir George (b. Halifax 1883), still living.

E

East, Michael (b. *c.* 1580, d. 1648), was an English musician, said to be the son of Thomas East. He took the degree of Mus.B. at Cambridge in 1606 and was organist of Lichfield Cathedral. He published seven sets of compositions. Two devoted entirely to madrigals are included in *The English Madrigal School;* the others contain instrumental music and anthems as wel as madrigals.

East, Thomas (d. London *c.* 1608), was an English music typographer and publisher. Amongst his publications were *The Whole Book of Psalms* in 1592 (the tunes being harmonized by Allison, Blancks, Cavendish, Cobbold, Dowland, Farmer, Farnaby, Hooper, Johnson and Kirbye) and the various volumes of madrigals republished in the present century as *The English Madrigal School.*

Eccard, Johann (b. Mülhausen 1553, d. 1611), was a composer mainly of church music. He was an important contributor to the development of the choral, and was highly esteemed as a composer by his contemporaries.

Eccles, Solomon (b. 1618, d. 1683), and his son, *John* (b. London *c.* 1650, d. Kingston 1735), were the most prominent members of a family of English musicians of the 16th and 17th centuries. John was chiefly a composer for the theatre.

Echo Organ, an organ, sometimes found on large church organs, consisting of quietly-voiced pipes, enclosed in a box and frequently placed apart from the main body of the organ. The incorporation of an echo organ was popular in old French and English organs from the late 17th century onwards, and influenced the church music of the time.

Ecossaise (Fr.), a dance form of Scottish origin, introduced into France towards the end of the 18th century. Ecossaises commonly consist of two repeated sections each of four or eight bars of quick two-four time.

Edwards, Richard (b. c. 1523, d. 1566), was an English musician. His madrigal *In going to my naked bed* is included in *The English Madrigal School*.

Eight-Foot Pitch, sounding in unison with the notation. This term is used particularly with reference to organ stops.

Eisteddfod (W.), a session. This name is applied to the national meeting of Welsh Bards, customary in some form since the 7th century. Local Eisteddfodau in the nature of general (not merely musical and literary) competitive festivals are now also popular.

Elegy, a composition of sad character, a name adopted with its meaning from poetry.

Elgar, Edward William (b. Broadheath 1857, d. Worcester 1934), was the son of a musician who kept a music shop and was organist of St George's Roman Catholic Church in Worcester. At his father's wish, Elgar made a willing but futile attempt to work as a clerk to a solicitor. He studied the violin and became proficient enough as an organist to deputize for his father. Apart from two short visits to London and Leipzig for study, Elgar remained at Worcester, making but prosaic progress as a professional musician; he became conductor of the Worcester Amateur Instrumental Society and in 1885 succeeded his father at St George's. Elgar married in 1889. In 1891 he moved to Malvern, devoting the next thirteen years mainly to writing. As his compositions gained performance at the Three Choirs' Festival, his ability became recognized. The production of the *Enigma Variations* in 1899 and *The Dream of Gerontius* in the next established his standing as a composer; though the full merit of the latter was not immediately recognized in England, it was particularly successful at the festival in Düsseldorf in 1902. Elgar moved to Hereford in 1904, and to London a few years later, remaining there till the death of his wife in 1920; both he and his wife are buried at Malvern.

Elgar received the degree of Mus. D. from Yale on his first visit to the United States, and also from Cambridge and Oxford. In

1905 he became the first Professor of Music at Birmingham University. He was knighted on the coronation of Edward VII, received the Order of Merit on the coronation of George V, and became Master of the King's Musick in 1924.

It is as an instrumental composer that Elgar has achieved most. Neither *The Apostles* nor *The Kingdom* has gained the same popularity as *The Dream of Gerontius*; apart from these three oratorios, and perhaps with the exception of his setting of *For the Fallen*, Elgar wrote no other choral works of importance. His vocal and instrumental chamber music, as a whole, cannot be compared with his orchestral music. Two symphonies, two concertos (for violin and violoncello), the *Enigma Variations* and the *Introduction and Allegro for Strings* are works of first importance. These and *Six Military Marches*, *Pomp and Circumstance*, the *Symphonic Study*, *Falstaff*, and *Cockaigne (In London Town)* are representative of his large-scale instrumental compositions.

Encore (Fr.), again. While English audiences use a French word for a repetition of a piece, the French and Germans use the Latin word 'bis'.

Ending, the inflexion at the end of a Gregorian chant.

English Madrigal School, a scholarly edition prepared by Fellowes of the volumes of madrigals by Allison, Bateson, Bennet, Byrd, Carlton, East, Farmer, Farnaby, Gibbons, Jones, Kirbye, Lichfield, Morley, Pilkington, Tomkins, Vautor, Ward, Weelkes, Wilbye and Youll, together with the madrigal writings of Cavendish, Greaves, Holborne, Mundy and Edwards and the volume *The Triumphes of Oriana*, which were originally published between 1588 and 1624.

English School of Lutenist Songwriters, a scholarly edition prepared by Fellowes of the volumes of songs, generally with lute accompaniment, by Attey, Bartlett, Campian, Cavendish, Corkine, Danyel, Dowland, Ferrabosco, Ford, Jones, Morley, Pilkington and Rossiter, which were originally published between 1597 and 1622.

Enharmonic, originally one of the Greek scale forms. This term is now used to describe melodic or harmonic changes which use, or imply the use of, two notes of different name but the same as each other on a keyboard, such as A♭ and G♯.

Ensemble (Fr.), together. Ensemble has been adopted into English musical terminology, and is used in the same sense as 'team work'.

Entr'acte (Fr.), between the acts. Commonly used in England for an orchestral interlude between the acts of a play or opera, frequently as a prelude to one of the acts rather than as an interlude between two of them.

Entrée (F.), entry. A movement or section of music forming an opening, particularly in ballet and opera, and consequently often march-like in character.

Episode, a subsidiary section of a movement, standing apart from the principal sections which are concerned with formal statements of the main subjects of the movement. In a fugue or a rondo the nature and purpose of episodes is particularly clear. In fugue, episodes offer relief from what might otherwise become a monotonous repetition of the subject; in a rondo the alternation of the principal subject with the episodes, the essential characteristic of the rondo, makes the episode a more clearly defined entity than it is in a fugue, in which it often grows out of and merges into the entries of the subject.

Equal Temperament, the system of tuning now used, which divides the octave into twelve equal semitones.

Equal Voices, voices having the same range.

Essential Notes, notes forming an essential part of the harmony, those not doing so being known as unessential notes.

Étude (Fr.), study. A composition evolved from one idea. An étude may be a purely mechanical repetition of some figure for the purpose of developing the technical efficiency of the performer. However, many études have a musical value above that of any executive value they may possess: such is the case, for instance, with the études of Chopin.

Eunuch Flute, an instrument now made only as a toy. It consists of a tube with a bell mouth and a membrane over the other end, having one hole near the membrane end into which the performer sings the notes he wishes to sound. The resulting sound differs considerably from that of the natural voice.

Euphonium, the highest of the tuba group of brass valve wind instruments.

Eurhythmics, a method of musical training through rhythmical physical action. It was devised by Jaques-Dalcroze at the Conservatory in Geneva and now has followers in many countries.

Euterpe, the patroness of music among the nine muses of Greek mythology.

Eximeno, Antonio (b. Valencia 1729, d. Rome 1808), was a Spanish Jesuit. He was a mathematician as well as a musician. In his writings the theories which later were more fully expounded by Wagner are anticipated in a remarkable way, and he was one of the first to expound the theory that the music of a country should be based on its national song.

Exposition, the initial statement of the subject or group of subjects upon which a movement is based.

Expression, the variations in quality, volume and duration which are still largely a matter of judgment on the part of the performer. Bach and Handel occasionally gave indications of speed and volume, but not until the 19th century did composers begin to give any considerable indications of their intentions in the matter of expression. Though the tendency has been to leave less and less to the discretion of the performer, the subtleties of expression at least remain with him.

Extemporization or *Improvisation*, the simultaneous invention and performance of music. Before the evolution of an exact musical notation, the creation of music was essentially extempore, and the repetition of a melody a matter of memory. Plainsong and folk song both originated in this way. After the invention of an exact notation, extemporization remained first in 'discantus supra librum', later in accompaniment from a figured bass (in opera, oratorio and concerted chamber music), and until recent times in the cadenza of a concerto. Apart from these special uses, extemporization has been a much admired art. Many of the foremost performers and composers of every period have excelled in extemporizing, particularly those whose duties as church organists have given them opportunities for its practice.

Extravaganza, a title used for compositions which embody some extravagant, fantastic, grotesque or like feature. It is particularly applicable to works for the stage.

F

Fa, the fourth note of the scale in solmisation.

Faburden, originally a primitive form of vocal composition, evolved about 1400, in which the melody was in the highest part instead of in the bass as had previously been the custom in organum. The harmony was in effect simply a series of triads in first inversion.

Faburden came to mean a setting, usually following the plainsong, of alternate verses of a psalm or canticle, the remaining verses keeping the plainsong.

Faburden is now sometimes used as a name for harmonizations of hymn tunes with the tune in the tenor.

Fah, the fourth note of the scale in Tonic Sol-fa.

Falla, Manuel de (b. Cadiz 1876, d. Córdoba 1946), was first taught by his mother, an able pianist. Later he studied composition with Pedrell. In 1905 he won a prize for a national opera with *Life is Short,* and from 1907 he lived in Paris, returning in 1914 to Madrid. Falla is the most important of modern Spanish composers, and his music is profoundly interesting. It has given expression to the traditional means of music-making of his country, and has shown the full merit of Spanish folk music. Among his compositions are the ballet *The Three Cornered Hat,* a concerto for harpsichord accompanied by six instruments, a number of piano pieces, songs, and a guitar solo in memory of Debussy, which shows how seriously he treats the guitar.

False Relation, the conflict between a note in one part and itself, chromatically altered a semitone, in another part (and therefore usually at another pitch) in the same or an adjacent chord.

Gradualia Lib. I. "Ave Verum Corpus"
BYRD

The conflict between different degrees of the scale a semitone apart does not cause false relation, and there can be false relation only in harmonic systems basically diatonic.

Falsetto, the high pitched notes, generally of poor quality and volume, which may be produced by men, as is done by the normal male alto.

Fancy, an English equivalent of fantasia. This form of the title is particularly associated with English composers of the 16th and early 17th centuries. Towards the end of the 17th century, the free fancy was superseded in popularity by the formal suite and sonata, and the title became obsolete.

Fandango, a Spanish dance, probably of South American origin, to a lively tune in triple time.

Fanfare (Fr.), a short flourish for trumpets such as is used on ceremonial occasions, or a passage of the kind occurring incidentally in concerted music, particularly opera.

Fantasia (It.), a composition of no prescribed form, and therefore essentially an instrumental composition. Unlike the English fancy, the continental fantasia had a continued life during the 18th and 19th centuries and, among other uses, it was commonly paired with a fugue.

Farandole, a national dance of Provence, usually danced at great feasts such as Corpus Christi. It is danced through the streets by as many as will. The music is in a moderate six-eight time.

Farce, originally an interpolation. In the 9th century, farcing in the musical performance of the liturgy became common. The interpolation of comic elements into religious drama gave origin to the present meaning of farce – an extravagant comedy.

Farjeon, Harry (b. New Jersey 1878, d. Hampstead 1948), came of English parents. He composed much interesting music of many kinds, and wrote extensively on musical matters.

Farmer, John (f. 1591-1601), was an English musician. His published madrigals are included in *The English Madrigal School*. He contributed to *The Triumphes of Oriana* and helped to harmonise the tune for the Psalter of 1592, published by Thomas East.

Farnaby, Giles (b. *c.* 1560, d. *c.* 1600), was an English musician. His published madrigals are included in *The English Madrigal School*. He helped to harmonize the tunes for the Psalter of 1592 published by Thomas East, and some fifty pieces by him are in the *Fitzwilliam Virginal Book*.

Farrant, John (f. *c.* 1600), of Salisbury, and *John* (f. *c.* 1600), of Christ Church, were two English composers of church music. The evidence is insufficient to distinguish between them with certainty.

Farrant, Richard (d. 1580 or 81), held appointments at the Chapel Royal and St George's Chapel, Windsor. He is remembered by several small but beautiful contributions to English church music.

Fauré, Gabriel Urbain (b. Pamiers 1845, d. Paris 1924), became distinguished both as a teacher and as a composer. He held a number of appointments as an organist. In 1896 he was appointed to the teaching staff of the Paris Conservatoire, nine years later becoming director, a post he held until his resignation in 1920. It is as a song-writer that Fauré is best known. His reputation as a composer rests mainly on his songs and concerted chamber music, some of each being among the best of its kind.

Faux Bourdon (Fr.), false bass. This term is the French equivalent of the English faburden; both forms are now used in England for the several kinds of composition which have been known by this name at various periods.

Fayrfax, Robert (d. 1521), was one of the leading English musicians preceding Tye and Taverner.

Ferrabosco, Alphonso (b. Greenwich *c.* 1575, d. there 1628), came of Italian parents. His published songs are included in *The English School of Lutenist Songwriters* and he contributed to *The Teares or Lamentacions* compiled by Leighton.

Fétis, François Joseph (b. Mons 1784, d. Brussels 1871), was the most learned writer about music of his time. He had a distinguished career, becoming director of the Brussels Conservatoire and 'maître de chapelle' to the King of the Belgians in 1833. Though containing, among other defects, many obvious inaccuracies, his *Dictionary of Musicians* and the fragment of his *General History* (ceasing at the 15th century) are indispensable authorities.

Fiddle, the old English name for bowed stringed instruments preceding the viol. It is now commonly used synonymously with violin.

Field, John (b. Dublin 1782, d. Moscow 1837), came of a musical family. During his lifetime he established a reputation as a pianist and composer; Chopin was pleased to be compared favourably with him when both were in Paris in 1832 and the following year. He is now remembered for the influence he had on Chopin, in particular for the form and style of the nocturne and the pianistic idiom for which Chopin and later composers are indebted to him.

Fife, a flute. The name now usually given to the B♭ flute, the chief instrument in the drum and fife band.

Fifteenth, an organ stop of diapason quality sounding two octaves above the unison, and therefore of 2-foot pitch on the manuals and 4-foot pitch on the pedals.

Fifth, the interval covering five degrees of the scale; three forms commonly occur.

(a) the diminished fifth, (b) the perfect fifth and (c) the augmented fifth. By fifth alone is generally meant the perfect fifth.

Figurante, a ballet dancer having an independent part.

Figure, the shortest musical idea, recognisable as an entity by its melodic, rhythmic and perhaps also its harmonic characteristics. The possibilities of developing a subject will depend largely upon the figures of which it is composed. However, a multiplicity of figures is by no means essential to the satisfactory construction of a movement, and many examples may be found in which one figure forms the basis of a whole composition.

Figured Bass, a bass part for a continuo player in which the harmonies of the part to be extemporized are indicated by figures. The realization of a figured bass, either at the keyboard or on paper, remained a feature of the study of composition after the practice of writing continuo figured basses had ceased. Each figure represents the interval between the bass and a note above it.

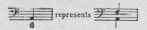

By convention, the note represented by the figure (in this case the F) may be realized in any octave. Thus this example could also be realized as

The full figuring of the common chord in its three positions is

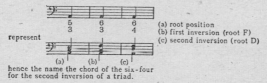

(a) root position
(b) first inversion (root F)
(c) second inversion (root D)

hence the name the chord of the six-four for the second inversion of a triad.

All the notes of a chord are not generally given in the figuring.

No figures implies	$\begin{smallmatrix}5\\3\end{smallmatrix}$	4 implies	$\begin{smallmatrix}5\\4\end{smallmatrix}$	7 implies	$\begin{smallmatrix}7\\5\\3\end{smallmatrix}$
2 „	$\begin{smallmatrix}6\\4\\2\end{smallmatrix}$	5 „	$\begin{smallmatrix}5\\3\end{smallmatrix}$	8 „	$\begin{smallmatrix}8\\5\\3\end{smallmatrix}$
3 „	$\begin{smallmatrix}5\\3\end{smallmatrix}$	6 „	$\begin{smallmatrix}6\\3\end{smallmatrix}$	9 „	$\begin{smallmatrix}9\\5\\3\end{smallmatrix}$

The arrangement of the resulting chord is left to the discretion of the performer.

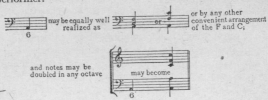

A stroke through a figure indicates that the note represented is to be raised chromatically a semitone; an accidental alone implies a corresponding change in the third from the base in the chord; a horizontal line indicates that the same harmony is to continue regardless of the bass.

Passing notes and other additions unessential to the harmony are not indicated in the figuring, and may be added at the discretion of the performer.

Figured Melody, a melody of florid character.

Final, the note on which a melody in a mode should finish. The final is the modal counterpart of the tonic in the major and minor key system.

Finale, the last movement of any composition consisting of a number of movements grouped together, particularly of opera and those instrumental compositions cast in the same form as the sonata.

Fine (It.), end. Indicates the end of a movement particularly after a 'Da Capo'.

Finger Board, the part of a stringed instrument against which the fingers of the player press the strings of the instrument to change their vibrating length, and consequently the pitch of the note sounded.

Fingering, the method of using the fingers on the keyboard, strings, pitch holes or keys of a musical instrument; also the numerals or signs indicating the fingers to be used.

For keyboard instruments the fingers are now generally numbered one to five from the thumb to the little finger, as they were in the 16th and 17th centuries. For a considerable time, the fingers were numbered one to four from the index finger to the little finger, using X or some other sign for the thumb; this system became common in Germany in the 18th century and later in England, where it remained in use until recently. The earlier system, now again in general use, became known in England as the continental system and the other as the English system.

For members of the violin family, the four fingers (excluding the thumb) are numbered one to four from the index finger, as in the so-called English system for keyboard fingering. An open string is indicated by 0 and, in the case of the violoncello, the thumb by φ.

For wind instruments there are but few alternative fingerings for a particular note on a particular design of instrument.

Fipple Flute, the generic name for flutes sounded with a whistle head, as is the recorder.

Firing, ringing the bells of a peal simultaneously.

First Movement Form (commonly but misleadingly called 'sonata form'), the most important extended musical form, the basis of most first movements of sonatas, symphonies, related forms and of many other extended instrumental and orchestral compositions. What is recognised as the mature standard form of first movement form was reached at the time that the sonata and symphony were being established as the prime instrumental and orchestral forms.

The standard pattern of first movement form has three main parts, the exposition, the development and the recapitulation. In older works, the end of the first section (at least) is clearly marked, and the first section was intended to be repeated. In the exposition, two groups of subjects, usually referred to as the first subject and the second subject, are announced. The first subject is in the tonic key; the second is in a related key, usually the dominant or, in the case of a minor key, the relative major. The addition of an introduction, modulating passages and a coda helps to round off the exposition in an artistic fashion. In the development, the possibilities of the subject matter of the exposition are displayed following no prescribed plan. The development leads to the recapitulation in which the two groups of subjects are stated again, this time both in the tonic key. As with the exposition, the recapitulation is rounded off in an artistic fashion, and the whole movement concludes with a coda.

Though by far the greater number of the first movements of sonatas, symphonies and the like may readily be referred to this standard form, examples differing in some respects are far easier to find than those conforming exactly to it. Among Mozart's pianoforte sonatas there are first movements in which the recapitulation reproduces the whole of the exposition with only slight changes necessitated by the change of key, in which the section corresponding to the development is nothing but a modulating series of scales and arpeggios of little intrinsic interest, and in which

introduction, episode or coda hardly exist. In Beethoven's treatment of the form, the development becomes the largest and most
important section of the movement; the introduction, episode and
coda play an important part in the design of the exposition; in
the recapitulation the subjects of the exposition appear in a
developed form, and the final coda becomes in itself an extended
and important section.

The objections to the use of the name 'sonata form' in this
connection are obvious. This form is the form of an individual
movement, not of a sonata as a whole, and it is as much associated
with the symphony, quartet and certain other extended compositions as with the sonata itself. For the same kind of reasons the
name 'first movement form' is not entirely satisfactory. First
movements are neither invariably nor exclusively in this form.

Fitzwilliam Virginal Book, the most important collection of music for
the virginal extant. This book is now in the Fitzwilliam Museum
in Cambridge. It contains music by a great number of composers,
mainly English, of the late 16th and early 17th century. Bull,
Byrd, Farnaby and Philips are particularly well represented.

Flageolet, a woodwind instrument similar to the recorder but having
two of its six main finger holes on the underside and so controlled
by the thumbs.

Flat, the sign ♭ which lowers a note one semitone from its natural
pitch, either as an accidental or as part of the key signature.

Florid, of a decorated character, particularly applied to a simple
melody or to part writing which has been varied by the introduction of a figure.

Flotow, Friedrich Freiherr von (b. 1812, d. Darmstadt 1883), was a
composer of opera. *Stradella* and even more *Martha* achieved
considerable popularity.

Flourish, the English name for a 'fanfare'. The name is commonly
reserved for the passages played by the trumpeters of the Household Cavalry on state occasions. The flourishes are played in
unison on E♭ trumpets without valves.

Flue-work, organ stops of pipes in which the sound is produced by a
stream of air being directed against an edge, as in the whistle head
of a recorder. Flue-work therefore includes all speaking pipe stops
other than those classed as reed-work.

Flute, a wind instrument in which the air column is set in vibration
by blowing across the edge of the tube.

In its simplest form the flute is one of the oldest of musical
instruments. Primitive flutes were sounded by blowing across one

open end of the tube, and the pitch was varied by the pitch holes in the side of the tube; such a simple flute is by no means easy to sound. Flutes developed in two ways, by the flute being held vertically and sounded by a whistle head, and by the flute being held sideways and sounded by blowing across a mouth hole in the side of the tube a short distance from one end which was blocked.

There have been numerous varieties of each kind of flute, differing in detail rather than principle. The vertical flute is by far the older of the two. Various names have been used for flutes of both kinds; a general name often being used quite unwarrantably to imply some difference in detail. The only essential later development in both kinds has been the addition of keys to facilitate the fingering. The two main modern representatives of each class are the recorder and the orchestral flute.

The modern orchestral flute is the high woodwind instrument of the orchestra. Though now often made of metal, it has changed

FLUTE MOUTHPIECES

wind directed across the open end
against the opposite edge.

(a)

(a) primitive flute

(b) recorder

(c) orchestral flute

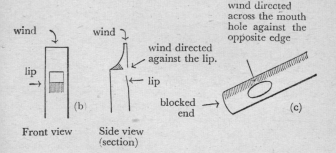

wind

lip
→

(b)

Front view

wind

wind directed
against the lip.

← lip

(section)

Side view

blocked
end →

wind directed
across the mouth
hole against the
opposite edge

(c)

little from the design with which Boehm is credited. Apart from
the head joint, which is parabolic, the flute has a cylindrical bore
and overblows the octave; it is sounded by the player directing
a stream of wind against the opposite edge of the elliptical mouth-
hole and the pitch is varied by the pitch holes which are covered
by open-standing keys. The natural scale of the flute is D, and its
compass is about three octaves from middle C upwards.

Flute, an organ stop of metal or wood, stopped or open, 8- or 4-foot
pitch, of flute-like quality.

Folía, an old noisy Portuguese dance. One extant folía melody has
been used by a number of composers, including Corelli and Bach.

Folk Dance, the dance counterpart of folk song.

Folk Song, the song of the common people. To a large extent folk
songs had their origin before the time of written music, beginning
as the spontaneous vocal expression of emotion by the uncultured
singer, and being polished as they were passed to each successive
generation. With the coming of written music, many songs of folk
origin were noted and so preserved. However, the great bulk of
folk song, neglected by serious musicians, would have been lost if
a conscious effort to record it by such as Cecil Sharp had not been
made during the last hundred years.

Ford, Thomas (b. *c.* 1580, d. Westminster 1648), was an English
musician. His published songs are included in *The English School of
Lutenist Songwriters* and he contributed to *The Teares or Lamentacions* compiled by Leighton.

Forkel, Johann Nicolaus (b. Meeder 1749, d. Gottingen 1818), was a
writer on musical history remembered as the first biographer of
Bach.

Forlana, an Italian dance in six-eight time popular with Venetian
gondoliers.

Form, the arrangements of melody, harmony, counterpoint and other
features of music which the ear may recognise as a series of similarities and contrasts, and so understand a composition as a sensible
organic and satisfying structure. The principles of form are as
equally apparent in the early simple designs of medieval hymn
tunes and folk songs as in the complex structure of later extended
composition. In fact the balance of the movements of a sonata or
symphony is as much a matter of form as the broad structure of
any one of its movements, the arrangement of the material in each
section, and the shape of a particular subject.

Two simple roots of form are commonly recognised, 'binary
form' and 'ternary form', to which were soon added primitive

varieties of 'rondo' and 'variation'. All these may be seen exemplified in the music of the Middle Ages. These patterns should, however, be considered as standard forms to which the great variety of later forms may be referred.

With the rise of polyphony this early sense of form became obscured, and compositions depended for their organic unity on the interplay of the vocal parts. This led to the two styles of canon and fugue.

The rise of homophonic music after the 16th century led to the development of all those extended forms associated with, and culminating in the sonata ('first movement form', 'minuet' and 'scherzo', 'rondo' and the large-scale treatment of 'variations'). At the same time a great number of dance forms were adopted as the basis for instrumental movements, grouped together as suites or used as part of operatic overtures. As soon as this was done the relationship between the movements of an extended composition became yet another consideration of form.

Formé, Nicolas (b. Paris 1567, d. there 1638), was a composer greatly esteemed in his day. His works have some historic interest.

Forte (It.), strong. Indicates volume of sound in the sense of loud. It is usually abbreviated to *f*.

Fortepiano (It.), loud-soft. This term is used for a rapid change from loud to soft indicated by *fp*. It was also an earlier form of the present name 'pianoforte'.

Fortissimo (It.), very strong. Indicates volume of sound in the sense of very loud. It is usually expressed by *ff*.

Fourth, the interval covering four degrees of the scale; three forms commonly occur.

(a)   (b)   (c)

(a) the diminished fourth, (b) the perfect fourth and (c) the augmented fourth. By fourth alone is generally meant the perfect fourth.

Franc, Guillaume (d. Lausanne 1570), was connected with the publication of the *Genevan Psalter* and other psalters of the same period.

Franck, César Auguste (b. Liège 1822, d. Paris 1890), came of an artistic family; a number of his ancestors were painters, and it was his father's intention that he should become a professional musician. Before he was eleven he studied at the Liège Conservatoire; later the family moved to Paris. Franck entered the Paris Conservatoire in 1837, leaving in 1842 after gaining considerable success. His next two years were spent mainly in pianoforte playing. He married in 1848, and had a routine life as a teacher and organist. He became organist at St Clotilde in 1858 and organ professor at the Paris Conservatoire in 1872. He died as the result of a road accident.

During his life his ability received remarkably little recognition. He died at a time when the future for him was full of promise; his health was good and his powers of invention were at their best.

The difference in quality between Franck's compositions is great. His reputation as a composer rests on relatively few of his works. His choral church music, mostly written on demand in unfavourable circumstances, is as a whole of poor quality; his small quantity of organ music has much merit. Among his best compositions are a sonata for violin and pianoforte, a string quartet, *Symphonic Variations* for pianoforte and orchestra, and a symphony in D minor.

Franco, Magister (probably 11th century), was the first writer on music to deal with music in which the notes had exact time values. There is considerable uncertainty as to the identity of a number of Francos, probably all the same person. Theorists of the 14th, 15th and 16th century all refer to the writings attributed to Franco of Cologne.

Frederick the Great, King of Prussia (b. Berlin 1712, d. near Potsdam 1786), was an able musical amateur. His connection with music is remembered mainly by the *Musical Offering* written for him by Bach after his visit to Potsdam in 1747.

French Horn, the early name, still in use, for the instrument commonly known simply as horn.

Frescobaldi, Girolamo (b. Ferrara 1583, d. Rome 1643), was a most distinguished organist and an important composer for the organ. He became organist of St Peter's, Rome, in 1608 and, except for a short period, remained there till his death.

Fret, each strip of wood or other material fixed on the finger-board of certain stringed instruments, such as the guitar, as a help to the fingers in stopping the strings.

Fugato, a movement or section of a movement of the nature of a fugue, but not displaying strictly the characteristics essential to a fugue.

Fughetta, a short fugue.

Fugue, a style rather than a form of composition, in which a melodic subject is treated contrapuntally and which exhibits certain clearly recognised features. A fugue is designed for a definite number of voices or parts; its most distinctive and regular feature is the exposition in which each voice enters in turn with the subject. The first voice to enter states the subject in the tonic key; the second enters with the answer, the subject in the dominant key; the voices enter in turn with the subject or answer until all the voices have entered. After the first voice has stated the subject it often continues with a counter-subject, a counterpoint to the subject (or answer). Sometimes a brief digression called a codetta is introduced before the third voice enters; sometimes extra entries (or a complete set of them forming a counter-exposition) occur after the exposition proper. If the subject has any marked statement or implication of tonic and dominant following each other, or a modulation from one to the other, the answer matches tonic with dominant and dominant with tonic (a tonal answer), rather than letting the answer be a straightforward transposition of the subject into the dominant key (a real answer).

"48" Bk. II, Fugue in C♯ major
BACH

S₁ subject, A tonal answer,
S₂ subject inverted (unusual in the exposition)

The exposition is followed by a series of modulations in the course of which entries of the subject may be interspersed with episodes. Generally the climax of a fugue is at the end of this middle section, as the return is made to the tonic key and the final entries of the subject occur.

During the course of the fugue the subject and counter-subject may be treated by augmentation, diminution, inversion or other device. The subject and counter-subject will normally be in double counterpoint with each other, and their judicious treatment by the less and more erudite contrapuntal devices is one of the main ways of making the interest grow. 'Stretto' and 'pedal' are common features of fugue, usually employed towards or at the end.

"48" Bk. I, Fugue in C major
BACH

P pedal, S₁ and S₂ entries of the subject in stretto
(the free parts are not shown)

Rules for the construction of fugue have been prescribed dog-
matically by many teachers. However, Bach, without rival the
greatest exponent of fugue, gives the style a variety and freedom
incompatible with the rules of Cherubini and later theorists.

Fuller Maitland, John Alexander (b. London 1856, d. Carnforth 1936),
was editor of the second edition of Grove's *Dictionary of Music*. He
was concerned in the transcription and publication of a great deal
of early English music, particularly for the keyboard.

Full Orchestra, the orchestra with a full complement of woodwind,
brass, drums and strings.

Full Organ, the full power of an organ generally to be obtained by
the use of the main stops of the Great Organ. Whether or not the
Swell Organ adds materially to the power of the Great Organ will
depend on the design of the instrument. In smaller organs the
effect of Full Organ can be obtained only from the combined
effects of both Great and Swell Organs; it is never necessary to
employ all the stops for Full Organ.

Fundamental, the distinctive tone by which the pitch of a note is
named, the first note of the harmonic series when referring to a
pure note.

Fuoco (It.), fire.

Furiant, used by Dvořák in his chamber music as the title of a fiery
movement.

Fux, Johann Joseph (b. near Gratz 1660, d. Vienna 1741), was a
prolific composer, particularly of church music. He was a master
of counterpoint, and, though contrapuntal devices are used with
discretion in his church music, the one exception, his *Missa
Canonica,* is a gorgeous display of every kind of canon. However,
Fux is remembered mainly as a teacher and for his *Gradus ad
Parnassum,* published in 1725, a comprehensive treatise on the
theory and practice of composition.

G

Gabrieli, Andrea (b. Venice *c.* 1510, d. there 1586), and his nephew
and pupil, *Giovanni* (b. Venice 1557, d. there *c.* 1612), were the
most important members of a distinguished family of Italian
musicians. Both were organists of St Mark's, succeeding Merulo,
and made important contributions to organ music as well as vocal

music. Giovanni had Prætorius and Schütz, amongst others, as his pupils.

Gade, Niels Vilhelm (b. Copenhagen 1817, d. there 1890), was the son of a musical instrument maker. He had a distinguished musical career and achieved some success as a composer.

Gagliano, Alessandro (f. *c.* 1695-1730), was the head of a family of violin-makers of Naples.

Gagliano, Marco da (b. Gagliano *c.* 1575, d. Florence 1642), was trained as a priest and became canon of St Lorenzo. In his time he was one of the leading musicians of Florence, and was one of the early group of opera composers.

Galilei, Vincenzo (b. Florence *c.* 1533, d. there 1591), was the father of the astronomer Galileo Galilei. Galilei was one of the most prominent figures in the musical life, surrounding Count Bardi, which saw the rise of opera.

Galliard, a merry dance of Italian origin, usually in three-two but sometimes in common time. The galliard was popular in England by the late 16th century. It appears to have been used as a contrast to the pavan, the galliard following the pavan, and often having music built on the same theme as that of the pavan.

Gallop, a lively dance of German origin in two-four time, very popular in the 19th century.

Galpin, The Reverend Francis William (b. Dorchester 1858, d. London 1945), was an authority on musical instruments.

Gamba, an open metal organ stop of stringy quality, generally of 8-foot pitch on the manuals.

Gamut, the plan of the musical scale associated with the hexachord. The name is a contraction of Gamma Ut, Γ (gamma), instead of G, being the bottom note of the whole scale and the ut of the lowest hexachord (see table 1, p. 110).

Gavotte, a dance form sometimes used as a movement in a suite. The dance was of French origin. The gavotte is in two sections, each repeated, and is written in four-four time beginning on the third crotchet in the bar (sometimes the signature ¢ is used).

Often the gavotte is followed by a second gavotte or a musette, after which the first gavotte is repeated.

Gay, John (b. 1685, d. 1732), was an English poet. Though not a musician, he is remembered in music as the writer of *The Beggar's Opera*. The brilliantly satirical libretto and cleverly chosen tunes (chosen by Gay with the assistance of Pepusch and arranged by the latter) made damaging fun of Italian opera and its conventions.

Gedackt (Ger.), covered. A name given to a stopped wooden organ stop of 8-foot pitch on the manuals.

TABLE I

The Gamut and the Seven Hexachords

	THE HEXACHORDS							THE GAMUT
	1	2	3	4	5	6	7	
E							la	E la
D						la	sol	D la sol
C						sol	fa	C sol fa
B						B♭ fa	B♮ mi	B fa, B mi
A					la	me	re	A la mi re
G					sol	re	ut	G sol re ut
F					fa	ut		F fa ut
E				la	mi			E la mi
D			la	sol	re			D la sol re
*C			sol	fa	ut			C sol fa ut
B			B♭ fa	B♮ mi				B fa, B mi
A		la	mi	re				A la mi re
G		sol	re	ut				G sol re ut
F		fa	ut					F fa ut
E	la	mi						E la mi
D	sol	re						D sol re
C	fa	ut						C fa ut
B	mi							B mi
A	re							A re
Γ	ut							Γ ut

* middle C

Gedackt-work, a sub-division of flue-work. Those flue-stops of stopped pipes. The larger pipes are generally of wood, the smaller ones of wood or metal. Stops of this kind were first made in Germany in the early 16th century.

Geigen, an open metal organ stop similar to the diapason or principal, but with a slight stringy quality.

Geminiani, Francesco (b. Lucca 1687, d. Dublin 1762), was a pupil of Corelli, and one of the most important representatives of his school. Geminiani was, however, very different from Corelli in his style both as a composer and performer.

Gemshorn, an open metal organ stop with pipes tapering in scale from the mouth upwards, of eight, four or two foot pitch on the manuals.

German, Sir Edward (originally *Edward German Jones*) (b. Whitchurch 1862, d. London 1936), achieved distinction as a composer particularly of light opera and other music for the stage. His incidental music to plays such as *Henry VIII* and *Nell Gwynn* made a notable contribution to raising the general level of theatre music. Of his operas *Merrie England* still enjoys popularity.

German Flute, the 18th-century name for the flute held sideways.

Gesualdo, Don Carlo, Prince of Venosa (b. Naples *c.* 1560, d. there 1615), was an important composer of madrigals. His treatment of both counterpoint and harmony was remarkably distinctive, showing him to be a modernist though he founded no school.

Gevaert, François Auguste (b. Huysse 1828, d. Brussels 1908), was a musical historian and theorist as well as a composer; he was also sometime director of the Brussels Conservatoire.

Gibbons, Orlando (b. Oxford 1583, d. Canterbury 1625), was the most distinguished of a family of musicians which also included his brothers Edward and Ellis and his son Christopher. Orlando was taken to Cambridge when he was about four years old. He was a chorister at King's College, Cambridge, and in 1605 was appointed organist of the Chapel Royal. He established for himself a reputation both as an organist and as a composer. He died suddenly during the time that the whole Chapel Royal was at Canterbury in attendance on Charles I, awaiting the arrival of the Queen, Henrietta Maria, married to Charles by proxy in Paris.

It appears that Orlando wrote only for the English rite of the Church. His church music represents two distinct styles. His service in F and many of his best-known anthems belong to the established full polyphonic style. His second service and the greater proportion of his anthems are in the verse style, having portions for solo voice and an independent organ part. *The Silver Swan,* the first of his one set of madrigals, is deservedly one of the best known of all madrigals. Much of his string music and keyboard music has also survived.

Edward (b. *c.* 1570, d. *c.* 1650), contributed to *The Triumphes of Oriana;* a little other music by him is also extant.

Ellis (b. Cambridge 1573, d. 1603), had two madrigals included in *The Triumphes of Oriana.*

Christopher (b. Westminster 1615, d. there 1676), became organist of Westminster Abbey. Some anthems and a large amount of string music by him are extant.

Gibbs, Cecil Armstrong (b. Great Baddow 1889), still living.

Gigue, a lively dance form commonly used as the last movement of the suite. The dance was of Italian origin. Its name is associated with the name of the early fiddle (either gigue or some variant of it). Gigues are usually in two sections, each repeated, the second conventionally built on an inversion of a subject of the first. Various time signatures are used indiscriminately, though

$$\flat \quad | \quad \flat \flat \flat \quad | \quad \flat \flat \qquad \text{and} \qquad \flat \quad | \quad \flat \quad \flat \quad | \quad \flat$$

and variations of them are characteristic figures of the gigue.

are typical examples. There are, however, some examples of gigues in common time, and many gigues begin on the beat instead of with a short note.

Giles, Nathaniel (b. Worcester *c.* 1558, d. Windsor 1633), was a Mus.D. of Oxford and Master of the Choristers at Windsor and the Chapel Royal. A number of anthems and a few motets and services by him are extant. He contributed to *The Teares or Lamentacions* compiled by Leighton.

Giocoso (It.), joyful.

Gittern, a medieval instrument similar to the guitar. In England it was the popular accompanying instrument before the introduction of the large lute in the 15th century.

Giusto (It.), just. Used in the sense of 'exact' or 'appropriate' with regard to speed.

Glazounov, Alexander Constantinovich (b. St Petersburg 1865, d. Paris 1936), was the son of a publisher and bookseller. He was reared in a musical atmosphere, became acquainted with Balakirev when he was fourteen and a year or so after studied under Rimsky-Korsakov. His music shows a preference for classical forms, separating him from certain other members of the modern Russian school, but like Rimsky-Korsakov he shows himself to be a master of orchestration. He has made notable contributions to orchestral and chamber music, but his few vocal works are of little importance.

Glee, a title particularly associated with the English vocal compositions of the 18th and early 19th centuries for solo men's voices, mainly in a homophonic style. The outstanding contributor to the glee form was Samuel Webbe.

Glière, Reinhold (b. Kiev 1875), still living.

Glinka, Michael Ivanovitch (b. Novospasskoi 1803, d. Berlin 1857), was reared in a cultured atmosphere and received music lessons from an early age. Though he showed a marked aptitude for music, it was not until 1828, when he resigned his official position in the government services, that music began to take the prime place in his life. From his childhood he appears to have been attracted by the possibilities of making use of traditional Russian music, and this bore fruit in his operas *A Life for the Tsar* and *Russlan and Ludmilla,* which marked the birth of a distinctive school of Russian music. In other circumstances Glinka's genius might have produced music which would have placed him in the front rank of composers. As it is, his importance was in paving the way for the new movement of which Balakirev became the leader.

Glissando (It.), sliding. In piano music, glissando indicates that a scale passage of white notes is to be played by sliding the back of the finger from each note to the next. On the harp, the glissando is an important effect. The harp glissando is similar to the piano glissando, but the actual scale played depends on the setting of the pedals.

Glockenspiel (as now used in the orchestra), a set of tuned metal bars rather than bells. Metal bars are easier to manipulate and tune than bells, and are free from the dissonant overtones common in bells. The bars are arranged in two rows corresponding to the white and black notes of the keyboard. The compass extends downwards from the C three octaves above middle C for a little over one octave, and sometimes for two octaves.

Gluck, Christoph Willibald, Ritter von (b. Weidenwang 1714, d. Vienna

1787), was the son of a member of the household of Prince Lob-kowitz. While he received musical training from an early age, musically his youth was in no way remarkable. In 1736 in the house of the Prince at Vienna he met Prince Melzi, a distinguished amateur, who engaged him as a member of his private band and enabled him to complete his studies in composition under Sam-martini. From 1741 Gluck regularly produced operas which from the first met with approval. In 1746 he visited London, where he met Handel and probably heard some of his oratorios. He subse-quently visited Paris, where he heard some of Rameau's operas.

Gluck was born in Germany, but his name is Czech rather than German. His musical education was firstly in Bohemia, and none of his large number of operas was in German, the more serious being in Italian and the lighter in French.

Gluck became the most important figure of the later part of the 18th century in the development of opera. Though he enjoyed the favour of the court at Vienna, and though the merit of his operas was undeniable, he suffered unreasonable criticism from his countrymen. Subsequently in Paris the animosity between his supporters and the supporters of Piccini, a Neapolitan composer of successful light operas, a far inferior figure, became a squabble of the first order (the war of the Gluckists and Piccinists). Gluck won, but after his return to Vienna the Parisian taste for senti-mental Italian opera prevailed.

His reforms, which made so great a contribution to operatic evolution, were mainly his great advance in the quality of the declamation, the importance he gave to the overture and his treatment of the orchestra. He left out the harpsichord, added the harp, used trombones and clarinets, and greatly increased the use of the orchestra to emphasise the drama. His compositions other than his dramatic works are quite undistinguished. Of his operas *Orfeo* is generally the best known and its success has been the most lasting; *Armide* is perhaps the most satisfactory and *Iphigénie en Tauride,* nearly his last work, was produced with great success.

Godfrey, Sir Dan (Daniel Eyers) (b. London 1868, d. Bournemouth 1939), was the most distinguished of a family of English band-masters, of which he belonged to the third generation. He is particularly associated with Bournemouth, where he raised the orchestra of the Winter Gardens to a high standard.

Goetz, Hermann (b. Königsberg 1840, d. Hottingen 1876), was a composer. His opera *Taming of the Shrew* has merit, though it has not achieved popularity. Some of his orchestral and chamber music also deserves, perhaps, more attention than it has received.

Goldberg, Johann Gottlieb (b. Danzig 1727, d. Dresden 1756), was a pupil of Bach, and was one of the finest clavier and organ players of his time. He is remembered by the set of variations which Bach wrote for him.

Gombert, Nicolas (b. Bruges f. 1520–37), was a pupil of Josquin de Près, and became one of the most important composers of his day.

Gong (as sometimes used in the orchestra), an Eastern instrument of bronze in the form of a disc with upturned edges. It is usually struck with a bass-drumstick.

Goossens, Eugene (b. London 1893), still living.

Gossec, François Joseph (b. Vergnies 1734, d. Passy 1829), was the son of a farmer. He is historically important for his contribution to the foundation of French symphonic and chamber music.

Goudimel, Claude (b. Besançon c. 1505, d. Lyons 1572), was probably living in Paris about 1550. He appeared first as a composer of songs. Though he wrote sacred music of all kinds, he is remembered chiefly by his harmonizations of Metrical Psalm tunes.

Gounod, Charles François (b. Paris 1818, d. Saint-Cloud 1893), came of a family of artists; his mother was an able pianist. He entered the Paris Conservatoire in 1836 and won the Grand Prix de Rome in 1839. In 1846 it appeared that he would take Holy Orders; he did not, but during this period acquired a marked literary ability. His first opera was produced in 1851 and for many years he was occupied mainly with music for the theatre. The production of his *Faust* in 1859 established him as one of the leading composers of his time. Besides a Solemn Mass, which was his first important work and which appeared first in London in 1851, he composed a considerable quantity of sacred music such as *Nazareth* and the extremely popular *Meditation* (*Ave Maria*) on the first Prelude of Bach's '48'. During the later part of his life, Gounod devoted himself mainly to the composition of sacred music. His style in such works as *The Redemption* had a particular appeal for the popular English taste of his time.

Grace Notes or *Graces,* the common English names for the ornaments in instrumental and vocal music.

Gradual, the Latin Service book containing the music sung at Mass. The *Antiphoner* is the complementary book.

Granados, Enrique (b. Lérida 1867, d. at sea 1916); was mainly a pianist, but his compositions, particularly those for the piano, have helped to increase the understanding and appreciation of serious Spanish music outside Spain.

Grandioso (It.), grandly.

Grand Opera, an opera of a serious nature in which the music is continuous, particularly French opera of this kind as opposed to opéra-comique.

Grand Piano, a pianoforte, the name being commonly used to distinguish the horizontal tailed pianoforte from the upright model.

Grave (It.), slow and solemn.

Gravicembalo, a harpsichord. The name is simply an Italian corruption of clavicembalo.

Grazia (It.), grace.

Great Organ, the first and most important manual organ of a modern English church organ. The name in the first instance was given to the large as distinct from the small church organ, it being customary in the 16th and preceding centuries to have more than one organ in any fair-sized church. The name presumably continued for the main department of the instrument after mechanical developments made it possible for the smaller instrument to be incorporated in the larger, each being played from a separate manual.

Great Stave, a stave of eleven lines illustrating the relation between the two staves of five lines (one with the treble clef, the other with the bass clef) which are now commonly used together for keyboard music.

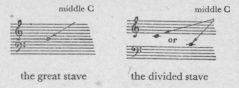

the great stave   the divided stave

Greaves, Thomas (f. 1604), was an English musician. His published madrigals are included in *The English Madrigal School.*

Greene, Maurice (b. London 1695, d. there 1755), became organist of St Paul's Cathedral, organist and composer to the Chapel Royal in 1727, and Professor of Music in the University of Cambridge in 1730.

Gregorian Music, the large collection of plainsong church music associated with the Church of Rome from early times, which became the dominant usage throughout most of the Roman Church, superseding most others. It is considered that St Gregory had a definite personal share in the formulation of this collection, during the latter part of the 6th century. The collection is thus justly named.

The collection falls into two main groups, the music of the Mass and the music of the Hours. The music of the Mass includes the Introits, the Graduals, Alleluias and Tracts, the Offertories and the Communions for the church's year; to these compositions for the choir were added the unvarying Kyrie, Gloria, Credo, Sanctus and Agnus Dei to be sung by the congregation. The later settings of these congregational portions and the tropes and sequences of the late Middle Ages do not form part of the Gregorian collection proper. The music of the offices originally consisted of antiphons, responds and the like. The cycle of hymns which was soon incorporated in the music of the Hours, and regularly enlarged, forms a separate collection.

The whole collection of Gregorian music was carefully preserved unmutilated throughout the Middle Ages, but during the 16th century the tradition of its performance was lost, and much of the music was altered almost beyond recognition. The re-establishment of Gregorian music in its original form at the beginning of this century was mainly the result of the labours of the Benedictines of Solesmes.

Gregorian Tones, the system of plainsong chants used in Gregorian music for the singing of the psalms, the canticles and the antiphons of the mass. Three forms of tone exist, the simplest being that for the psalms. Eight psalm tones correspond to each of the eight modes and a ninth tone, exceptionally, does not conform to the strict modal pattern. Each tone consists of two parts corresponding to the two halves of a verse of a psalm; at the beginning and end of the first part are the intonation and mediation, and at the end of the second part the ending; these three inflexions are separated by two reciting notes, the dominant of the mode, to which that part of each verse not fitted to the inflexions is sung. There is one intonation and mediation to each psalm tone, though a number of endings, the number varying among the tones.

Grétry, André Ernest Modeste (b. Liège 1742, d. near Montmorency 1813), was the son of a violinist. He was a prolific composer of operas, and in his day achieved very considerable success.

Grieg, Edvard Hagerup (b. Bergen 1843, d. there 1907), was the son of the British Consul General in Bergen. His mother, Gesine Hagerup, was a cultivated amateur musician who encouraged his musical ability from an early age. From 1858 to 1862 he studied at the Leipzig Conservatorium, and afterwards at Copenhagen. In 1867 he founded a music society in Christiana, and was its conductor until 1880; and he visited Italy in 1865 and again in 1870. He performed his own pianoforte concerto at Leipzig in 1879 and in England in 1888; he revisited England a number of times, receiving the degree of Mus.D. from Cambridge in 1894. Between his foreign visits, he lived a quiet life in the country near Bergen. Grieg married his cousin Nina Hagerup, a singer, who became a most successful interpreter of his songs.

The quantity of Grieg's compositions is small. His songs and pieces show him at his best. Among his orchestral music are two suites arranged from his incidental music for Ibsen's play *Peer Gynt*. His one pianoforte concerto, deservedly well known, is his only large-scale work. He wrote no symphonies. He wrote a number of pieces for string orchestra and his chamber music includes one string quartet. Grieg made extensive use of melodies hardly differing from genuine folk tunes. He is foremost among the composers who developed a Norwegian national style.

Grossvater-Tanz (Ger.), grandfather dance. A German family dance of the 17th century, used by Schumann in *Carnaval* and *Papillons*.

Ground Bass, a repetition of a bass theme with varied melodies, figures and harmonies above. In a strict ground, the theme remains in the bass and is itself unvaried. More often than not, however, ground bass is employed during only part of a composition, or is one of the characteristics used freely in certain variation forms. The ground bass was particularly popular during the 17th century, Purcell among others making considerable use of it.

Grove, Sir George (b. Clapham 1820, d. Sydenham 1900), was the first director of the Royal College of Music, and editor of the first edition of the *Dictionary of Music and Musicians* which bears his name. He had a distinguished career as a civil engineer, and played a prominent part in various projects concerned with Biblical research. In 1875 he received the honorary degree of D.C.L. from the University of Durham for his services to literature, no mention being made of his services to music, though he had already begun work on the *Dictionary of Music and Musicians*. From this time onwards he became concerned primarily with music. He accepted the appointment of Director of the Royal College of Music in 1882 and was knighted when the college was opened the following year.

Grovlez, Gabriel (b. Lille 1879, d. Paris 1945), had a distinguished career as a composer, conductor and teacher.

Guarneri, Guiseppe Antonio (b. Cremona 1687, d. there 1745), was the most important member of a family of violin-makers. A senior member of the family, *Andrea* (b. *c.* 1626, d. Cremona 1698), was a fellow pupil with Stradivari under Amati. The work of Giuseppe has been rated second only to that of Stradivari. He became known as Giuseppe del Gesù from the I.H.S. which he added after his name on his labels. ·

Guerre des Bouffons (Fr.), War of the Comedians. This famous quarrel between two parties of Parisian musicians and opera enthusiasts began in 1752. One party supported the national French serious opera of Lully and Rameau, the other the Italian opera buffa of Pergolesi. The trouble started over an opera of Destouches, and was fostered by a subsequent performance by a troupe of Italian comedians of Pergolesi's *La Serva Padrona*. It was waged with surprising acrimony, and became almost a national issue. The national party was of the aristocracy with the King as its champion, while the Italian party was of the intelligentsia with the Queen as its champion. The latter party considered the Italian opera superior because it was more melodious and less contrapuntal than the French. The efforts of French musicians to compete with Italian opera buffa resulted in a new style of French comic opera.

Guido d'Arezzo (b. Arezzo *c.* 990, d. Pomposa *c.* 1050), was a musical theorist of very considerable importance. It was he who adopted the names ut, re, me, fa, sol and la for the notes of the hexachord. He is credited with the invention of the stave by spacing the neumes accurately according to their pitch, and drawing through them a yellow line for C, a red line for F and a green line for B♭.

Guitar, a plucked stringed instrument, the modern representative of the large family of instruments which includes the lute and cither. The characteristics of the guitar are its flat back, and its sides curving inwards.

The guitar, both name and instrument being of Eastern origin, was brought to Spain by the Moors; the earliest known Spanish instruments of the kind date from the 12th century. With the rise of homophonic music at the end of the 16th and beginning of the 17th century, the Spanish guitar grew in popularity. During the 17th century it received attention in France and Italy as well as in Spain. At the end of the 18th and beginning of the 19th century it became fashionable throughout Europe. An inferior variety of instrument which became known as the English guitar was introduced to England in the mid-18th century, but was superseded by the Spanish guitar towards the middle of the 19th century.

The modern guitar has six strings tuned

It is played with the fingers, and its music written an octave higher than sounding.

Outside Spain, the guitar has not received that attention from composers which it deserves. The few serious works which have been written for it indicate its possibilities. Further, 16th- and 17th-century lute music might be played on it most effectively.

Gurney, Ivor (b. Gloucester 1890, d. Dartford 1937), achieved some distinction as a poet and composer of songs. Mental ill health following the 1914–18 war prevented the fulfilment of his early promise.

Gusto (It.), taste.

Gymel, a primitive form of vocal two-part harmony, the melody being in the upper voice, and the harmony being essentially a chain of thirds.

H

Habanera, a song and dance which originated in Africa and reached Spain from Cuba, where it had been introduced by the Negroes. The dance, though stately and graceful, is alluring and suggestive. The music has a distinctive rhythm, using the figures

$\frac{2}{4}$ ♪.♪♪♪   and   ♪♪♪♪   ♪♪

It consists of an introduction and two sections, the second commonly in the major if the first is in the minor. The habanera is generally known by Bizet's use of it in *Carmen*.

Hadley, Patrick (b. Cambridge 1899), still living.

Hadow, Sir William Henry (b. Ebrington 1859, d. London 1937), achieved distinction as a writer on musical subjects.

Halévy, Jacques François Fromental Elias (b. Paris 1799, d. Nice 1862), studied at the Paris Conservatoire, won the Grand Prix de Rome in 1819, and subsequently had a distinguished career as a composer of opera.

Half-close, an imperfect cadence.

Hallé, Sir Charles (b. Hagen 1819, d. Manchester 1895), achieved distinction as a pianist and conductor. He is remembered by the orchestra and concerts named after him which he established.

Halling, a characteristic Norwegian dance. The dance is usually performed by a single dancer accompanied on a kind of violin. The music is generally lively, in two-four time, and in a major key.

Hammer, the implement, forming part of the action, by which the strings of a pianoforte are made to vibrate. The hammers are scaled down in size and weight from the bass to treble. Both the head and shank of the hammer must be elastic. Both are made of wood, the head of mahogany, the shank of cedar (now more commonly birch, hickory or pear-tree). The heads are covered with felt, or felt and leather.

Hammerclavier, the early German name for the pianoforte.

Hammerschmidt, Andreas (b. Brüx 1612, d. Zittau 1675), was a composer who contributed to the chorals in use in the Lutheran Church.

Hand Bassel, an obsolete bowed string instrument, apparently either a small form of violoncello or double bass.

Hand Bells, small bells fitted with clappers and springs. They are used for change-ringing practice, and hand bell ringing has been a pastime enjoyed particularly in the North of England.

Handel, George Frederic (b. Halle 1685, d. London 1759), was the son of a barber-surgeon. His father had little interest in the arts, and while allowing his son organ lessons, did not encourage his interest in music. Handel was educated at the local grammar school and, after his father's death in 1696, completed at the university the study of law for which his father had intended him. He left Halle in 1703 for Hamburg, set upon a musical career.

At Hamburg he was appointed violinist and later harpsichordist at the opera, and while there wrote four operas and a setting of the St John Passion. He left in 1706 and appears to have been in Rome in 1707, staying in Italy until 1710 composing and assimilating the style of his musical surroundings. He left Italy to become Kapellmeister to the Elector George of Hanover, and almost immediately visited London. Two years later, in 1712, he failed to return from a second visit to London and was still there when his master succeeded Queen Anne in 1714, as George I. Handel made England his home, being reconciled to his master within a year or two. He accompanied the King on a visit to Hanover in 1716, and became a naturalized Englishman in 1726. He visited Aix-la-Chapelle in 1737, hoping for a cure from the paralysis which had afflicted him; later mental disorders added to his discomfort, and from 1751 onwards his sight troubled him; by 1753 he was quite blind. His last illness came suddenly. He enjoyed Royal patronage most of his life, and was buried in Westminster Abbey.

In England, Handel found Italian opera well established and his life centred round the composition and production of opera in the Italian style, writing over thirty operas during the next twenty years. He refused to satisfy public taste for entertainment of the kind given by The Beggar's Opera, first performed in 1728, and persisted in the Italian style of which the public was tired. The accent changed from opera to oratorio, some twenty oratorios being written and produced during the next thirty years; the oratorio Messiah was written in twenty-three days during 1741, and produced during one of his most successful periods the next year. The Messiah alone among his operas and oratorios has had, to any great extent, more than initial success, though many of the arias from both the operas and oratorios have achieved popularity. Neither his opera nor oratorio projects were an unqualified financial success; he was bankrupt at least once.

Besides the operas and oratorios, Handel's compositions include his harpsichord suites and pieces, no doubt following from his appointment as music master to the daughters of George II; his organ concertos, which were written for performance during intervals in his oratorios; his twelve grand concertos of 1739 for strings; his Water Music, pieces written at different times and collected together in 1740, and his Fireworks Music, performed during the celebration for the peace of Aix-la-Chapelle in 1749; and a considerable amount of sacred music including the Chandos anthems written while he was Master of Music to the Duke of Chandos, 1718–21, and the four coronation anthems written for George II in 1727.

Handel borrowed extensively from the works of others. More charitably this may be considered as a matter of arrangement for immediate performance, so preserving the work of others, rather than a conscious use of the work of others as his own.

The little of Handel's music commonly known is in odd contrast to the honourable place he holds in popular esteem. His operas and oratorios are a store of lovely music and some of them would justify a revival combining scholarly faithfulness to the score with an imaginative production. Some have already been so revived.

Handel's family spelt its name in many ways. Handel himself used Händel, Haendel, Hendel and Handel. He began to use

Handel soon after he came to England, and used it when he was naturalized. The forms Händel and Haendel are generally used on the Continent.

Harmonic, a term used to describe organ stops consisting of pipes twice their speaking length. Such pipes are assisted in over-blowing their octave by a small hole half-way up each pipe.

Harmonica, an instrument consisting of a set of glasses from which the sound is produced by stroking them with the moistened fingers. The pitch of the notes produced is regulated either by the size of the glasses, or, earlier, by the amount of water in glasses of the same size. Such instruments were invented towards the middle of the 18th century, and were in vogue until the early years of the 19th century. Although both Mozart and Beethoven wrote one composition each for it, the harmonica must be counted as a musical curiosity.

Harmonic Flute, an open metal organ stop of four foot pitch on the manuals. The pipes overblow an octave (that is, sound their first harmonic) and are therefore twice the length of their speaking pitch length.

Harmonichord, a keyboard string instrument in which the strings were set in vibration by a revolving wheel, as in the hurdy-gurdy. The instrument was invented in 1810, and the following year Weber wrote one composition for it.

Harmonic Minor, the form of the minor scale in which the leading note is sharpened.

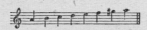

It was generally adopted during the second half of the 19th century as better representing the characteristics of the minor scale than the 'melodic minor'.

Harmonics, the notes of the harmonic series, other than the funda-mental, which may be sounded on string and wind instruments. Wind instruments, particularly the brass, normally use harmonics in forming their scale; harmonics, therefore, refers particularly to the production of the upper harmonics on string instruments, especially by members of the violin family and by the harp. These harmonics are produced by touching the string lightly at the appropriate nodal point.

Harmonic Series, in its musical sense, is a succession of sounds whose frequencies are in proportion to the whole numbers.

The notation is only approximate, those harmonics marked *
being distinctly flatter than the notation. The series may readily
be obtained from a stretched string by sub-dividing it into two,
three, four or more parts; and a column of air in a tube may be
made to vibrate so as to sound this same series.

A whistle head attached to a tube open at the other end gives
the full series, as does a reed attached to a tube of conical bore; a
whistle head attached to a tube closed at the other end gives only
the odd members of the series, as does a reed attached to a tube of
cylindrical bore. All instruments of the horn, trumpet and closely
related families give the full series.

Harmonium, a keyboard free reed instrument. The reeds are set in
vibration by wind from an air reservoir supplied from bellows
worked by the feet of the player. During the early part of the 18th
century a variety of instruments of simple design conforming to
these essential characteristics of the harmonium were constructed.
These instruments may claim the Chinese cheng and the regal as
ancient and indirect ancestors.

No one instrument-maker may fairly be claimed as the inventor
of the harmonium. Alexander Debain incorporated the work of his
predecessors in his harmonium patented in Paris in 1840, in which
he advanced the design of the instrument further by using a
number of sets of reeds under the control of stops, as on the
organ.

A number of important inventions and refinements followed.
The expression stop brought the pressure of the wind supplied to
the reeds directly under control of the player. Various devices gave
predominance to the melody or bass, and the incorporation of
double touch enabled individual notes to be made predominant at
the will of the performer. Other inventions improved the prompt-
ness of speech of the reeds, and improved the steadiness of pressure
on the reservoir.

The harmonium has a keyboard of five octaves, from the C two
octaves below middle C upwards, as in the organ. The stops are
divided, the bass stops acting up to the E above middle C, and
the treble stops upwards from the F above middle C. Further,

the stops are divided into front and back organs, the front organ containing the full-toned foundation stops and the back organ the reedy-toned imitation stops. Four stops, one of sixteen-foot pitch, two of eight and one of four, bass and treble, are the normal minimum complement of the harmonium. A full organ stop or knee attachment, by which the full power of the instrument is brought into play at once, and a swell, similar to the Venetian swell on the organ, controlled by a knee attachment, are usual features of the modern harmonium.

Harmony, one aspect of the simultaneous combination of notes, the other being counterpoint. Harmony and counterpoint have been likened to vertical and horizontal aspects of the same thing. They are not independent and neither can be effective without due regard for the other.

The drone of primitive bagpipes, and the parallel fourths, fifths and octaves between voices singing the same melody at a different pitch probably led to the rise of harmony and counterpoint. The earliest compositions showing a genuine harmonic sense date from the 9th century. Fourths, fifths and octaves are used as concords; all other intervals (including the third) are treated as discords which must be explained contrapuntally by their context. The style of this primitive harmony is shown by these examples from *Musica Enchiriadis*, a late 9th- or 10th-century treatise.

By the 13th century the fourth was being treated as a discord, while the third and sixth were being treated with increasingly greater freedom. By the 15th century the common chord (the triad) and its first inversion were treated as concords, and had taken a prominent position in harmony. The two famous English compositions *Sumer is icumen in* and *Deo gracias Anglia* give some idea of what was achieved during this period.

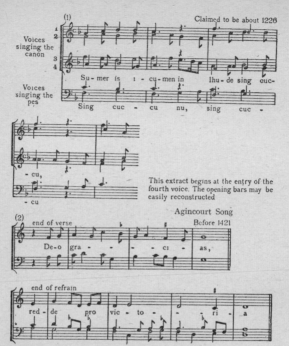

Claimed to be about 1226

Voices singing the canon

Voices singing the pes

Su - mer is i - cu - men in   lhu - de sing cuc-

Sing cuc - cu nu, sing   cuc -

- cu,

- cu

This extract begins at the entry of the fourth voice. The opening bars may be easily reconstructed

Agincourt Song
Before 1421

(2) end of verse

De-o gra - - - ci - as,

end of refrain

red - de pro vic - to - - ri a

The canon *Sumer is icumen in* has an unprecedented polish and technical ingenuity for the date commonly ascribed to it. *Deo gracias Anglia* is more typical of the style of its time, though Dufay and Dunstable achieved better artistic results.

During the 16th century the first contrapuntal style matured. The harmonic conventions on which this style was based treated the common chord and its first inversion as a concord. The style was no longer tied to the medieval modal system, but was not yet bound by the major and minor key system. A sense of tonality was sufficiently developed to recognise the value of the perfect authentic cadence, and to have a feeling for modulation.

During the 17th century the harmonic basis of 16th-century technique was developed at the expense of the counterpoint with which it had previously been inseparably interwoven. The example (given in the article on consecutives) from a song by Hume shows the simple harmonic style which was being developed at the end

of the 16th and the beginning of the 17th century. In this song
Hume uses only the tonic, dominant and subdominant triads.
Example (a) in the article on suspensions (from a madrigal by
Monteverdi) shows a deliberate exploitation of a harmonic effect
contrapuntally derived. In contrast, this example from the lute
music of Dowland shows a technique more often associated with
the early 18th century than with Dowland's own time.

"Forlorne Hope"
DOWLAND

By the end of the 17th century the simple harmonic basis of
the 16th-century polyphony had been considerably broadened.
Harmonic effects which had been derived contrapuntally were
separated from their contrapuntal context and treated as having
their own harmonic implications. Harmonies were organised in
relation to the major and minor key system which dominated
musical composition during the next two centuries. Within the
tonal framework of the key system, the harmonic resources were
further enriched. Purcell in the later part of the 17th century and
Bach in the first part of the 18th century each used the accepted
harmonies of their day, but they freed those harmonies from their
contrapuntal derivation and in turn used them as a vehicle for
new contrapuntal writing which created fresh harmonic effects.
Example (b) in the article on suspensions (from a setting of a
choral by Bach) and this example from Purcell's string music show
the deliberate use of harmonies (chords of the seventh in particular)
which previously were derived contrapuntally from a simpler
harmonic basis.

Fantasia No. 3, for Strings
Middle Section
PURCELL

Bach represents the culmination of this second contrapuntal style of composition.

Developments in style during the remainder of the 19th century were concerned mainly with form. Harmonic values remained much the same; development of them was mainly in the nature of disguising the preparation and resolution of discords by means of the figuration possible on keyboard and other instruments.

Towards the end of the 19th century and during the present century there have been several kinds of harmonic development. Some composers have developed still further traditional harmonic idioms, while others have invented idioms which appear (at least) to have no roots in the past. Some idioms, described as neo-modal, suggest the flavour of the medieval modal system by using traditional or new modal melodies often combined with predominantly diatonic harmony. Other idioms exploit the effect of simultaneous harmonic streams which move with considerable independence, though not entirely regardless of one another. Idioms in which two or more tonalities are suggested simultaneously by two or more melodic or harmonic streams are described as polytonal. Idioms which make no pretence of key have been described as atonal. Several harmonic idioms have been based on other than the traditional scales. Debussy used the whole tone scale, Scriabin a scale derived from the harmonic series, while others have used as scales series of notes chosen arbitrarily from the chromatic scale. The 'twelve note music' of Schönberg is one of the most convincing attempts to discard completely the traditional tonal basis of melody and harmony.

Harp, a plucked stringed instrument. In its more primitive forms the harp is probably the earliest of plucked string instruments, the principle of combining a number of pipes or strings of different sizes to give a musical scale being more elementary than that of having sound holes in one pipe or stopping one string. The earliest records of harps are Egyptian, and may be of the 13th century B.C.

The beautiful distinctive triangular form of the harp, and the simplicity of the essential features of the instrument are readily recognised in the various forms of the instrument to be found from the most ancient models to those now used in the modern orchestra. The soundboard, usually next to the player, forms one side of the triangle, the curved neck the top side of the triangle, and the front pillar the third side. The strings, stretched from the neck to the soundboard, are parallel to the front pillar.

The ancient Egyptian harps were invariably without front pillars, so limiting the tension possible in the strings. They varied considerably in size (from large six-foot models to small instruments easily held by a seated player), number of strings and ornament. The medieval harps were diatonic instruments and would have been unlikely to survive long after the introduction of modulation into Western music. Chromatic harps were tried in the 18th century, but the difficulty of playing them was too great. In Bavaria about the year 1820 was first made a pedal mechanism which instantaneously raised each string a semitone. The production of a satisfactory pedal action is credited to two Frenchmen, father and son, Cousineaus, who by about 1782 made the first double-action pedals and changed the open scale from E♭ to C♭.

The harp was brought to perfection by Sebastian Erard who, during the close of the 18th and the beginning of the 19th centuries, invented a fork mechanism for stopping the strings, and later combined it with double action throughout the instrument, and his instrument of 1810 has remained the model for the modern orchestral harp.

The compass of the Erard double-action harp is six-and-a-half octaves upwards from the C♭ three octaves below middle C. The open strings are tuned to the scale of C♭, two strings to each pitch. Each of seven pedals raises the pitch of notes of the same name either a semitone or a tone, so enabling tuning in every major and minor key possible, as well as a number of peculiar tunings possible, since adjacent pairs of strings may be made to sound the same note.

Harp Lute, one of the first of a number of instruments invented at the beginning of the 19th century, intended to replace the guitar. Edward Light of London designed a harp lute in 1798 following it with a harp-lute-guitar, and later his British lute-harp and dital harp.

Harpsichord, the most important of the keyboard stringed instruments in which the strings are set in vibration by jacks. The names of the various instruments of this kind are loosely associated with their shapes (these are shown in the diagram).

Shape (a) may be considered as that proper to the harpsichord, and by harpsichord is invariably meant an instrument of this shape. Shapes (b) and (c) are those commonly associated with the name spinet and virginal, the latter being shape (c) rather than (b). Shape (d) was that of the clavicytherum. Though instruments of shapes (b) and (c) were never called harpsichord, those of shape (a) were often called spinet or virginal.

Harpsichords were developed by the addition of a second keyboard and by having more than one string to each key, each set of strings being controlled by a stop as on the organ. More rarely a pedal board and a third keyboard were added. Commonly the second keyboard was essentially of octave pitch while the larger instruments had stops of 16-, 8- and 4-foot pitch on the principal keyboard.

The harpsichord was adopted as the accompanying instrument of the orchestra in opera and oratorio from the beginning of the 16th century, and held its place in the orchestra until the close of the 18th century. It was the principal solo keyboard instrument until it was superseded by the pianoforte during the second half of the 18th century.

Harrison, Julius (b. Stourport 1885), still living.

Harty, Sir Herbert Hamilton (b. Hillsborough 1879, d. Brighton 1941), achieved distinction primarily as an orchestral conductor.

Harwood, Basil (b. Olveston 1859, d. Clifton 1949), was organist of Christ Church, Oxford from 1892 to 1907, when he retired. Some of his church music is well known, and he made several notable contributions to the repertory of the organ.

Hassler, Hans Leo (b. Nuremberg 1564, d. Frankfort 1612), was the most distinguished member of a musical family. He achieved considerable eminence as an organist and composer.

Hautboy, the English corruption of the French haut-bois, used by Shakespeare. In Handel's time the name became spelt hoboy, and more recently the Italian form oboe has been commonly adopted.

Hautboy, a reed stop on English organs, of 8-foot pitch on the Swell Organ.

Hawkins, Sir John (b. London 1719, d. there 1789), was a musical historian who, like his contemporary Burney, made an out-

THE HARPSICHORD

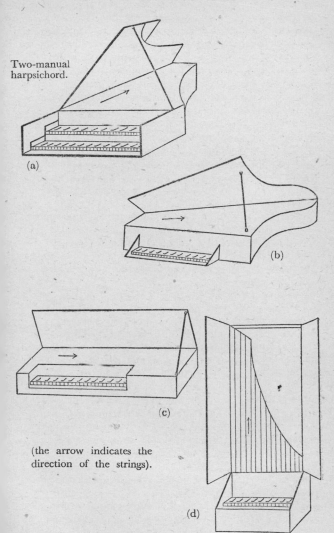

Two-manual harpsichord.

(a)

(b)

(c)

(the arrow indicates the direction of the strings).

(d)

standing contribution to musical research. His *General History of the Science and Practice of Music* was published in 1776, the year in which the first volume of Burney's *General History of Music* appeared.

Hay or *Hey*, a figure occurring in dances, often mentioned in the 16th and 17th centuries, in which the dancers wind about one another in a figure of eight.

Haydn, Franz Joseph (b. Rohrau 1732, d. Vienna 1809), was the son of a master wheelwright. There is evidence that he was of Croatian, not Teutonic, origin; in either case his parents were of low estate, and their apparent fondness for music was uncultured. Haydn showed a liking for music from his early youth. He was taken to school at Hainburg by a relative who was a schoolteacher and choirmaster there, and in 1740 was noticed by the Kapellmeister of St Stephen's, Vienna, and taken into his choir. Five years later Haydn's brother Michael joined the choir and by 1749, when Haydn left, had taken his place as leading chorister. Though his musical and general education at Vienna was better than it had been at Hainburg, Haydn had little help in writing music. His next few years after leaving St Stephen's were, therefore, largely spent in acquiring a formal knowledge of the principles of composition. His first study was of the clavier sonatas of C.P.E. Bach.

From the first Haydn obtained recognition in his profession. He wrote the music for a farce which was first performed in 1752 and often repeated, was engaged by Porpora as accompanist (an association which enabled him to make a regular study of the standard theoretical books on music), obtained various small teaching appointments, and by 1755 had a reputation which gained for him an invitation for a long visit to the home of an eminent physician and musical enthusiast at Weinzirl. In Vienna Haydn was in request as a performer and teacher. He married in 1760; he had no children and parted from his wife after a few years.

In 1761 he was appointed second Kapellmeister to Prince Esterhazy, and after five years, when the senior Kapellmeister died, became solely responsible for the music of the prince's household. A little later he moved with the main body of the musical establishment to the prince's new summer residence, Esterhaz, in Hungary. The disadvantages of the seclusion at Esterhaz were more than balanced for Haydn by the demands it made on his own originality, the opportunities it gave him for experiment, his happy relations with his musicians, and the use made by the prince of his musical establishment. On two occasions, in 1769 and 1777, the whole musical establishment visited Vienna. The prince died in 1790, leaving Haydn a pension, provided he kept the title of Kapellmeister. The new prince, while he increased Haydn's pension, dismissed nearly all the musical staff; and, though the establishment was reconstituted later, Haydn, while continuing his association with Esterhaz, did not resume his duties. For the remainder of his life Haydn enjoyed the fruits of the reputation he had established among the nobility during his service with the prince. He accepted invitations to London in 1791 and in 1794, received the degree of Mus.D. from Oxford and was welcomed at court. After 1801 he wrote little; his last few years he spent in retirement, having deservedly gained full recognition of his genius.

Most of Haydn's music was written in the course of his duties for the singers and players in the prince's household and, as his fame grew, in response to particular requests, such as that by the cathedral of Cadiz for music for Good Friday, in response to which he wrote *The Seven Words*. Of his oratorios *The Seasons* and *The Creation* are well known. His other sacred music includes fourteen masses. His operas and music for the stage are now almost forgotten. Among his instrumental compositions are over a hundred symphonies, nearly as many string quartets, over fifty clavier sonatas and an equally large number of concertos, for clavier or other instruments, trios and the like. It must be remembered, however, that these compositions are very much slighter than those of later writers; the early symphonies, for instance, are scored for strings with but few wind instruments, are simple in form and short in duration. These compositions were, however, a contribution of first importance to the establishment and early development of those forms associated with the sonata and symphony.

Hely-Hutchinson, Christian Victor (b. Cape Colony 1901, d. London 1947), was on the staff of the South African College of Music at Cape Town before he joined the B.B.C. in 1926. He followed Sir Granville Bantock as Professor of Music at Birmingham University in 1934, returning to the B.B.C. as Musical Director in 1944. As a composer he is known chiefly for his settings of Nonsense and Nursery Rhymes.

Henschel, Sir George (b. Breslau 1850, d. in Scotland 1934), achieved distinction as a singer, conductor and composer.

Hérold Louis Joseph Ferdinand (b. Paris 1791, d. Les Ternes 1833), studied at the Paris Conservatoire, won the Grand Prix de Rome in 1812, and subsequently had a distinguished career as an opera composer. His successful opera *Zampa* is now remembered by its overture.

Heseltine, Philip (b. London 1894, d. there 1930), is commonly known by the name Peter Warlock under which he composed. He received no special musical training, apart from learning music at Eton, where he was educated. Perhaps his main contribution to music was as a song-writer, but his *Capriol Suite*, delightful settings of tunes from Arbeau's *Orchésographie*, is well known. He made a valuable contribution to the revival of English songs by Dowland and his contemporaries by his faithful transcriptions from the original song books. He gained a Carnegie award in 1923 for *The Curlew*, a song cycle for tenor voice, flute, cor anglais and string quartet, but his merit as a composer is probably not yet fully realized.

Hexachord, a group of six sounds forming a scale. The hexachord was associated with the gamut, and played an important part in the evolution of the scale during the 11th and following centuries. A table showing the seven hexachords is given in the article on the gamut.

Hidden Fifths and *Hidden Octaves*, the consecutive fifths and consecutive octaves which were considered (from the 17th to the 19th century) to be implied or hidden when two parts approach the fifth and octave by similar motion.

Highland Fling, a dancing step of the Scottish Highlands, and commonly the name of the dance itself. The dance is performed to the music of the Strathspey by three or more persons, and is characterized by dancing alternately on each leg, flinging the other behind or in front.

Hiller, Johann Adam (b. near Gorlitz 1728, d. Leipzig 1804), was an eminent conductor and teacher. As a composer of the lighter style of opera he achieved considerable success.

Hilton, John (f. 1601), was an English musician. He contributed to *The Triumphes of Oriana*, and was almost certainly the composer of the anthem *Lord for thy tender mercies' sake*, sometimes attributed to Richard Farrant.

Hilton, John (b. 1599, d. 1657), was probably the son of the older John Hilton.

Hindemith, Paul (b. Hanau 1895), still living.

Hipkins, Alfred James (b. Westminster 1826, d. London 1903), was an authority on old keyboard instruments.

Hocket, a device used in its primitive form particularly in the 13th and 14th centuries. The melody was either interspersed with rests, remaining in one part, or divided between two parts, each part singing alternate notes. Though unseemly in its primitive forms and use, the emotional effect at which it aimed was genuine. Later forms of precisely the same device have produced perfectly satisfactory results.

Hoffman, Ernst Theodor Amadeus (b. Königsberg 1776, d. Berlin 1822), was an eccentric composer and novelist, the hero of Offenbach's *Tales of Hoffman.*

Holborne, William (f. 1597), was an English musician. His published madrigals are included in *The English Madrigal School;* the original publication containing his madrigals also contained instrumental music by his brother *Antony* (d. 1602).

Holbrooke, Joseph (b. Croydon 1878), still living.

Holmes, John (f. 1601-1610), was an English musician. He contributed to *The Triumphes of Oriana.*

Holst, Gustav Theodore (b. Cheltenham 1874, d. London 1934), was of predominantly English ancestry, though his family was originally Swedish. He entered the Royal College of Music in 1895, with an open scholarship for composition. After three years' study he began his professional career playing trombone in the Carl Rosa Opera Company. He was later music master at St. Paul's Girls' School, and in 1919 joined the teaching staffs of the Royal College of Music and University College, Reading.

Among his compositions for full orchestra are *The Planets, Egdon Heath* and a *Double Concerto* for two violins. The *St Paul's Suite* and *Brook Green Suite* are two delightful simple essays for strings alone. Among his compositions for chorus and orchestra are *Choral Hymns from the Rig-Veda* and *The Hymn of Jesus.* A number of settings of folk songs and carols and a variety of smaller choral compositions display a sympathetic and imaginative treatment of voices. He also wrote for the stage and contributed a little music to the repertory of the brass and military bands.

Homophony, plain harmony, without contrapuntal features in the part writing, the melodic interest being confined to one part.

Honegger, Arthur (b. Havre 1892), still living.

Hook, James (b. Norwich 1746, d. Boulogne 1827), became organist of Vauxhall Gardens. He is remembered for *The Lass of Richmond Hill,* one of his numerous songs.

Hooper, Edmund (b. Halberton *c.* 1553, d. London 1621), contributed to *The Teares or Lamentacions* compiled by Leighton.

Horn (in its broadest sense), any wind instrument descended from the natural horn fashioned from the horn of an animal. The variety of animal horns enabled an equal variety of primitive instruments of this kind. In this sense, therefore, horn includes the trumpet (and with it the trombone) and the tuba, as well as a great many older and more modern instruments. In all these instruments the lips of the player pressed together and held against a cupped mouthpiece act as a double reed.

Conveniently, the horn may be taken in the more limited sense of brass instruments with a bore mainly conical, played with a cupped mouthpiece which is funnel shaped, and which sound far less brilliant than the trumpet. Horns of metal were made by the Romans (buccina and cornu), if not before. The essential proportions of the horn as it is now known were established by the beginning of the 18th century; from then it began to take its place in the orchestra.

The orchestral horn was originally without valves. The horn with valves superseded the horn without valves during the 19th century. Early orchestral music took advantage of horns built in (or adapted by means of a crook to) a variety of keys covering a range of an octave from B ♭ to B♭. Although the key of a horn with valves may be changed by means of a crook, the horn is now usually used in F, other keys specified in older music being obtained by using the valves rather than by changing the crook.

The notes obtained from the horn in F without the use of the valves are:

that is, the notes of the harmonic series. Apart from the fundamental, which is difficult to obtain, and the notes marked *, these are the harmonics normally used. By use of the three valves, the complete chromatic scale may be produced over the two and a half octaves. By placing the hand in the bell (known as 'stopping') both the tone and the pitch may be modified.

The horn is treated as a transposing instrument. Music for it is written on the treble clef and sounds a fifth lower than written.

For low notes the bass clef is sometimes needed, and in older music the notes were then written an octave lower than normal; thus notes on the bass clef for a horn in E would sound a third higher than written, while notes on the treble clef would sound a sixth lower than written.

Horn Pipe, a dance, well known in the 16th century in England. The music was then in triple time. Many examples of the music have survived, though the steps of the dance itself are now forgotten. During the 17th century the hornpipe changed its character. From then on it was usually written in four-four time, began on the last crochet in the bar, ended with three crotchet repetitions of the final note, and had ♪│♩♩♩ and ♪│♫♫♩ as characteristic figures. It was introduced into the theatre and became commonly associated with sailors, probably because as now danced it can be performed in little space and does not require partners.

Howells, Herbert (b. Lydney 1892), still living.

Hucbald (b. *c.* 830, d. *c.* 930), a monk of St Arnaud, was the writer of an early treatise on music.

Hughes, Herbert (b. Belfast 1882 d. Brighton 1937), achieved distinction as a composer. He played a prominent part in founding the Irish Folk Song Society, and his compositions include many charming settings of Irish folk songs.

Hume, Tobias (d. 1645), was an Englishman; details of his life are negligible; he finished his days suffering from mental delusions in the Charter House. Most of his music is of little interest, but his setting of the anonymous poem *Fain would I change that note* is incomparable.

Humoreske, a name used by Schumann, Grieg and others, particularly for pianoforte pieces of light character. The name has no special aptness or meaning.

Humfrey, Pelham (b. 1647, d. Windsor 1674), became Master of the Children of the Chapel Royal. He studied with Lully in France. Humfrey left several fine anthems and a quantity of secular vocal music.

Hummel, Johann Nepomuk (b. Pressburg 1778, d. Weimar 1837), was the son of the Director of the Imperial School of Military Music at Pressburg. He had a distinguished career as a pianist and his influence on the development of keyboard technique was considerable. He suggested a logical system of fingering and a number of changes in the method of performing trills and turns.

Humperdinck, Engelbert (b. Siegburg 1854, d. Neustrelitz 1921), was a composer, mainly of dramatic music, and a teacher. He gained outstanding success with his masterpiece, the opera *Hansel and Gretel*.

Hunt, Thomas (f. 1601), was an English musician. He contributed to *The Triumphes of Oriana*.

Hurdy Gurdy, a keyboard stringed instrument in which the strings are set in vibration by a rosined revolving wheel. In so far as three or four strings sound continuously as drones while the melody is played on the higher strings, the hurdy gurdy is a string counterpart to the bagpipe.

Hydraulus, the organ invented in Egypt in the third century B.C., which became associated with the Roman gladiatorial displays of the early centuries of the Christian era. The details of its construction were forgotten during the Middle Ages. The detail in a clay model of the hydraulus, found in 1885 in the ruins of Carthage, made possible the construction of a working model by Francis Galpin. The steady pressure of the wind supply was maintained by water pressure: hence the name of the instrument. The Carthage organ had nineteen pivoted keys operating three ranks of metal fluepipes tuned at the unison, octave and super octave, which could be brought into play at will.

Hymn, originally any sung act of praise to God. The name became limited to exclude the psalms and canticles, and to be applied with few exceptions to metrical poems only. To St Ambrose is the credit for the introduction of the metrical hymn into the services of the Western Church, and a comprehensive cycle of Latin metrical hymns with plainsong melodies evolved during the early centuries of the Christian Church. With the rise of polyphony, these tunes were constantly used as canti fermi for masses and motets, and Palestrina's *Hymni Totius Anni* are an outstanding example of the contrapuntal treatment of these hymns. The Reformation encouraged the singing of vernacular hymns. In Germany this resulted in the Lutheran Choral which reached its peak of refinement and embellishment in the hands of Bach. In France, followed by England, the Metrical Psalms supplied the same need.

The present conception of the hymn, and the numerous English hymn books of to-day followed the Church revival of the mid-19th century. The English metrical psalter was succeeded by hymnals which included material from the three sources, Latin hymns, German chorals and metrical psalms, as well as numerous lesser sources, and a great deal of later religious poetry and music, much of it of an inferior quality. The *Historical Edition of Hymns Ancient and Modern* indicates the remarkable variety of the sources from which both the words and melodies have come. Unfortunately the manner in which a prosaic succession of minims was substituted for the varied note values of the original melodies, and the harmonies were brought into line with the current English vocal part-writing, destroyed the distinctive features of the various styles of the originals. Later hymn books, the *English Hymnal* in particular, under the musical editorship of Vaughan Williams, have restored the original character of the material from old sources, rejected much of the old that was bad and incorporated much new that is good.

Hyper and *Hypo* (Gr.), over and under. These prefixes were used in the Greek modal system, and were adopted from it to the modal system evolved during the Middle Ages. The use of these terms in the two systems was not identical.

I

Idyll, a title, borrowed from poetry, sometimes used for compositions of a pastoral nature.

Imitation, the strict or free repetition of a melody or figure in another voice or part. Imitation includes, therefore, the most free use of a theme in various voices or parts as well as the employment of the strictest forms of canon.

Impromptu (It.), a name used by Chopin, in particular, for pianoforte pieces. The name would imply that the compositions were in the nature of extemporizations.

Improvisation, another name for extemporization.

Incidental Music, music occurring during the action of a play as opposed to such as an overture or interlude.

Inflexion, any melodic variation in an intonation which is mainly on one note. Inflexions are mainly associated with the chanting of religious services. The Gregorian chants, for instance, illustrate clearly the nature and purpose of inflexions in what would otherwise be a pure monotone.

In Nomine, apparently an exclusively English type of instrumental composition popular during the 16th and early 17th centuries. In every case the plainsong *Gloria Tibi Trinitas* is used as a canto fermo. The reason for this peculiar title has only recently been discovered. In Taverner's Mass on the plainsong *Gloria Tibi Trinitas,* the words 'in nomine Domini' in the Benedictus are set in four parts in duple measure with the plainsong entire in the alto part. At a time when concerted string playing was in its infancy and the supply of music for strings meagre, this excerpt proved suitable as a short piece for strings in four parts, and as such it became the prototype of many similar compositions.

Inscription (at the beginning of a canon), the sign or motto or both indicating how the canon may be worked out. Many of the extravagant inscriptions attached to canons composed in the 15th and 16th centuries added to the perplexity of the solver rather than helped him.

Instruments. Musical instruments may be classified in several more or less elaborate ways. The classification adopted here is by no means comprehensive, but it should be sufficient to indicate the relation between the principal types, particularly those in common use at the present time.

TABLE II

A Classification of Musical Instruments

(a) Stringed Instruments

Sub class	Type		Typical Examples
1. By plucking	Without a neck	Open strings	Harp, Lyre, Psaltery
		Fretted strings	Zither
	With a neck		Lute, Cither, Guitar
2. By striking			Dulcimer
3. By friction (bowed)	Without a neck		Crwth
	With a neck		Rebec, Viol, Violin, Marine Trumpet

Note – The Harp, Guitar and members of the Violin family are the chief modern representative of this class.

(b) Wind Instruments

Sub class	Types			Typical Examples
1. Flue-voiced	Whistle mouthpiece			Recorder
	Blown across open end	Open pipe		Nay
		Closed pipe		Pandean Pipe
	Blown across side hole			Flute
2. Reed-voiced	Single reed	Cylindrical tube		Clarinet
		Conical tube		Saxophone
	Double reed	Cylindrical tube		Aulos
		Conical tube		Oboe, Cor Anglais, Bassoon
	Both types of reed and tube, the reeds enclosed			Bagpipe
3. Lip-voiced	Tube of fixed length (natural)			Bugle, Horn, Trumpet
	Tube of variable length	By finger holes or keys	Wood	Serpent
			Metal	Ophicleide
		By slide		Trombone
		By pistons		Horn, Trumpet, Tuba

Notes – (i) Modern instruments of sub classes 1 and 2 are commonly known as woodwind, those of sub class 3 as brass.

(ii) The Nay, Pandean Pipe and Aulos are primitive instruments; modern instruments of this type are not used.

(iii) The natural forms of the Horn and Trumpet are no longer in general use.

(c) Percussion Instruments

Sub class	Type		Typical Examples
1. Stretched membranes	Non-melodic	Rim frame	Tambourine
		Cylinder frame	Bass drum, Tabor, Side drum
	Melodic		Kettledrum
2. Various materials	Non-melodic		Castanets, Cymbals, Gong, Triangle
	Melodic		Glockenspiel, Xylophone

(d) Keyboard Instruments

Sub class	Type	Typical Examples
1. Stringed	By striking	Chekker, Clavichord, Pianoforte
	By plucking	Harpsichord
	By bowing	Hurdy-Gurdy
2. Wind	Flue and Reed pipes	Organ
	Free reeds	Regal, Harmonium
3. Various materials	By striking	Celesta, Dulcitone

Interlude, a composition played between the acts or scenes of a drama, church service or performance of any kind. The interlude has been, and still is an important part of the musical decoration of church services, particularly those of the Roman Catholic Church.

Intermezzo, a title used in a number of senses. Light dramatic entertainments between the acts of an opera or dramatic performance, to allow rest for the performers, relief from strict attention to the audience, and time for the preparation of stage effects, were known as intermezzi. Those for one opera or drama gradually became a connected group forming a subordinate and continuous but independent drama on their own. The performance of intermezzi as a continuous piece led to the independent development of opera buffa.

Orchestral interludes in an opera, indicating the passing of time, and played without lowering the curtain, are known as intermezzi, as also are short movements, instrumental or vocal, between larger movements in large-scale composition. This title has been used by Mendelssohn and others as the name for a large-scale movement, and by Schumann, Brahms and others as the name of small-scale independent compositions.

Interrupted Cadence, a cadence in which the expected chord succession of dominant followed by tonic is interrupted by some other chord sounding where the tonic was expected.

interrupted cadence

An interrupted cadence has an element of surprise rather than the element of rest naturally expected in a cadence.

Interval, the difference in pitch between two notes. Intervals are named by the number of the degrees of the scale they cover.

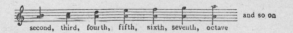

second, third, fourth, fifth, sixth, seventh, octave   and so on

The octave, fifth and fourth from the key note in either the major or minor scale (these intervals are the same in both scales) are described as perfect. Two sizes of second, third, sixth and seventh occur (within the octave) in the major scale; in each case the larger interval is described as major, the smaller as minor. An interval a semitone less than perfect or minor is described as diminished, while an interval a semitone more than perfect or major is described as augmented. This system of nomenclature is sufficient for most purposes. Several intervals for which it allows, such as the diminished second and the augmented third, do not usually occur.

In several instances two of these intervals are identical on the keyboard, though harmonically and melodically they receive different treatment.

	Intervals	Size in tones
(a)	major second, diminished third	1
(b)	augmented second, minor third	1½
(c)	major third, diminished fourth	2
(d)	augmented fourth, diminished fifth	3
(e)	augmented fifth, minor sixth	4
(f)	major sixth, diminished seventh	4½
(g)	augmented sixth, minor seventh	5

Scientifically an interval is measured by the ratio of the frequencies of the two notes concerned. For instance, the sizes of the successive pairs of notes of the harmonic series are

$$2 \quad 3/2 \quad 4/3 \quad 5/4 \quad 6/5 \quad 7/6* \quad 8/7* \quad 9/8$$

and so on. The octave is represented by 2 and the unison by 1. In the octave divided into twelve equal semitones, the intervals of the unison, one semitone, two semitones, and so on up to the octave are represented precisely by the values

$$2^{\frac{0}{12}} \quad 2^{\frac{1}{12}} \quad 2^{\frac{2}{12}} \quad 2^{\frac{3}{12}} \text{ and so on to } 2^{\frac{12}{12}}$$

It so happens that these values (the first twelve powers of the twelfth root of 2) approximate closely to the values of certain simple ratios. With the exception of those marked *, the intervals between the first nine notes of the harmonic series can be closely represented on the scale of twelve equal semitones to the octave (the equal temperament scale). The ear is willing to accept the intervals of the equal temperament scale as sufficiently good approximations to these intervals of the harmonic scale. These two facts make possible the combination of melody, harmony and modulation as we know it.

In practice it is convenient to express the size of an interval in either savarts or cents. Whereas to add intervals their ratios must be multiplied, savarts or cents need only be added. An octave is represented by 301 savarts or by 1200 cents. Both savarts and cents are logarithmic units. One savart is approximately equal to four cents. Savarts are simply logarithms correct to three decimal places with the decimal point omitted. Cents conveniently represent each equal semitone as 100.

Intrada, a name used by Beethoven and Mozart for an opening movement and by Bach for an independent movement.

Introduction, an initial section of a composition before the first statement of the main subject or subjects. It is commonly used of this section in symphonic music, which may vary from a few bars to an extended section.

Invention, a name used by Bach for fifteen short keyboard pieces in two-part counterpoint. They are commonly known as the two-part inventions to distinguish them from the pieces of a companion set in three-part counterpoint (named symphonies by Bach) which are commonly known as the three-part inventions.

Inversion, a term used in various senses:

(a) An interval is inverted by raising the lower note or lowering the top note an octave.

(b) A chord is inverted when one of its notes other than the root is in the bass.

(c) A pedal point is inverted when it is placed in an upper part.

(d) Counterpoint is inverted when the upper part is placed
below.

(e) A melody or a phrase is said to be inverted when it is
imitated by contrary motion.

Intonation, the inflexion at the beginning of a Gregorian chant.

Ireland, John (b. Bowden 1879), still living.

Isaac, Heinrich (b. *c.* 1450 d. 1517), was the most important German
composer of his time. Nothing is known of his early life, and but
little with certainty of the rest of it. He lived a good deal of his
life in Florence, and was appointed to the court of Maximilian
shortly after he had become sole ruler of Germany. Isaac's
sacred and secular compositions place him in the front rank of
late 15th- and early 16th-century composers.

J

Jack (in the action of instruments of the harpsichord family), the
plectrum which sets a string in vibration. The jack consists of a
short rod of wood, resting vertically on the back end of the key-
lever, with a thorn or quill on a movable tongue set in the rod.
The quill twangs the wire as the key is depressed and the jack
at the other end of the key-lever rises. The movable tongue
allows the quill to pass the string without twanging it as the key
is released and the jack returns to its normal position.

Jacob, Gordon (b. London 1895), still living.

Janáček, Leoš (b. Hukvaldy 1854, d. Ostrau 1928), achieved distinction as a conductor, teacher and composer.

Jannequin, Clément (16th century), was a Frenchman and a follower of Josquin des Près. His most important contributions to music were his songs for four voices which appear to have gained considerable popularity.

Jaques-Dalcroze, Émile. See appendix.

Järnefelt, Armas (b. Viborg 1869), still living.

Jew's Harp, the English name for an instrument found throughout Europe and Eastern Asia. Its name in Europe is commonly some form of 'trump'. The instrument consists of a small horse shoe of metal with a metal tongue between, free to vibrate when touched by the fingers. The instrument is held between the front teeth and the note produced varied by altering the cavity of the mouth. The name does not appear to have been derived from either Jews or jaws.

Jig, a lively tune of no characteristic rhythm or form. The English jig thus differs from the 'gigue', by name its Italian counterpart.

Jingles, the discs of metal fastened round the sides of the tambourine.

Joachim, Joseph (b. Kittsee 1831, d. Berlin 1907), was the foremost violinist of his time and a musician of real artistry. The numerous distinctions he received testify to the general admiration in which he was held. His quartet was founded in 1869 and continued with some changes until his death; each member of it played with a Stradivari of the same period.

Virtuoso compositions were excluded from his repertory. By his example and direct teaching, his influence in forwarding the cause of a faithful performance of the best in music rather than a display of virtuosity was great. His compositions have merit and reflect his serious approach to his art.

Jodel, the abrupt change from chest voice to falsetto which is a characteristic feature of the performances of Tyrolese singers.

Johnson, Edward (f. 1592-1601), was an English musician. He contributed to *The Triumphes of Oriana* and helped to harmonise the tunes for the Psalter of 1592 published by Thomas East.

Johnson, Robert (d. before 1634), was an English musician. He contributed to *The Teares or Lamentacions* compiled by Leighton.

Jommelli, Niccolo (b. Aversa 1714, d. Naples 1774), was one of the more distinguished of the many Neapolitan composers of the 18th century who followed in the wake of A. Scarlatti. His compositions included both opera and sacred music.

Jones, Robert (f. 1597–1615), was an English musician. He took the degree of B.Mus. at Oxford in 1597. He was one of the more prolific writers of ayres contemporary with Dowland. He published five volumes of songs, which are included in *The English School of Lutenist Songwriters*. His style is simple and his vocal parts are particularly suitable for the voice. He published a volume of madrigals which are included in *The English Madrigal School*, contributed to *The Triumphes of Oriana* and to *The Teares or Lamentacions* compiled by Leighton.

Jongen, Joseph (b. Liège 1873), still living.

Jongleur, the instrumentalist attendant on a 'trouvère'.

Josquin des Près (b. c. 1445, d. Condé 1521), was one of the greatest composers of his period. The details of his life are uncertain. He served in the Sistine Chapel from 1456 to 1494; he appears to have then been appointed to Louis XII of France and later to the Emperor Maximilian. In his earlier works he achieved mastery over the problems of canon. His later works achieve a combination of melodic beauty with contrapuntal skill. His extant compositions include seventeen masses, a large number of motets (amongst them a *Stabat Mater* for five voices), and a number of settings of secular songs.

Jota, a typical north Spanish dance, similar to the waltz.

Jubal, the Biblical inventor of stringed and wind instruments.

Just Intonation, tuning according to what have been accepted as the true intervals between the notes of the diatonic scale. Only one such key can be so tuned; the closely related keys are then passably in tune while the more distant keys are unbearably out of tune. This results from the discrepancy of the comma between compound intervals calculated in different ways.

K

Karg-Elert, Sigfrid (b. Oberndorf-am-Neckar 1877, d. Leipzig 1933), achieved distinction as a composer for the organ. His choral improvisations are a notable contribution to the organ repertory.

Keeners, the mourners at an Irish funeral who sang the caoine.

Keiser, Reinhard (b. Teuchern 1674, d. Hamburg 1739), achieved success mainly as an opera composer. He had an important influence on German opera.

Kettledrum, the basin-shaped drums used in the orchestra which give a musical note. Formerly two drums only were used. Towards the end of the 19th century a third drum became commonly used. Before Beethoven the pair of kettledrums were commonly tuned to the tonic and dominant of the key, being retuned where necessary during the course of a movement. Further, the drums were treated as transposing instruments, being written for in C. From the time of Beethoven any convenient tuning of the kettledrums became common.

The usual compass of the three kettledrums now employed is

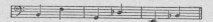

It has long been the custom to write the actual notes sounded. Both single taps and rolls are effective on the kettledrums. Though normally played with felt-headed cane sticks, various special effects, such as playing with side drum sticks and muffling the drums with a cloth, are occasionally employed.

Kettledrums are of Arabian origin and were probably introduced into Western Europe during the Crusades. They were known in England during the 14th and later centuries as nakers, a corruption of their Arabian name.

Key, the levers of the mechanism of musical instruments operated by the fingers of the performer. The keys of various keyboard instruments and those of woodwind instruments perform differing though related functions. The keys of keyboard instruments, the clavichord, harpsichord, pianoforte and organ, are each identified with a particular note; either directly or indirectly, they effect the sounding of the particular note with which they are associated by causing a particular string to vibrate, or by allowing wind to reach a particular pipe. The keys of woodwind instruments open or close sound holes, so altering the effective or sounding length of the tube and the pitch of the note produced on sounding the instrument. Keys have been applied to brass instruments, but keyed brass instruments are either obsolete or rarely used.

Key, properly the position on the scale in which European music in either the major or minor mode is written. The term key is, however, invariably used indiscriminately for the two distinct conceptions of key and mode. The twelve semitones in the octave of the European scale enable each of these two modes to be reproduced at twelve positions, giving rise to the twelve major and twelve minor keys.

Keyboard, the set of keys by which the organ, pianoforte and numerous other modern and older instruments are played. The origin of the keyboard is uncertain. Though the hydraulus had a primitive keyboard, it is most probable that the keyboard was re-invented or re-discovered after the principles on which the hydraulus was constructed had been forgotten. The keyboard of levers may have been invented and first applied to strings, or it may have replaced push-pull rods by which wind was let to the pipes of primitive organs.

The earliest keyboards were doubtless diatonic. Whatever the order in which the sharps were introduced, the complete chromatic arrangement of the naturals and sharps as we now know it had been evolved by the later part of the 15th century.

The crude mechanism of the primitive large organ necessitated clumsy and widely spaced keys. The small keyboard applied to strings (probably for the first time during the 14th century) when applied to pipes severely limited the size of pipes which could be used. With improvements in mechanism, the keyboard of the large organ reached a manageable size towards the beginning of the 16th century, and from the 16th century onwards the size of the keyboard has remained almost the same. Various attempts to design keyboards which would recognise the difference between sharps and flats have met with no success.

Key Bugle, Kent Bugle or *Regent's Bugle,* simply a keyed modification of the natural bugle. It was a popular and prominent member of military bands sometime during the first half of the 18th century.

Keyed Guitar, a guitar having keys of some kind to pluck or strike the strings. Keys were devised for English guitars towards the end of the 18th century.

Key Note, the note by which a key in the modern key system is named. It corresponds to the final of the older melodic modes.

Key Signature, the group of sharp or flat signs placed after the clef at the beginning of a composition, or after a double bar in the course of it. The sharps or flats of a key signature are effective throughout a composition unless contradicted by a new key signature and apply to all notes of the same name at any pitch except when temporarily altered by accidentals. The key signatures and the major and minor keys associated with them are shown in the Table of Key Signatures.

It will be noticed that the first three sharp keys and the last three flat keys are equivalent, at least so far as the keyboard is concerned, the most convenient generally being chosen. Needless to say, the key signature of C flat major is not used.

TABLE III

A Table of Key Signatures

| Key | major | C sharp | F sharp | B | E | A |
| | minor | A sharp | D sharp | G sharp | C sharp | F sharp |

| Key | major | D | G | C | F | B flat |
| | minor | B | E | A | D | G |

| Key | major | E flat | A flat | D flat | G flat | C flat |
| | minor | C | F | B flat | E flat | A flat |

Kirbye, George (d. Bury St Edmunds, 1634), was an English musician. His published madrigals are included in *The English Madrigal School*. He contributed to *The Triumphes of Oriana* and helped to harmonise the tunes for the Psalter of 1592 published by Thomas East.

Kit, an extremely small violin used particularly by dancing masters. The English kit of the 17th century was the counterpart of the slightly earlier French pochette (so called because it could be carried in the pocket) and Italian sordino (so called because of its diminutive quality of sound).

Köchel, Ludwig Ritter von (b. Stein 1800, d. Vienna 1877), made an invaluable contribution to the study of Mozart. He numbered Mozart's compositions in chronological order (Mozart not having used Op. numbers as have most later composers). Mozart's works are now invariably identified by their K. numbers.

Kodály, Zoltán (b. Kecskemet 1882), still living.

Korbay, Francis Alexander (b. Budapest 1846, d. London 1913), began his musical career as an opera singer. He later studied the pianoforte and achieved distinction as a singer, teacher and composer. His compositions include many settings of Hungarian songs.

Krakoviak, a Polish dance originating from the district of Cracow.

Kreisler, Fritz (b. Vienna 1875), still living.

Kreutzer, Rodolphe (b. Versailles 1766, d. Geneva 1831), achieved distinction as a violinist and composer. He is remembered particularly for the sonata for violin and pianoforte which Beethoven dedicated to him and for his outstanding contribution to the repertory of violin studies.

Kuhnau, Johann (b. Geising 1660, d. Leipzig 1722), was the most important German composer for the clavier before Bach.

Kullak, Theodore (b. Krotoschin 1818, d. Berlin 1882), was an important teacher of the pianoforte, for which he wrote valuable teaching music.

L

La, the sixth note of the scale in solmization.

Lah, the sixth note of the scale in Tonic Sol-fa.

Lalande, Michel Richard de (b. Paris 1657, d. Versailles 1726), was in the service of the court of Louis XIV and Louis XV for forty-five years. He was the most successful French composer of church music of his period.

Lalo, Victor Antoine Édouard (b. Lille 1823, d. Paris 1892), was of Spanish origin. He was one of the most distinguished French composers of his day, particularly of orchestral and instrumental chamber music. His *Spanish Symphony* for violin and orchestra is one of his most successful works.

Lament, a name common in Scottish and Irish folk music for those airs used on occasions of mourning and misfortune.

Lancers Quadrille, a dance for eight or sixteen pairs claimed to have been invented at the beginning of the 19th century by a Joseph Hart.

Landino, Francesco (b. Florence *c.* 1325, d. there 1397), was an organist and composer of importance. He was blind from his childhood.

Ländler, an Austrian, Bavarian, Bohemian and Styrian dance similar to the waltz, but danced rather more slowly.

Large, the longest note of the medieval time system, equal to two or three longs according to the mood.

Larghetto (It.), the diminutive of 'largo'.

Largo (It.), broad. An indication of style rather than speed, though usually implying a slow pace as well as a dignified style.

Lassus, Orlande de (b. Mons *c.* 1530, d. Munich 1594), was taken to Sicily and Milan in 1544 by Gonzaga, Viceroy of Sicily, into whose service he had been taken on account of the beauty of his voice. Little is known of the earlier years of his life. Later, Lassus was choirmaster at St John Lateran in Rome for a few years, but he had settled in Antwerp by 1555. By this time he had gained an extensive experience of life. His first publications, dating from this time, show him to have acquired a developed technique of composition and a distinctive style. A year or two later he was appointed to the musical establishment of Duke Albert of Bavaria. In 1570 the Emperor Maximilian gave him a patent of nobility. Lassus visited Paris in 1571 and subsequently enjoyed the favour of the French court, though remaining for the rest of his life in the services of Duke Albert and his successor Duke William. In 1574 he visited Rome and was invested in the Papal Chapel as a Knight of the Golden Spur.

A large proportion of Lassus' compositions, volumes of motets, madrigals and the like, were published during his lifetime. In 1604 his sons Ferdinand and Rudolf published in six volumes, entitled *Magnum Opus musicum O. de Lasso,* all the motets, sacred and secular, already published and nearly a hundred more. His settings of the penitential psalms are perhaps the most often quoted examples of Lassus' finest work. Four settings of the Passion are interesting early examples of their form. Lassus, however, contributed to all the purely vocal forms sacred and secular of his time.

By the quantity, quality and variety of his compositions, Lassus ranks with Palestrina and Byrd as one of the great composers of his age.

Lautenclavicymbal, an instrument designed in 1740 by Bach with quality of sound so like that of the lute that it is said to have deceived even professional lutenists.

Lawes, Henry (b. Dinton 1596, d. London 1662), was the most important member of a family of English musicians flourishing in the 17th century. Lawes was a pupil of Cooper and in 1626 became a gentleman of the Chapel Royal. He was buried in the cloisters of Westminster Abbey. He wrote music for a number of dramatic works, the most important being that for Milton's masque *Comus.* He supplied new tunes for a paraphrase of the psalms by George Sandys, and with his brother William set another collection of psalms to music, adding to the collection some elegies, set by themselves and others, and some canons by

William. The most important of Lawes' sacred compositions was the anthem *Zadok the Priest* for Charles II's coronation. During his life Lawes had a high reputation both as a performer and composer.

Lay Clerk, a man singer in an English Cathedral choir, sometimes called 'lay vicar' or 'vicar choral'.

Leader (of an orchestra), the chief player amongst the first violins, who is considered responsible, under the direction of the conductor, for a variety of duties, such as preparing parts and supervising rehearsals in the conductor's absence.

Leading Note, the seventh note of any scale in the modern key system. In the modal systems the note next below the final was in some cases at an interval of a semitone, in others a tone. With the evolution of the modern key system the leading note was invariably at a semitone below the tonic in the minor as well as the major keys.

Leclair, Jean-Marie (b. Lyons 1697, murdered Paris 1764), was an eminent violinist and composer for the violin.

Legato (It.), connected. Describes execution without a perceptible break between each note and the next. Unless indicated otherwise, a legato performance is presumed. As a special warning, legato is sometimes placed at the beginning of a passage or movement.

Leger lines, short lines added when necessary above or below the staff.

Leggiero (It.), lightly.

Legrenzi, Giovanni (b. Clusone, 1626, d. Venice 1690), was an eminent organist and composer associated with St Mark's, Venice. Bach and Handel treated themes taken from his works.

Lehar, Franz (b. Komaron 1870, d. Bad Ischl 1948), was the son of a military bandmaster. He studied at the Prague Conservatory as a violinist, and for a while became a bandmaster like his father. Later he devoted himself to composition and achieved enormous success with operetta, proving himself a worthy successor to the Strauss family.

Among his most popular stage works are *The Merry Widow,* composed in 1905, and since revived many times, and *The Land of Smiles,* composed in 1931.

Leighton, Sir William (d. before 1617), was an English musician. He published in 1614 *The Teares or Lamentacions of a Sorrowfull Soule,* a compilation of fifty-four metrical psalms set variously for voices and instruments. Eight settings are by Leighton himself, the remainder are by Bull, Byrd, Cooper, Dowland, Ferrabosco,

Ford, Gibbons, Giles, Hooper, Johnson, Jones, Kindersley, Lupo, Milton, Peerson, Pilkington, Ward, Weelkes and Wilbye.

Leitmotiv (Ger.), guiding theme. A figure, melody or harmony associated with a person or idea throughout a composition. Guiding themes are a feature appropriate to both programme music and opera. Wagner employed the device consistently throughout his operas, and it is with him that the device is particularly associated.

Lento (It.), slow.

Leo, Leonardo (b. near Brindisi 1694, d. Naples 1744), was a prolific composer of opera, oratorio and sacred music. He held an important place in the evolution of the modern key system from the modal system, and the development of academic counterpoint in it.

Leoncavallo, Ruggiero (b. Naples 1858, d. Montecatini 1919), was a composer, mainly of opera. He is remembered for his opera *I Pagliacci;* most of his operas were of light character.

Lesson, a title commonly used in the 17th and 18th centuries for compositions, generally for the harpsichord, which, in groups, might well have formed a suite. The individual items in a collection of lessons commonly had their own titles.

Libretto (It.), a little book. The name now commonly used for the text of an opera or oratorio.

Lichfield, Henry (f. 1613), was an English musician. His published madrigals are included in *The English Madrigal School.*

Lieblich (Ger.), lovely. Used to describe organ stops such as the flute and gedact.

Ligature, groups of two or more notes sung metrically to one syllable. The ligatures were adapted from the earlier neumatic notation as the rise of polyphonic music made consideration of precise time values necessary.

Lira, a name given in the Middle Ages to certain stringed instruments such as the rebec and hurdy gurdy. During the 15th and 16th centuries the name was particularly used for bowed stringed instruments having more than their normal complement of strings.

Lisley, John (f. 1601), was an English musician. He contributed to *The Triumphes of Oriana.*

L'istesso Tempo (It.), the same time. Indicates a continuation at the same pace when a change might otherwise seem intended.

Liszt, Franz (b. Raiding 1811, d. Bayreuth 1886), was the son of a steward in the household of Prince Esterhazy. He received his early instruction in pianoforte playing from his father; his success as a pianist at the age of nine earned for him enough patronage to guarantee his being able to study for a number of years. His first public appearance in 1822 was an outstanding success. During the next few years he visited England and Switzerland and finally settled in Paris, where, in 1834, he formed an intimacy which lasted ten years with the Countess d'Agoult. By her he had three children; one of them, Cosima, was to be the wife first of Bülow, then of Wagner. His generosity, one of the outstanding features of his character, began to display itself during this period. The instances of the monetary fruits of his genius being given to charitable purposes were innumerable. In 1842 he began his connection with Weimar and settled there in 1849 for twelve years; two years earlier Princess Karolyne zu Sayn-Wittgenstein became associated with him and their house in Weimar became a centre of musical culture. In 1847 Liszt gave his last appearance for his own benefit and then appeared for others. During his stay in Weimar, Liszt made it the centre of musical life in Germany. From 1859 he made Rome his centre, sharing his time between Rome, Budapest and Weimar. In 1879 he received an honorary canonry and, though not a priest, could enjoy the privilege of wearing the priestly garb and so publicly display his profession of the faith to which he had had strong leanings in his youth. He visited England again in the last year of his life and his reception was overwhelming.

As a virtuoso who placed art before mere brilliance, Liszt was pre-eminent. He was the first to use the title Symphonic Poem, and in his compositions of this kind presented an advanced development of the theory of programme music. His arrangements and transcriptions of music of all kinds and all qualities, apparently all made with equal care, form a comparatively large part of his output, and a great many of his original works appeared in different forms. Liszt achieved his most satisfactory results in his orchestral and pianoforte programme music, and perhaps his least satisfactory results in his sacred music, much of which has been described as incongruous in the extreme. As a pianist, composer and philanthropist, the Abbé Liszt was one of the outstanding figures of the 19th century.

Lloyd, Charles Harford (b. Thornbury 1849, d. Slough 1919), achieved distinction as an organist and composer particularly of Anglican church music.

Locke, Matthew (b. Exeter c. 1630, d. 1677), was a chorister in

Exeter Cathedral under Edward Gibbons. In 1661 he was appointed composer in ordinary to the King for the instrumental music he wrote in honour of Charles II at the time of his coronation. Many vocal and instrumental compósitions by him appeared in the various collections of music published towards the end of the 17th century, and several anthems by him have survived. His most important contribution to music was in his music for the stage. With Christopher Gibbons he wrote the music for the masque *Cupid and Death* by Shirley; he wrote some of the music for the *Siege of Rhodes* by Davenant, nearly all the music for *Psyche* by Shadwell, and music for a number of other dramatic works. These place him as the chief predecessor of Purcell as a composer of music for the English stage.

Loco (Lat.), in place. Indicates that the pitch is as printed.

Loeillet, Jean Baptiste of Ghent (f. late 17th and early 18th century), *John of London* (d. 1728) and *Jaques* (d. Paris c. 1746), were the most important members of a distinguished family of Flemish musicians. Their biographies have become confused. Both Jean Baptiste and John were flautists and oboists, and left several groups of sonatas for these instruments.

Loewe, Johann Carl Gottfried (b. Lochejuen 1796, d. Kiel 1869), was a composer credited with creating the German dramatic ballad.

Long, the second longest note of the medieval time system, equal to two or three breves according to the mood.

Lorenzani, Paolo (b. Rome 1640, d. there 1713), achieved distinction as a musician both at the French court, in the time of Lully and Louis XIV, and in his native Rome. As a composer his motets enjoyable considerable favour.

Lotti, Antonio (b. Venice c. 1667, d. there 1740), was an eminent organist and composer associated with St Mark's, Venice.

Loure (Fr.), originally a variety of bagpipe and later a country dance slower than the gigue, but similar to it.

Ludford, Nicholas (f. late 15th and early 16th centuries), was an English composer of church music.

Lully, Jean-Baptiste (b. near Florence 1632, d. Paris 1687), was naturalized a Frenchman. Little is known of his earliest years. He was brought to France when ten or eleven by a certain Chevalier de Guise and employed by his niece at the Palais d'Orléans as a scullion. The ability he displayed on a violin earned him a place in the household band, but he disgraced himself and was dismissed. He was favourably noticed by the young King,

Louis XIV, and shortly given a place in the band of twenty-four violins, and subsequently the perfection of his playing so impressed Louis that a new band was formed for him to train. From then on Lully enjoyed the King's favour increasingly through his life; he had the intellectual ability and the character to profit to the full from his fortunate position. He was particularly successful in composing music for the court ballets. The two royal appointments (and the salaries attached to them) which he received in 1661 were a reflection of the popularity he had achieved. In 1672 he obtained the transfer to himself of certain privileges which had been originally granted to the Abbé Perrin. Lully's genius was apparently not matched by his honour or morals. However, the privileges gave him an unrivalled opportunity for the production of musical dramatic works, and he proved himself to be an artist of outstanding merit, producing the earliest notable French opera *Les Fêtes de l'Amour et de Bacchus* as the first of a series of twenty to appear in the following fourteen years.

Lully's immense success was due in no slight degree to his collaboration with Molière, for whose comedies he provided the dances and other music, and with Quinault, whose librettos were of a high quality. Though Lully is said never to have mastered French, his recitatives have been described as models of declamation at its best. He appears to have been a master of the stage, and this more than balanced the formality of his music.

Lupo, the name of a family, originally of Milan, associated with the English court during the late 16th and early 17th century. Thomas Lupo contributed to *The Teares or Lamentacions* compiled by Leighton.

Lur, a prehistoric bronze wind instrument. Examples have been found in the peat bogs of Denmark and Sweden.

Lute, a plucked string instrument, now obsolete. The characteristics of the lute are its pear-shaped back and concave sides unlike those of the guitar.

The lute is of oriental origin; it became known throughout Western Europe during the Crusades, and flourished particularly during the 16th century. Though both Handel and Bach wrote for it on rare occasions, it fell into disuse during the course of the 18th century. The number of strings and their tuning varied considerably. With the larger instruments there appears to have been a broad division between the strings lying over the frets, and the lower strings which were not stopped, the latter commonly having longer strings with pegs for them on a second higher neck.

The main strings were commonly six in number tuned

The lower strings, some seven in number, were tuned diatonically below the lowest of these six. This tuning was, however, by no means general.

The large lutes were generally known as theorbos or archlutes and chitarones.

Lute-Harpsichord, the English equivalent for Lautenclavicymbal.

Luther, Martin (b. Eisleben 1483, d. there 1546), the well-known religious reformer, was the establisher of congregational singing in Germany. Some three dozen or so hymns (translations of Latin hymns, arrangements of earlier hymns and so on, as well as original poems) and some dozen tunes are ascribed to him.

Lyre, a plucked string instrument used by the ancient Greeks. The strings of the lyre were stretched partly over a hollow body, partly between two arms fixed to the body, and held at each end by a cross bar, one on the body and the other between the bars. The lyre was played with a plectrum. It had fewer strings than the harp and no fingerboard.

Lyre-Guitar, a guitar built on the lines of the ancient lyre. Such instruments appeared in France towards the end of the 18th century.

Lyric, a name (derived from Lyre, and now used with considerable confusion) which might properly be considered simply as implying music. In relation to the stage this is its customary meaning. In poetry, lyrical and dramatic are thought of as different branches of poetry, regardless of any musical considerations, and this use has been extended to music.

M

Macdowell, Edward Alexander (b. New York City 1861, d. there 1908), was a composer and pianist who is generally known for some of his slighter pianoforte compositions.

McEwen, Sir John Blackwood (b. Hawick 1868, d. London 1948), was the son of a Presbyterian minister. He took an arts degree at

Glasgow University in 1888, and studied at the Royal Academy for two years from 1891. He joined the staff of the Academy in 1898 and was its Principal from 1924 to 1936. Oxford made him an honorary Mus.D. in 1926, and he was knighted in 1931.

His compositions include several symphonies and other large-scale works, but his chamber music, including some fifteen string quartets, represent him at his best.

Macfarren, Sir George Alexander (b. London 1813, d. there 1887), achieved distinction as a teacher and composer. He became Professor of Music in the University of Cambridge in 1875, and Principal of the Royal Academy of Music in the following year.

Mackenzie, Sir Alexander Campbell (b. Edinburgh 1847, d. London 1935), achieved distinction as a teacher and composer. He became Principal of the Royal Academy of Music in 1888, and held the office until 1924. He has been considered as one of the leaders of the revival of English music.

Madrigal, a secular vocal composition for two or more voices often of a polyphonic character. The name madrigal is generally taken to include all the more or less specific forms, composed during the 16th and early 17th century, having the essential features of the madrigals, such as the canzonet and ballet. The completeness of the vocal parts and their independence of an accompaniment distinguishes them at once from the English ayre or its foreign counterpart.

The use of contrapuntal devices in the part-writing is by no means an essential characteristic of the madrigal. Though frequently the melodic interest is shared equally between the voices, often the chief melody is in the top part, the other parts being melodious though less important.

The derivation of the name is presumed to be from matricale, a medieval Latin name for a country song. The composing of madrigals began in the 14th century in North Italy. During the 16th and early 17th centuries the madrigal became popular throughout most of Europe. English composers in particular reached a remarkable eminence in the composition of madrigals.

Maestoso (It.), majestically. Used as an indication of speed, rather slower than 'andante'; also used as an indication of style when qualifying some other speed.

Maggiore (It.), major. Used as a warning of a sudden change into the major key, especially in sets of variations.

Maggot, a name used in old English keyboard music for fanciful pieces, often with someone's name attached.

Mahler, Gustav (b. Kalischt 1860, d. Vienna 1911), was a conductor and symphonic composer. His nine symphonies are characterized by their length and heavy orchestration.

Major and *Minor,* complementary terms used in music in a number of senses. They are applied to the greater and lesser forms of an interval when these are both concordant or both dissonant. According to physical theory there are major and minor tones, but the difference between them (known as a comma) is so small that it is ignored on the modern keyboard. Triads are called major or minor according as the interval between the lowest notes of the triad is a major or minor third. The scales

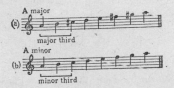

are called major and minor respectively.

Malipiero, Gian Francesco (b. Venice 1882), still living.

Mandoline, a small plucked string instrument similar to the lute, but having a relatively deeper back. The commonest form of mandoline, the Neapolitan, has four pairs of strings tuned in fifths like the four strings of the violin. The mandoline is played with a plectrum, commonly of tortoiseshell, and the fingerboard is fretted.

Mandore, a small plucked string instrument similar to the lute, popular with the 12th- and 13th-century jongleurs. It was known in England from the 14th-century, and a 16th-century collection of music for it is extant.

Manual, a keyboard for the hands. This name is used mostly in connection with the organ.

Marcato (It.), marked. Used as an indication of expression, drawing attention to the melody or subject, particularly when it is in the bass or in an inner part.

Marcello, Benedetto (b. Venice 1686, d. Brescia 1739), achieved distinction as a composer, though not a professional musician. His settings of 50 Psalms are notable.

March, a title used for instrumental compositions of no definite form, merely having the characteristics of a march, and also for compositions designed specifically for military purposes. Military marches now commonly have a main section followed by a trio, after which the main section is repeated.

Marenzio, Luca (b. near Brescia 1553, d. Rome 1599), was an Italian musician. Little is known of his youth, and what is known of his life is uncertain. He was esteemed both in Rome and at the court of Poland, at which he held a musical appointment probably for two years about 1590. He is said to have been maestro di cappella to the Cardinal d'Este before going to Poland, and after his return to Rome is said to have been appointed to the Papal choir. He wrote a large number of motets, but his most important compositions are his madrigals. Among his secular vocal music are one set of madrigals for four voices, nine for five voices and six for six voices, as well as five sets of less serious part-songs which are (with the exception of one piece for four voices) for three voices. Marenzio brought the madrigal to perfection in Italy; his madrigals were first made known in England by the publication of *Musica Transalpina* in 1588.

Marimba, an instrument in use in the Southern parts of Mexico. It consists of a set of tuned wooden blocks, suspended upon wooden resonators, played with drumsticks.

Marine Trumpet, a bowed stringed instrument of one string; that is, a portable bowed monochord. The instrument was commonly about 6 ft long and the open string tuned to sound the C two octaves below middle C. Though the instrument could be played by stopping in the usual way, it was properly played using the natural harmonics only. Some form of the marine trumpet was probably the oldest bowed instrument known. The name marine trumpet was probably given to the instrument when it was introduced into Italy on account of its similarity in shape to the speaking trumpets used on Italian ships. The instrument became disused during the 18th century.

Marson, George (b. *c.* 1570, d. Canterbury 1632), was one of the English composers who contributed to *The Triumphes of Oriana.*

Martini, Giovanni Battista, commonly known as *Padre Martini*, (b. Bologna 1706, d. there 1784), was a priest trained in the Franciscan Convent at Laco. He was the most scientific of the 18th-century writers about music.

Mascagni, Pietro (b. Leghorn 1863, d. Rome 1945), was the son of a baker. After a prosaic beginning to his musical career he achieved success at the age of thirty-seven with his opera *Cavalleria Rusticana,* on which his fame now rests.

Mass, as a musical form, a setting of the Ordinary of the Mass, that is the Kyrie, Gloria in Excelsis, Credo, Sanctus and Agnus Dei.

Until the close of the Middle Ages the settings of these portions of the Liturgy were independent. From then onwards settings of these portions of the Liturgy as an organic whole became common. One of the earliest and amongst the best known of the plainsong settings of mass is the *Missa de Angelis.* Later the polyphonic composers of the 15th, 16th and 17th century left numerous masses, mostly based on traditional plainsong melodies, but not a few on secular melodies and many on original themes, often those of a motet previously composed, by which the mass was named. The Credo had tended to keep to its original plainsong setting, while varied settings of the Kyrie, Gloria, Sanctus and Agnus Dei were associated with it. Further, the use of the plainsong melody as the basis of a polyphonic setting tended to continue longer with the Credo than with the other movements. In both the Credo and Gloria the custom of the opening phrase being sung by the celebrant to the traditional plainsong remains, even when the remainder of the setting bears no relation to plainsong.

Massenet, Jules Émile Frédéric (b. Montaud 1842, d. Paris 1912), was a composer of operas. He was particularly successful with a style of composition popular with a large portion of the public of his day; this style is to be seen at its best in the opera *Manon,* for which he is generally remembered.

Matassins, (Fr.), or *Bouffons* (Fr.), a dance popular in the 16th and 17th century. It was usually danced by four men in armour, and included mimic fights between the sections of the dance. It is described by Arbeau.

Matelotte, a dance of Dutch sailors similar to the hornpipe.

Matthay, Tobias (b. London 1858, d. Haslemere 1945), was a successful teacher of the pianoforte. He was on the staff of the Royal Academy of Music. His own school was founded in 1900.

Maxima (Lat.), largest. A name given to the longest note in the medieval time system.

Mazurka, a Polish national dance, dating from the 16th century or earlier. The dance is characterised by considerable latitude in varying the steps. The mazurka was adopted by Russia, but the Russian and Polish forms of the dance differ. The music is in three-four time, but is much slower than that of the waltz; it is in two or four sections each repeated. The melody should end on the second beat of the bar, and there is often a strong accent on

the third. In the earlier mazurkas the bass was commonly limited
to the tonic note. The mazurkas of Chopin differ considerably, by
their elaboration and refinement, from the simple tunes to which
the mazurka was commonly danced.

Me, the third note of the scale in Tonic Sol-fa.

Meantone, the system of tuning which prevailed before the present
system of equal temperament.

If the fifths at (a) are tuned perfect and the D and F♯ of (b) are
tuned to match those of (a), then the third at (b) will be considerably greater than a perfect third. In the meantone system the
third at (b) is tuned perfect and all the fifths at (a) made equally
flat so that the D and F♯ match those at (b).

A series of these fifths (meantone fifths) and their inversions
(meantone fourths)

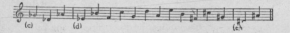

produce an A♭ and a G♯ differing from each other by a third of a
semitone. Hence if the notes in (d) are tuned to this plan the six
major scales of B♭, F, C, G, D and A and the three minor scales of
G, D and A are equally in tune. Other scales, requiring the notes
at (c) or (e), simply do not exist, as these notes differ so greatly from
the sharps and flats in (d) with which in the equal temperament
system they are identical. The chords formed by treating say G♭
as though it were A♭ are extremely rough; the sound of them was
likened to the howling of wolves and their occurrence in a composition referred to as a wolf.

Various tuning devices were tried to overcome the unsatisfactory
effect of the less usual keys. However, the inherent weakness of
the system was simply that, while the good keys were all equally
in tune, the others did not really exist; F♯, say, was tuned as F♯,
not as a compromise between F♯ and G♭, consequently the keys
requiring G♭ were not really there.

Measure, originally any dance with a well-marked rhythm, but later
a dance of a solemn and stately character. The term is also used
for the period from one bar to the next.

Medesimo Tempo (It.), in the same time.

Mediant, the third note of any scale in the modern key system. In the various modal systems the position of the mediant varied.

Mediation, the inflexion half way through a Gregorian chant.

Medtner, Nicolai Raslovitch (b. Moscow 1880), still living.

Méhul, Étienne Henri (b. Givet 1763, d. Paris 1817), was a successful composer of opera. He holds an important place in the continuity of the tradition of French opera.

Meistersinger, the middle-class counterpart of the Minnesinger. The Meistersinger flourished from the 14th to 16th centuries.

Melba, Dame Nellie (b. near Melbourne 1861, d. Sydney 1931), was one of the most successful operatic sopranos of her day.

Melisma, a group of notes sung to one syllable in plainsong. It is also used for a melodic as against a declamatory passage.

Melodic Minor, the form of the minor scale in which both the sub-mediant and the leading note are sharpened 'ascending' and both natural 'descending'.

A minor

'ascending'   'descending'

Melodrama, a dramatic composition in which the spoken part is accompanied by music, simple or elaborate.

Melody, a musically pleasing succession of notes. Melody is used in a less precise sense than either phrase or tune. Melody is a complementary term to harmony, whereas tune is complementary to accompaniment.

Mendelssohn, Jakob Ludwig Felix Mendelssohn-Bartholdy (b. Hamburg 1809, d. Leipzig 1847), came of Jewish parents. His father was a prosperous banker, keenly interested in art and literature, who had his children baptised as Protestant Christians and later, with his wife, was received into the Protestant Church. The family escaped to Berlin in 1811, during the French occupation of Hamburg, and there Felix with his brother and two sisters was reared. Felix married, in 1837, the daughter of a clergyman and by her had five children.

The musical gifts which Mendelssohn displayed from an early age were encouraged to such purpose that his overture to *A Midsummer Night's Dream* was written when he was seventeen, and the first performance of the *St Matthew Passion* since the death of Bach was given at the Singakademie in Berlin under his direction, and as the result of his enthusiasm, when he was twenty. He visited London for the first time in 1829 and on his return to Berlin was offered the newly-founded Chair of Music in the University. He declined in favour of continuing his travels. He visited Vienna, Rome and Paris, as well as many lesser centres of musical culture, and London again before returning to Berlin in 1832.

He failed to obtain the Directorship of the Singakademie and his first definite appointment was in 1833 as conductor of the Lower Rhine Festival at Düsseldorf, and in 1835 he was appointed conductor of the Gewandhaus Concerts in Leipzig. In 1841 he received the title of Kapellmeister to the King of Prussia in connection with his work for the formation of an Academy of Arts in Berlin under the patronage of William IV. In 1843 the conservatorium in Leipzig, which he had proposed some years earlier, was opened with himself leading the staff. These last three appointments made concurrent demands on his energies as conductor, composer and teacher. The first performance of his oratorio *Elijah*, conducted by himself at the Birmingham Festival in 1846, may be considered as the climax of his career as a composer.

Amongst the best of his numerous compositions are the oratorio *Elijah*, the overture *The Hebrides (Fingal's Cave)*, the overture and incidental music to *A Midsummer Night's Dream* and the Violin Concerto. Of his piano music the *Songs Without Words* have the most popular appeal. His three preludes and fugues and six sonatas for the organ have proved a most useful contribution to the organ repertory. His chamber music includes an octet written when he was sixteen, six string quartets and two piano trios. But perhaps even more important to music than his compositions is the influence he had on musical culture in Germany and England, most of all by his revival of Bach.

Meno (It.), less.

Merbecke, John (d. Windsor c. 1585), was an English musician. Little is known of the details of his life. He was lay-clerk and organist of St George's Chapel, Windsor, in 1541. He was condemned for heresy in 1544 but was pardoned. A mass, two motets and a carol which are included in *Tudor Church Music* are all that survive of his compositions, with the exception of his outstanding contribution to English church music *The Booke of Common Praier Noted*, 1550.

Merkel, Gustav (b. Oberoderwitz 1827, d. Dresden 1885), was an organist and composer of organ music.

Messa di Voce, a term used in singing for a crescendo followed by a diminuendo on a long note.

Metamorphosis, a term used in music for the modification of an idea from one form to another. Liszt made notable use of the metamorphosis of themes in his symphonic poems. The 'idée fixe' of Berlioz and the 'leitmotiv' of Wagner are akin to the metamorphosis of themes as used by Liszt.

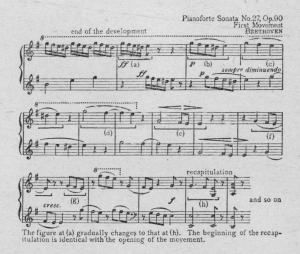

Pianoforte Sonata No.27, Op.90
First Movement
BEETHOVEN

end of the development

The figure at (a) gradually changes to that at (h). The beginning of the recapitulation is identical with the opening of the movement.

Metastasio, Pietro Antonio Domenico Bonaventura (b. Rome 1698, d. Vienna 1782), was the most famous of Italian opera libretto writers.

Metre, the regular grouping of notes with regard to their accent and duration. The analogy invariably made between literature and music has led to confusion in the musical use of the term. Both accent and duration (stress and quantity) have at times governed the metrical analysis of poetry. The difference between the Prayer Book version and the metrical versions of the Book of Psalms draws nicely the distinction between what is usually meant by non-metrical and metrical so far as literature is concerned. This feature of metre which commonly distinguishes poetry from prose may also be recognised in music. The fact that the various forms of the foot, into which the syllables are grouped in a metrical analysis of poetry, may be identified in prose does not make the prose metrical. It would appear reasonable that this same distinction may be carried into music. Further, in the same way that an alternation of accented and unaccented syllables may be recognised as either trochaic or iambic (groups of strong-weak or of weak-strong) so a distinction may be drawn in music between

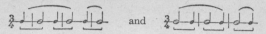

Time is a feature of music grafted on to metre, and both should be distinguished from rhythm. Unfortunately the meanings of all three terms are often confused.

Metrical Psalter, a book of Psalms paraphrased in verse. The practice of paraphrasing the psalms into metre became popular towards the middle of the 16th century with the rise of congregational participation in worship.

The Genevan Psalter was first published in 1542 and completed twenty years later; Marot and Bourgeois were responsible for the paraphrases and the melodies respectively. What became the accepted English Psalter began from a small volume of Psalms in metre by Sternhold, published in 1549, without tunes. A psalter by Sternhold and others was published in Geneva in 1556 for the English Protestants who had taken refuge there; for the first time melodies were included in the collection. Sternhold was by no means the only, or first writer in England to paraphrase the psalms. The first complete edition of the English Psalter was published in 1562 and, with but few changes, the melodies in this edition remained the established church tunes which were harmonized and set many times during the next hundred years. The psalter of Playford in 1677 was the last complete setting.

The Psalter of Sternhold, usually known as 'Sternhold and Hopkins' or the 'Old Version', lasted until the early part of the 19th century. A later paraphrase 'Tate and Brady', otherwise known as the 'New Version', lasted some thirty years longer. These psalters were superseded by the hymnals now in use, and in which occur examples of metrical psalms, and settings of their tunes taken from the various psalters.

The origin of the old tunes is mostly uncertain. Generally speaking they were taken from the Genevan Psalter, but they were not always set to the same psalms in the English Psalter as in the Genevan. The large number of fresh tunes and settings of the 18th century contributed little that was good to the English Psalter.

The majority of what was new was quite unfitted for church use, and most of it has failed to survive. The Scottish Metrical Psalter diverged from the English from rival editions of 1651, and unlike the English Psalter has survived in use, as a whole, until the present time.

Metronome, an instrument for giving the speed. Primitive instruments to serve this purpose were designed towards the end of the 17th century. The principle of the instrument now used was invented during the early part of the 19th century by Winkel, though Maelzel, who patented the invention in his own name, is now generally credited with it. Maelzel set up a metronome factory in 1816. The metronome is simply a double pendulum, operated by clockwork, which may be made to vary its speed of oscillation by adjusting a movable weight on the upper arm. The ticks of the pendulum are audible, and may be adjusted according to a scale from 40 to 208 a minute.

Meyerbeer, Giacomo (b. Berlin 1791, d. Paris 1864), came of wealthy Jewish parents. He was a composer mainly of opera. His most successful opera was *The Hugenots* and his best, from the musical point of view, was *L'Africaine.* The lavish settings required for his operas have probably been largely responsible for even the best of them now being neglected.

Mezza Voce (It.), half voice. Indicates a quality of tone between normal singing tone and 'sotto voce'.

Mezzo (It.), half. *Mezzo Forte* and *Mezzo Piano* are used in the senses of 'moderately loud' and 'moderately soft' respectively and are abbreviated to *mf* and *mp.*

Mi, the third note of the scale in solmization.

Middle C, the note most commonly taken as the point of reference for naming other notes. It is approximately in the centre of the range of human voices; it is the C corresponding to the C clef; it is sounded by a flue pipe approximately two feet long and its frequency is approximately 512 (a figure adopted for the convenience of mathematical calculations and rather less than the standard of pitch now in use).

Milhaud, Darius (b. Aix-en-Provence 1892), still living.

Milton, John (b. *c.* 1563, d. London 1647), was an English musician and father of the poet who wrote *Paradise Lost.* He contributed to *The Triumphes of Oriana* and to *The Teares or Lamentacions* compiled by Leighton.

Minim, half a semibreve. It is written ♩ and its corresponding rest ⏬.

Minnesinger, the counterpart in Germany of the troubadour of

Southern France. The Minnesinger flourished in the 12th and 13th centuries.

Minor, the complement to 'major'.

Minor Canon, a priest in a cathedral or collegiate church whose duties are associated with the performance of the daily services, and who, by statute, should be skilled in music.

Minore (It.), minor. Used as a warning of a sudden change into the minor key, especially in sets of variations.

Minstrel, commonly used in the sense of musician, but originally the instrumentalist attendant on a 'troubadour'.

Minuet, a slow stately dance of French origin, in triple time and beginning usually on the first, sometimes on the third beat of the bar. The old minuet was in two parts, each repeated, originally each part being of eight bars. This simple form became enlarged by the addition of a complementary second minuet, similar in form but different in character from the first, and by an increase in the number of bars, particularly of the second part of each minuet. As a dance the minuet continued to flourish until towards the end of the 18th century.

The musical importance of the minuet, above that of other old dances, arises from its incorporation in the sonata and symphony. In the suite the minuet is one of the more important of the movements sometimes introduced. The minuets of Bach show a great variety of form and treatment. Sometimes the second minuet is in a different key from the first. The second minuet is sometimes called a trio, though only in those cases where it is actually in three part counterpoint. In one instance, a definite indication is given that the first minuet is to be repeated after the second. According to later custom the second minuet is always in a contrasted key, is always called a trio (whether appropriately or not) and is always followed by a repetition of the first minuet without repeats.

The minuet was adopted as the usual third movement of the sonata and other compositions in the same form, and numerous examples of it may be found in the sonatas, quartets and symphonies of Haydn and Mozart. Though the form of the minuet was generally retained, its character became changed. The slow stateliness was lost and a quicker lightness became customary, a development which finally, in the hands of Beethoven, led to the transformation of the minuet into the scherzo.

Mixed Voices, a combination of male and female voices.

Mixture, an organ stop in which from two to five pipes, tuned to certain of the harmonics of the note struck, sound together, so reinforcing certain of the natural sounding harmonics and increasing the brightness of the quality. The harmonics commonly found in a mixture are the 4th, 6th and 8th. These harmonics are generally discontinued in turn in the extreme upper range and replaced by lower harmonics, as the higher harmonics tend to pass beyond the limits of audition. Every such change in a mixture is known as a break.

M.M., Maelzel's Metronome. At one time M.M. was placed before the figures indicating a metronome setting.

Mode, a characteristic succession of intervals forming a scale. After a long period of evolution eight modes were formulated to which, in general, plainsong and polyphonic music may be referred. These modes are appropriately commonly called the ecclesiastical modes.

The modern key system distinguishes twelve major and twelve minor keys. The difference between major and minor is essentially one of character; the difference between the individual twelve members is one of pitch.

Of these three scales, (a) and (b) are the same in character but different in pitch while (a) and (c) are different in character but the same in pitch. It would be convenient to describe the difference in character as mode, and that of pitch as key. However, neither mode nor key have been used in these mutually exclusive senses.

There is reason to suppose that Greek scale forms named Dorian and Lydian differed from each other in key, not, as has at times been commonly supposed, in mode. In the formation of the medieval modal system, a great deal of borrowing (particularly as regards name and classification) took place. The character of a mode is determined by the sequence of its intervals and by the position of the fixed (two principal) notes, the dominant and the final. The two intervals of a semitone are either a fifth or fourth apart; it follows that all the modes may be reproduced on the white notes of the keyboard. The eight church modes with their finals and dominants, and the Greek names by which they are sometimes known are:

Number	Range	Final	Dominant	Name
I	D – D	D	A	Dorian
II	A – A	D	F	Hypodorian
III	E – E	E	C	Phrygian
IV	B – B	E	A	Hypophrygian
V	F – F	F	C	Lydian
VI	C – C	F	A	Hypolydian
VII	G – G	G	D	Mixolydian
VIII	D – D	G	C	Hypomixolydian

The modes run in pairs. I, III, V and VII are called authentic, II, IV, VI and VIII plagal, II being derived from I and so on. The range of each mode, it will be noticed, is an octave; in the case of the authentic modes the final is the lowest note of the range. This scheme may be completed by adding:

IX	A – A	A	E	Aeolian
X	E – E	A	C	Hypoaeolian
XI	B – B	B	G	Locrian
XII	F – F	B	E	Hypolocrian
XIII	C – C	C	G	Ionian
XIV	G – G	C	E	Hypoionian

Moderato (It.), moderately. Used as an indication of speed; also used to qualify other indications of speed.

Modulation, passing from one key to another. Modulation is therefore a feature of music based on the major and minor key system, but is hardly applicable (at least in its traditional sense) to modern harmonic systems which do not retain the main features of tonality of this key system.

Four types of modulation are readily recognised.

(1) Diatonic, in which the modulation is effected by means of chords, diatonic in each of the keys concerned.

* chords diatonic in both
C major and G major

(2) Chromatic, in which the modulation is effected by means of chords, chromatic in the keys concerned.

(3) Enharmonic, in which the modulation is effected by ignoring the theoretical difference between notes identical on a keyboard.

(4) In these three types the process of changing key can be identified with a definite succession of chords, and at least one chord common to the two keys forms a pivot. Modulations between keys having no chord in common are often effected by treating the note or notes common to two chords, one in each key, as a pivot, while a change is made from the chord in the first key to the chord in the second.

While a great proportion of the modulations to be found in music of the 17th, 18th, and 19th centuries may be explained in terms of these four types, many deliberate changes of key may be found in music of the latter part of this period which it would be pedantic to attempt to explain in terms of them.

The most difficult aspect of modulation is the establishment of the new key. This is often done by some obvious form of dominant harmony.

Moeran, Ernest John. See appendix.

Molto (It.), very.

Monochord, a single vibrating string, which being divided in simple ratios gives the main notes of the musical scale. The monochord has been the most important piece of apparatus in the development of acoustical theory. The octave is sounded from $\frac{1}{2}$ the string, the fifth from $\frac{2}{3}$ of the string, the fourth from $\frac{3}{4}$ of the string, and the tone difference between the fourth and the fifth by $\frac{8}{9}$ of the string. This scientific basis of music is especially associated with Pythagoras in the 6th century B.C. who possibly obtained his first knowledge of it from Egypt.

Monody, music in which the melody is in one part only. The name has, therefore, almost the same implications as homophony.

Monotone, one note. This term is used particularly of the recitation of portions of the liturgy on one note without inflexion.

Monteverdi, Claudio (b. Cremona 1567, d. Venice 1643), was a pupil of Ingegneri. From about 1590 until 1612 Monteverdi was in the services of Duke Vincenzo I at the Mantuan court, first as a violinist and then, after some ten years, as 'maestro di cappella'. In 1613 he was appointed 'maestro di cappella' at St Mark's in Venice, and in 1633 became a priest. Monteverdi's importance and genius was in his use of, rather than his invention of, new techniques and effects. He advanced the use of voices in his madrigals, more dramatic than earlier examples, and the use of both voices and instruments in his operas. His opera *Orfeo* produced in Mantua in 1607 is one of the first landmarks in the early history of opera. He was master of polyphony as it had been evolved during the 16th century, but developed the new style of homophony. In his operas he made advances in the organisation of the orchestra, and made effective use of pizzicato and tremolo for the strings. Among his madrigals are eight sets for five voices, all of which have survived. *Orfeo* and *L'incoronazione di Poppea*, his first and last important dramatic works, both survive, though the music of most of his operas is lost. Some sacred music by him is also extant and his lengthy and interesting *Vesperes* has recently been revived.

Mood, the relation between the large, the long and the breve in the medieval time system.

Morales, Cristobal (b. Seville *c.* 1500, d. Marchena 1553), was a priest and an important early Spanish composer, held in high esteem by his contemporaries.

Mordent, a melodic ornament in which the principal note is alternated rapidly with the note above it. The mordent may be short or long (the grace note occurring once or twice) and may be applied to any note in a chord. It is indicated by the sign $\mathbf{w}$.

Morendo (It.), dying. Indicates a gradual diminuendo. Its use is limited, as a rule, to the end of movements.

Morley, Thomas (b. 1557, d. *c.* 1603), was an English musician. Few details are known with certainty about his life. He is said to have been a pupil of Byrd; about 1590 he was organist of St Paul's

Cathedral, and in 1592 was made gentleman of the Chapel Royal. He held a leading place in the musical culture of Elizabethan England. In 1598 he was granted a monopoly for printing song books, and his publications included his own notable *A Plain and Easie Introduction to Practical Music*, 1597, *The Triumphes of Oriana to 5 and 6 voices: composed by divers severall authors*, 1601, in which were two madrigals by himself, his canzonets for two, three and more voices, and one set of lute songs. His madrigals and songs are included in *The English Madrigal School* and *The English School of Lutenist Songwriters*. A little keyboard and church music by him is also extant.

Morris Dance, a dance introduced into England probably towards the end of the 16th century, in which bells played a big part, and in which the dresses and acting were the most important features. The Morris dance was commonly incorporated in pageants of Robin Hood performed during May celebrations. The Morris Dance may have been derived from the Matassins or possibly from a Moorish dance, the Morisco.

No particular steps or rhythms appear to have been associated with the dance as originally introduced into England. Various tunes, some with words, and various dances, each with its own peculiarities, have survived in various parts of England.

Mosso (It.), moved. Used after 'più' and 'meno' to indicate a change in speed.

Moszkowski, Moritz (b. Breslau 1854, d. Paris 1925), was a pianist and composer. He is commonly known by such works as his colourful Spanish dances for four hands on a pianoforte.

Motet, originally an early form of polyphonic composition. In the early motet a given part of words and music, the tenor, was decorated by the addition of two or three parts; the added parts differed from the given part in words as well as music. In this form the motet was closely associated with the trope. During the 15th century the tenor gradually lost its distinctive character and the words of the added parts became the same as those of the tenor. By the beginning of the 16th century, the motet had reached its final form of a short vocal composition for liturgical use. Motet is conveniently used to distinguish compositions with a Latin text, generally without accompaniment, from the anthem, and to distinguish the extended unaccompanied composition from the accompanied one, as is the case with the motets and cantatas of Bach.

Motif, commonly used as an abbreviation for 'leitmotiv'. It is also used in the senses of 'subject' and 'figure'.

Motion, the movement of a succession of notes with regard to their pitch. Movement is described as conjunct or disjunct according to whether the successive notes are adjoining degrees of the scale or not. The motion of two simultaneous parts is described as similar or contrary according to whether they are both rising or falling, or one rising and one falling, and as oblique when one part is stationary while the other rises or falls.

Moussorgsky, Modeste Petrovich (b. Karevo 1839, d. St Petersburg 1881), was the son of musical parents. Moussorgsky's musical ability showed itself from an early age; however, he began a military career. In 1857 he resigned from the army to devote his life to music and to begin a struggle with poverty which lasted all his life, and was no doubt responsible for his early death. Moussorgsky spent most of his life in St Petersburg. For a while after 1870 he lived with Rimsky-Korsakov. Promise of better days came too late when his health was already undermined by his poverty and careless mode of life.

To some extent, particularly in his orchestration, Moussorgsky's technique was insufficient for the demands of his inspiration. For this reason, his songs are perhaps the best expression of his imagination and description powers. The number of his compositions is small. The ten musical sketches *Pictures from an Exhibition* are perhaps the best known of his compositions for the piano. His reputation as an operatic composer rests on *Boris Godounov.*

Mouthpiece, that part of a wind instrument placed in or applied to the mouth. With few exceptions, the mouthpiece is also the speaking part of the instrument, and by it the player exercises direct control over the volume, pitch and quality of the sound produced. An extreme exception is the bagpipe in which neither quality, volume nor pitch are controlled through the mouthpiece; with the recorder, broadly speaking, only the volume is controlled through the mouthpiece. The orchestral flute, oboe, clarinet, horn and trumpet are representative of the five kinds of mouthpiece which are also the speaking parts of the instruments. A mouthpiece of the horn or trumpet variety is called a 'cupped mouthpiece', that of the oboe or clarinet a 'reed'.

Mozart, Wolfgang Amadeus (b. Salzburg 1756, d. Vienna 1791), was the son of an able musician, Leopold Mozart, who attained to the post of Vice-Kapellmeister to the Archbishop of Salzburg. Though Leopold may justly be accused of exploiting his children's precocity, he must be credited with systematically training the remarkable musical ability (frequently misrepresented by sentimental biographers) which Mozart showed from his early youth. In 1762 the family went on tour, exhibiting in the courts of Vienna, Munich, Paris and London the undoubted (though exaggerated) ability of Wolfgang and his sister Marianne. The family returned to Salzburg in 1766, and two years later Mozart was appointed Konzertmeister to the Archbishop. The next nine years were spent in study and touring, during which time Mozart's ability as a composer rapidly developed. His opera *Mitridate* was produced for the first time in Milan in 1770 with him conducting. This opera is but a small portion of all the music (symphonies, concertos, church and chamber music) he wrote before he was twenty-one.

In 1777 Mozart left Salzburg, his mother accompanying him; she died the following year, and a year later, in 1779, he returned to Salzburg, where he remained for a year fulfilling the duties of Konzertmeister and organist to the court and cathedral. His opera *Domenico* was produced for the Munich carnival in 1781; in the middle of the festivities, he was summoned to join the Archbishop who had moved from Salzburg to Vienna. His treatment at the hands of the Archbishop appears to have been disgusting, in contrast to his treatment by the Viennese nobility (at whose musical gatherings he made his reputation as a performer). A few months later, when the unpopular prelate left Vienna, Mozart resigned his appointment. For a while Mozart lived with the Webers where he probably met Haydn for the first time and formed a friendship with him which lasted till Mozart's death and influenced beneficially the music of both. Later in 1782 Mozart married Constanze Weber, cousin of Carl Maria von Weber.

Mozart failed to obtain any permanent appointment and neither he nor his wife appear to have had the ability to manage successfully on his irregular earnings. His weak constitution was undermined by the strain of work and his financial difficulties, and a general breakdown of his health followed. He died of malignant typhus and was buried in a pauper's grave.

The quality and quantity of Mozart's compositions, achieved in only thirty-five years of life, is truly prodigious. Among the best of his operas are *The Marriage of Figaro, Don Giovanni, Così fan tutte,* and *The Magic Flute.* Of his thirty-nine symphonies the three masterpieces those in Eb major, G minor and C major (*The Jupiter*) were all written in 1788. His chamber music includes over twenty string quartets and a particularly lovely quintet for clarinet and strings. His pianoforte sonatas, in contrast to his pianoforte concertos of the Viennese period, do not represent Mozart at his best. Some fifteen masses and the *Requiem* (completed by Süssmeyer) give some idea of his sacred compositions. These named compositions are, however, only representative of the best of his vast output of over six hundred works.

Mundy, John (d. 1630), was an English musician. His published madrigals are included in *The English Madrigal School*, and he contributed to *The Triumphes of Oriana*.

Muris, Johannes de (f. early 14th century), was a musical theorist as well as a mathematician and astronomer of considerable reputation. There appears to be little justification for the claim that he was English. He lived part of his life in Paris.

Musette, a composition of simple style appropriate to the instrument from which it takes its name, generally having a pedal bass. (An example of a musette is quoted in the article on 'ternary form'.)

Musette, a name given indiscriminately to a small double reed wind instrument of the shawm variety, and to the various kinds of shepherd's pipe.

Musica Ficta, the convention of leaving the insertion of certain accidentals to the competence of the performer. This convention lasted throughout the centuries during which polyphony evolved. The rules governing the insertion of accidentals during this period are still largely a matter of surmise. The rules probably varied from time to time according to the current feeling for tonality, becoming more stable as the medieval modal systems gave way to the modern key system.

Musica Figurata (Lat.), figured music. This name was given in the early part of the polyphonic period to music having a second melody added to, and decorating, the plainsong.

Musical Bow, a crude musical instrument found among primitive peoples in various parts of the world. The form of the instrument is simply that of the weapon, generally with the addition of some hollow vessel to act as a resonator.

Musica Mensurata (Lat.), measured music. This name was given in the early part of the polyphonic period to music in which the notes of the plainsong (having a melody added in counterpoint to them) had a definite time duration, and were no longer free to follow the rhythm of the words at the discretion of the singer.

Musica Transalpina, a collection of Italian madrigals with an English translation compiled by Nicholas Yonge and published by Thomas East in 1588. The collection contains fifty-seven madrigals, including sixteen by Ferrabosco and ten by Marenzio. Palestrina,

Monte, Lassus and a number of lesser composers are represented, and two stanzas set by Byrd are also included. A second volume of twenty-four madrigals under the same title was published in 1597, Ferrabosco and Marenzio being the most important composers represented.

Mutation Stop (on an organ), any register sounding a note of different name from that of the key pressed down. The mutation stops found are those sounding the fifth and rarely the third above the key name, that is, those sounding a G or E when a C key is depressed. The most commonly found mutation stop is the twelfth, sounding an octave and a fifth above the unison.

Mute, the name now commonly used for the mechanical device for restricting the sound of members of the violin and brass families. A three-pronged grip fixed over the bridge is used with members of the violin family, and a pear-shaped piece of wood or metal placed in the bell for members of the brass family. A device on early square pianofortes (operated at first by stops and later by pedals) and on certain upright pianofortes, in which the quality is muffled and reduced with felt, may be classed with the mutes of the violin and brass families.

The English term 'mute' is really a misnomer. On the pianoforte it would be more properly applied to the dampers which stop the strings sounding after the key is released. The Italian term 'sordino', now equivalent in usage to the English mute, was in fact used by Beethoven, most misleadingly, to indicate the release of the dampers.

It is customary and convenient to use mute and sordino as equivalent to each other, and as referring to the devices used with the strings and brass of the orchestra. The two pianoforte pedals, the one controlling the dampers and the other now usually an 'una corda' are best considered as quite distinct from mute and sordino. The damping of unstruck strings, so prohibiting the resonance with the struck strings, cannot fairly be likened to the effect commonly associated with the term muting.

N

Nail Violin, an instrument invented in 1740 by Johann Wilde, a German violinist. Nails mounted on a wooden sounding-board are sounded with a bow.

Naker, the old English name for the kettledrum.

Nanini, Giovanni Mari (b. Tivoli *c.* 1545, d. Rome 1607), and his brother, *Giovanni Bernardino* (b. Vallerano *c.* 1560, d. Rome 1623), were both important musicians. Giovanni Maria was the first Italian to establish a public Music School in Rome and was one of the most outstanding Italian composers of both sacred and secular vocal music of his time.

Nardini, Pietro (b. Fibiana 1722, d. Florence 1793), was a composer and violinist and the most important of Tartini's followers.

Natural, the sign ♮ which restores to its natural pitch a note otherwise sharp or flat by reason of the key signature or some previous accidental.

Nay, the primitive Egyptian flute. It is a typical example of the vertical flute played without a whistle mouthpiece. It is sounded by blowing across the upper open end, and has about six finger holes.

Nefer, an Egyptian hieroglyph which has been thought to be the name of the ancient Egyptian long-necked guitar.

Neo-Modal, a style of modern melody and harmony incorporating certain features of modal music.

Neri, St Philip (b. Florence 1515, d. Rome 1595), was the founder of the Congregation of Oratorians, closely associated with the rise of oratorio.

Neumes, the signs used in the system of musical notation which had arisen by the 9th century, and was the forerunner of the present notation. In the first instance, the neumes were intended merely to remind the singer of the melody which he was already supposed to know. By the 13th century the neumes had been grafted on to a stave, so indicating relative pitch precisely. The neumatic notation has survived for the notation of plainsong, and the forms used by the Benedictines of Solesmes follow directly from the earlier tradition. The neumes, though rhythmical, have no time values, the words being sung with a natural duration as they would be spoken.

Nicholson, Richard (b. *c.* 1570, d. Oxford 1639), was one of the English composers who contributed to *The Triumphes of Oriana*.

Nicholson, Sir Sydney Hugo (b. London 1875, d. Ashford 1947), became organist of Westminster Abbey in 1918. He founded the School of English Church Music in 1927 for training organists, choirmasters, and clergy in the musical work of the Church. The institution of a diploma for church musicians by Archbishop Lang in 1936 was a sequel to the success of Nicholson's work. In 1945 the school became the Royal School of Church Music. Nicholson received the Lambeth Doctorate in 1928, and was knighted in 1938.

Nicolai, Carl Otto Ehrenfried (b. Königsberg 1810, d. Berlin 1849), was a conductor and composer. He is generally remembered for his opera *The Merry Wives of Windsor*.

Ninth, the interval covering nine degrees of the scale. It is simply the interval of a second compounded with the octave, and like it may be major or minor.

Nobile (It.), noble.

Noble, Thomas Tertius (b. Bath 1867), still living.

Nocturne, a name used by John Field for pianoforte compositions of a quiet reflective character and adopted, with the style of composition, from him by Chopin. The name meant originally a kind of serenade.

Node, a point of rest or least motion on a vibrating string, column of air, metal plate or other body. The ends of a vibrating string are generally not referred to as nodes.

Noël, the French form of the English Nowell.

Nonet, a composition for nine voices or instruments.

Norcome, Daniel (b. Windsor 1576, d. before 1626), was one of the English composers who contributed to *The Triumphes of Oriana*.

Nota Cambiata (It.), changing note.

Notation (of music), the art of representing musical ideas in writing. Musical notations are of two main kinds. In phonetic notations (such as those of the Hindus, the Chinese, the ancient Greeks, the Arabs, various tablatures and Tonic Sol-fa), the notes are represented by the names of the degrees of the scale. In diastematic notations (such as those used in the early Western Church, in the Greek Church, in the classical notation of Japan, in the music of the Middle Ages and in the modern European notation descended from this last), the notes are represented by signs placed to follow the rise and fall of the melody.

The Greek system of notation appears to have fallen out of use during the 3rd, 4th, and 5th centuries, and subsequently the plainsong music of the Christian Church survived for some centuries by a purely oral tradition. Probably by the end of the 7th century, the system of neumes, which became fully organised by the 9th century, had started to evolve. The neumes were grafted on to a stave during the 12th, 13th and 14th, centuries; in the first instance the stave was but one or two lines. The practice of placing letters at the beginning of the lines to indicate which note the neumes on each line represented (the forerunners of the modern clefs), and the adoption of the ♭ and ♯ signs soon followed. Thus the problem of a notation indicating the relative pitch of each note exactly was solved in principle. Later additions were mainly a matter of detail and refinement. The rise of polyphony made it necessary for each note to have a precise relative duration. Certain neumes were adopted and became the long ◢ , the breve ■ and the semibreve ◆ . To these were added, one at each end, the large ◢◣ and minim ♩ . Some of the compound neumes were also adopted as ligatures.

As would be expected, there were many variations in the notation. Whether a particular note was two or three times the time value of the next shorter was not always certain, in spite of the rules which often became complicated. The rhythmic modes were one of the first systems of controlling the mensural structure of the music. A note equal to three of the next shorter notes (described as perfect) became distinguished in cases of doubt from one equal to two of the next shorter notes (described as imperfect) by the point of perfection added after it. Experiments were made in colouring or filling in notes to indicate changes from a perfect to an imperfect relation between the notes of various time duration. Finally various signatures were adopted to indicate unambiguously the relationship between the various time values. The relation of the large to the long was shown by the signature of the mood major; that of the long to the breve by the mood minor; that of the breve to the semibreve by the time, and that of the semibreve to the minim by the prolation.

The stave became stabilized at five lines for vocal music during the 15th century, though instrumental music continued using larger staves until the 17th century. Also during the 15th century, the lesser note value of crochet was introduced, and the introduction of the quaver and semiquaver soon followed. Rests corresponding to the various note values came into use at the same time as the notes. Ledger lines came into use in the 16th century, and expression signs in the 17th. The bar was used during the 16th century as a guide to the eye; not until the 18th century did the relation between the time signature and the bar become close. The modern use of the accidentals and key signature evolved during the 16th and 17th centuries. The great variety of clefs at first used became restricted to three and their shapes were conventionalized. From the early 17th century the number of lines on which they could be used was gradually limited.

TABLE IV

The signs commonly used in modern musical notation

1.	stave bar double-bar brace repeat

2.

   G clef   now invariably placed on the second line and known as the treble clef.

   F clef   now invariably placed on the fourth line and known as the bass clef.

   C clef   known as the soprano, alto or tenor clef when on the bottom, middle or fourth line respectively.

   (and other forms) a variant of the G clef sometimes used for the vocal tenor part.

     (see also the article on clef)

3.

sharp   natural   flat   double sharp   double flat

(see also the articles on key signature and accidental)

4.

$\frac{2}{4}$, $\frac{3}{4}$, $\frac{4}{4}$, $\frac{6}{8}$ and the like, also C and ¢

various time signatures.

5.

Note	Name	Rest
	breve	
	semibreve	
	minim	
	crotchet	≀ or ⌐
	quaver	
	semiquaver	
	demisemiquaver	

6.

         ♩♩♩   or   ♫♪   and the like.

          triplet

    (see also the article on time)

7.

        <   >

      crescendo   diminuendo

8.

    >   –   . !   ⌢

    accent   staccato   pause

9.

Uses of the curved line.

(a)   tie or bind

(b)   slur

         (indicating legato or, in string music, the
         bowing or, in wind music, the tonguing)

(c) The curved line is also used, often unnecessarily,
to indicate the phrases, and in vocal music to
indicate the grouping of notes to each syllable.
It is also used to indicate a portamento.

10.

         ♪♩   acciaccatura

         ♪♩   appoggiatura

11.

         w   mordent

         ẇ   inverted mordent

         ~   turn

         tr ⁓   trill

12.

                                  arpeggio

The degrees of the major and minor scales are known by the names:

I	Tonic
VII	Leading Note
VI	Submediant (or Superdominant)
V	Dominant
IV	Subdominant
III	Mediant
II	Supertonic
I	Tonic

The tonic is always the key note, the supertonic one degree above the key note, and so on, regardless of which key (major or minor) is under consideration.

The triads on each degree of the scale may be referred to by the appropriate Roman numeral. The type of triad, certain chords derived from the triads, and the position of the chord may be indicated by an extension of this notation.

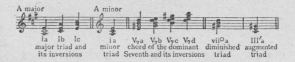

A major   A minor

Ia Ib Ic i a V₇a V₇b V₇c V₇d vii°a III′a
major triad and minor chord of the dominant diminished augmented
its inversions triad Seventh and its inversions triad triad

The value of this notation is limited.

The methods of indicating the notes of different octaves are unfortunately various and confusing. The following method, however, is unambiguous

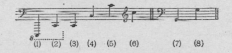

(1) (2) (3) (4) (5) (6) (7) (8)

(8) Fiddle G (the lowest note on the violin)
(7) Gamut G (the bottom note of the gamut)
(6) 1 foot C (or Treble C)
(5) 2 foot C (or Middle C)
(4) 4 foot C (or Tenor C)
(3) 8 foot C (or Double C)
(2) 16 foot C (or Great C)
(1) 32 foot C

Other systems in use are:

(1) (2) (3) (4) (5) (6) (7) (8)

Note	(a)	(b)	(c)	(d)	(e)	(f)	
(8)	c^{IV}	c^4	ccccc	c^{111}	c^3	cccc	Upper group of C's
(7)	c^{111}	c^3	cccc	c^{11}	c^2	ccc	
(6)	c^{11}	c^2	ccc	c^1	c^1	cc .	
(5)	c^1	c^1	cc	c	c	c	
(4)	c			C	C_1	C	Lower group of C's
(3)	C			CC	C_2	C_1	
(2)	C_1			CCC	C_3	C_2	
(1)	C_{11}			CCCC	C_4	C_3	

The alternatives (a), (b) and (c) for the upper group of C's all have the same notation for the lower group of C's. The alternatives (d), (e) and (f) for the upper group of C's are associated in various ways with the alternatives (d), (e) and (f) for the lower group. Columns (a) and (d) as they stand are the most usual forms. The confusion between these systems is obvious. In some older books, notations of this kind run from G to G (following the gamut) instead of from C to C.

The terms 'in alt.' may refer to the seven degrees of the scale upwards from

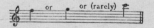

In the first two cases the octave above may be referred to as 'in altissimo'.

That the various systems do not take A (the first letter of the alphabet!) as the first note of the musical scale is in itself confusing. The notes A and B are not followed by C and D, as might be expected, but by c and d; G is not above A but below it.

TABLE V

The common English, French, German and Italian names for certain terms and symbols used in musical notation

English	French	German	Italian
1.			
Stave, Staff	Portée	System	Sistema
Clef	Clef	Schlüssel	Chiave
Key Signature	Armature Signes Accidentales	Vorzeichnung	Armatura
Time Signature	Fraction	Taktzeichen	Tempo
Bar (Line)	Barre	Taktstrich	Stanghetta
Bar	Mesure	Takt	Misura, Battuta
Note	Note	Note	Nota
Rest	Silence, Pause	Pause	Pausa
2.			
G	Sol	G	Sol
F	Fa	F	Fa
E	Mi	E	Mi
D	Re	D	Re
C	Ut	C	Do
B	Si	H (B)*	Si
A	La	A	La

* In German, B is equivalent to the English B♭. At one time B flat and B natural were indicated by the round (Roman) b and the square (Gothic) ♭ respectively. Their use was extended to indicate the flattening and correction to natural of other degrees of the scale besides B. The similarity of the Gothic ♭ to an h explains the German use of H for B natural.

English	French	German	Italian
3.			
Natural	Bécarre	Quadrat	Bequadro
Sharp	Dièse	Kreuz *	Diesis
Double Sharp	Double-Dièse	Doppelkreuz *	Doppio Diesis
Flat	Bémol	Be *	Bemolle
Double Flat	Double-Bémol	Doppel-Be *	Doppio Bemolle

* In German, particular notes are named by adding the suffixes -is, -isis, -es and -eses for sharp, double sharp, flat and double flat respectively.

English	French	German	Italian
4.			
Breve	Carrée	Doppel-taktnote	Breve
Semibreve	Ronde	Ganz-taktnote	Semibreve
Minim	Blanche	Halbe	Minima, Bianca
Crochet	Noire	Viertel	Semiminima, Nera
Quaver	Croche	Achtel	Croma
Semiquaver	Double-Croche	Sechzehntel	Semicroma
Demisemiquaver	Triple-Croche	Zweiunddreistigstel	Biscroma

English	French	German	Italian
5.			
Major	Majeur	Dur	Maggiore
Minor	Mineur	Moll	Minore

Note, a sign indicating a musical sound. Its shape indicates its duration. The notes generally in use since the beginning of the

17th century are breve, semibreve, minim, crochet, quaver, semi-quaver and demisemiquaver, each having half the duration of the previous, the duration being purely relative, not absolute.

Note, a musical sound recognised as having the attributes of pitch, volume and quality. A note may be described as pure or complex. A pure note, as is obtained from a stretched string or a pipe, has overtones which approximate closely to the harmonic series. A complex note, as is obtained from a bell, has overtones which are only indirectly related to the harmonic series.

Novák, Vitězslav (b. Kamenice-on-Lipa 1870, d. Prague 1949), was a pupil of Dvořák at Prague Conservatory where later he became a teacher. With Suk he was one of the leaders of modern Czech music.

Novello, Vincent (b. London 1781, d. Nice 1861), was the son of an Italian father and English mother. He achieved distinction as an organist and composer, and made a considerable contribution to the revival of old English music by his editing and arranging. In 1811 he founded the firm of Novello, music publishers, of London.

Nowell, the English form of the French Noël, properly a French popular song in honour of the birth of Christ and so now commonly included under the general name of carol. Noëls emerged as a type towards the end of the 15th century.

Nut (of a bow), the piece of ivory or ebony over which the hairs pass. It is attached to the end of the bow by a shank, and is movable by means of a screw, so tightening or slackening the hairs.

Nut (of a violin), the slip of ivory or ebony over which the strings pass at the upper end of the finger board.

Nyastaranga, a musical instrument of brass used in the N.W. provinces of India. The instrument placed over the throat of the performer acts as a resonator to the humming of the performer.

O

Obbligato (It.), necessary. Indicates that the part, vocal or instrumental, is essential.

Oblique Motion, the movement of a second part against a first which is stationary.

Oblique Pianoforte, an upright pianoforte with the strings arranged diagonally, so obtaining a greater length of string. This refinement was patented in 1811 by Robert Wornum of London, adopted early by French makers and later by German and American makers.

Oboe, the high double reed woodwind instrument of the orchestra. The oboe has a conical bore and overblows the octave. It is sounded from a double reed mouthpiece, and the pitch is varied by the pitch holes in the tube. The natural scale of the oboe is D. Its normal compass is about two and a half octaves from the B♮ (sometimes B♭) below middle C.

Crude double reed wind instruments were known in ancient times and by the 16th century two families were established, those with conical bores, and those with cylindrical bores. The conical bore family consisted of shawms and pommers, the oboe developing from the shawms, the smaller instruments, and the bassoon from the pommers. Many have contributed to the perfection of the present instrument, and the system of fingering evolved by Boehm for the flute has been adapted to it.

Obrecht, Jacob (b. Utrecht *c*. 1430, d. Ferrara 1505), was one of the most important composers of the 15th century. His Passion Music is a notable early contribution to the evolution of oratorio based on the Passion story.

Ocarina, a family of small wind instruments having a large interior and no bell.

Occasional Music, music written for, and generally appropriate to a particular occasion.

Octave, the interval covering eight degrees of the scale, and therefore between two notes of the same name. The octave is the most perfect of consonant intervals.

Octave, an organ stop an octave higher than the diapason but otherwise similar to it. On the manual organs this stop is generally called principal and matches the open metal diapason. On the pedal organ, as with the diapason, the octave is often of wood.

Octet, a composition for eight voices or instruments.

Octo Basse, an outsize variety of double bass invented in Paris by Vuillaume in 1849. Two specimens are known to exist.

Ode, a form of poetry of Greek origin. In its various forms the ode has proved most suitable for musical setting.

Odington, Walter de (13th century), was an English musical theorist, known by one work, *De Speculatione musices*.

Offenbach, Jacques (b. Cologne 1819, d. Paris 1880), was the son of the cantor of the synagogue at Cologne. He was the most successful and brilliant composer in his day of the lighter type of opera. All told he wrote some ninety operas in twenty-five years. He was still working on his best opera *The Tales of Hoffmann* when he died; it was completed by Guiraud, and produced the year after Offenbach's death.

Okegham, Jean de (b. *c.* 1430, d. Tours 1495), was one of the most important Netherland composers of his time, and is commonly considered the founder of a new school following the older school of Dufay.

Open, a term used to describe organ stops consisting of open pipes. The complementary term is 'stopped'.

Open Notes (on brass wind instruments), those notes produced without the use of valves, slides, or, in the case of the horn, by the insertion of the hand in the bell; that is, the notes forming the harmonic series proper to the tube of the instrument.

Open Notes (on members of the violin family), those notes produced from unstopped strings.

Open Score, a score in which a stave is allotted to each part. The complementary term is 'short score'.

Opera, a musical dramatic entertainment in which the music plays an essential and not merely incidental part. While excluding a great variety of musical stage productions, opera includes a wide range of styles from the most serious to the most light, in which the music may be continuous throughout a scene or be broken up into recitatives, songs and choruses, or even have the dialogue spoken.

Opera arose in Florence at the end of the 16th century. The creators were mainly noblemen, musicians and other learned men accustomed to meet at the home of a certain Count Bardi who attempted to revive the style of Greek tragedy. The earliest opera to survive complete is *Euridice,* by the poet Rinuccini and the musician Peri, which was produced in 1600, three years after the first attempts at producing opera. The first musically important figure of opera was Monteverdi.

Early in the 17th century a comic element began to appear in opera. The first opera house was opened in Venice in 1637 and the popularity of the new art soared. As a result, opera became standardised. From Venice opera spread to other cities throughout Europe, in particular Vienna, where the Imperial Court was the most splendid in Europe, and later to Paris where, in the days of Louis XIV, opera became a Court function established musically by Lully (an Italian) whose operas invariably started with a prologue in praise of the King. Opera was less readily established in England, but Purcell's *Dido and Aeneas,* produced in 1689, is among the masterpieces of early opera.

Alessandro Scarlatti was the next most important figure in the history of opera. His career was divided between Rome and Naples. Opera became one of Italy's main exports, as much on account of its singers, particularly the male soprano, a castrato, as the music. Handel established the Italian style of opera in England. Opera had become a highly conventionalized form of entertainment and became to some extent a singing competition between the performers, particularly as the excellent librettos by Metastasio were set repeatedly, some of them more than once by the same composer.

From the 18th century onwards lighter styles of opera became more important. Previously opera was the entertainment of the privileged few, the cultured aristocracy, and so was of a serious and dignified character. Both Italy and France began to develop opera with a comic vein, having in England its counterpart *The Beggar's Opera*, a social satire by John Gay, with music borrowed (or stolen!) from a variety of sources and arranged by Pepusch. In the late part of the century, the reforms of Gluck are the dominant feature, and, as Vienna became the centre of musical life, Mozart made his incomparable contribution to opera.

At the beginning of the 19th century stand Rossini, whose later operas, including *William Tell*, were produced in Paris, and Weber, who was the pioneer of romanticism in German opera. From this time onwards the orchestra played a continually more important part in German opera, leading to the prodigious contribution of Wagner.

The latter part of the 19th century saw an increase in the lighter types of opera (perhaps best classed together as operettas, though that term is commonly defined otherwise). Offenbach in Paris, Johann Strauss in Vienna and Sullivan in England produced operas (operetta, comic opera by name as the case may be) and, at the end of the century, England saw the production of the most trivial variety of operetta, musical comedy.

Verdi was the one great opera composer surviving after the death of Wagner. A number of lesser figures are remembered by individual operas: Gounod's *Faust*, Bizet's *Carmen*, Mascagni's *Cavalleria Rusticana*, Puccini's *Madame Butterfly*, Smetana's *The Bartered Bride* and Humperdinck's *Hansel and Gretel*, for example. The emergence of Russian opera is another feature of the latter part of the 19th century. Richard Strauss, writing at the beginning of the present century, is best regarded as the last composer in the old style.

Though opera in England has been largely imported, repeated efforts have been made during the last fifty years or so to establish national opera. There are at last signs that the revival of British music is bearing fruit in the sphere of opera. Rutland Boughton, Vaughan Williams and now Benjamin Britten have made contributions which promise more than temporary success.

Generally speaking, modern composers are producing operas of distinctive national character. Debussy in France, Falla in Spain, Berg in Germany and Rimsky-Korsakov in Russia have all made notable contributions to the operatic repertory in the last fifty years.

Even the least stereotyped operas are a mass of conventions. The most important of the operatic conventions, beyond those inherent in any stage dramatic performance, is that the performers sing instead of speak their parts. The action may be held up, even at the most urgent dramatic moments, while the performers sing solos or join in choruses commenting on the situation, describing the actors' emotions or simply making an extended musical performance on the most trivial dramatic pretence.

At first, the story of an opera was carried on in recitative. During the 17th century the emotional importance tended more and more to be concentrated in the arias and choruses, and the recitative became more and more dull, particularly when it was left to be accompanied by the harpsichord. Recitative accompanied by the orchestra gave a much greater emotional potentiality to these portions of the opera. In Wagner's operas, not only do the scenes and acts become continuous but also the distinction between recitative, aria and chorus no longer exists and the fullness of musical treatment is the same throughout.

Particular styles of light opera have been dignified with specific names – opéra-comique, opera buffa, comic opera, operetta and the like. Such distinctions are, however, more confusing than helpful. In the 18th century one of the chief differences between French and Italian comic opera was that the French preferred the dialogue to be spoken. In Paris grand opéra and opéra-comique have always been separated (the distinction became mainly one of size, as spoken dialogue is convenient only in a small theatre), and a wide social distinction has always existed between the two. Opera covers a wide range and distinctions are no longer sharp; the modern repertory company presents all types to audiences drawn from all classes.

Opéra Bouffe, a comic French opera designed on a trivial scale, lighter in character than an opéra-comique.

Opera Buffa, a variety of Italian opera, having a more or less extravagantly comic plot. The arias, duets and choruses form the main attraction of an opera buffa; the dialogue is in 'recitativo secco'.

Opéra-comique, a variety of French opera. Originally having amusement as its aim, it was characterised by the humour of its plot, the simplicity of its music, and its spoken dialogue. Opéra-comique arose at the beginning of the 19th century; it became one of the most popular forms of dramatic art in France and finally the humour and spoken dialogue were discarded: a romantic plot, and music which though serious was never solemn remained its distinguishing features.

Operetta (in England), usually a musical dramatic work better classed as comic opera.

Operetta, an Italian opera of small scale and short duration, otherwise usually having the features of an opera buffa.

Ophicleide, a keyed brass instrument invented towards the end of the 18th century. The established form of the instrument had eleven or twelve keys, was played with a large cup mouthpiece and had a range of about three octaves upwards from two octaves below middle C. Though having good intonation and a distinctive quality, the ophicleide did not mix well with other instruments of the orchestra. It fell into disuse towards the end of the 19th century, being replaced by the improved valve brass instruments.

Oratorio, a musical setting of a large-scale dramatic poem or prose of a sacred character. Evidence of dramatic presentation of scenes from the Scriptures dates from the 12th century. The present name and popularity of such performances must be credited to St Philip Neri, founder of the Congregation of Oratorians, who introduced them in the oratory of his own church in Rome, after the sermon. Because of their popularity, these performances were continued after his death in 1595.

Conveniently and justifiably the rise of oratorio may be traced from about the same time as the rise of opera in Florence. In the first instance, dress and scenery were probably as much a feature of oratorio as of opera, and the difference of subject matter made little or no difference to the musical treatment or mode of production. The close association between Italian opera and oratorio remained evident from the dramatic character and flavour of earthly entertainment in oratorios, whether or not they were actually intended for dramatic presentation. Alessandro Scarlatti wrote oratorios scarcely distinguishable from his operas, and there is no great difference in design and treatment between Handel's operas and many of his oratorios.

In Germany oratorio started on a far loftier religious plane with the spirit of Passion music and undoubtedly inherited much from the medieval mystery plays. In the first instance, it was strongly influenced by the plainsong tradition of the Roman Church, as exemplified in the oratorios of Schütz, though this readily gave way to the influence of the chorale so extensively used by Bach. Innumerable settings of the Passion story were made by the predecessors and contemporaries of Bach; Telemann for instance wrote forty-four!

Stress is often laid on the reflective character of Bach's oratorios and the dramatic character of Handel's. This distinction, partly true, is exaggerated and misleading. To deny the dramatic element in Bach's and the reflective in Handel's oratorios would be unjustifiable. The difference in character is a reflection of the devotional setting and religious tradition in which Bach produced his compositions, and the secular background to those of Handel. However, Bach and Handel between them established the characteristic features of modern oratorio now recognised as a type quite distinct from opera, a religious, non-liturgical work, devotional or not, and not intended for stage production.

Haydn made many fine contributions to oratorio. In contrast, Mozart's work in this field is negligible, as also is Beethoven's, compared with their work in others. During the 19th and present centuries, oratorio has received as much, if not more, attention, than opera; but relatively few oratorios have achieved lasting popularity. In England, the oratorios of Mendelssohn, Brahms' *German Requiem* (which ranks with the finest of oratorios) and, as the climax of the revival of English oratorio, those of Elgar are representative of the more important contributions to oratorio which are at present held in popular esteem.

The boundaries of oratorio are clearly ill-defined. Generally speaking, settings of the Mass, Requiem Mass and smaller definitely liturgical compositions, even though intended for non-liturgical performance, are not classed as oratorio.

Orchestra, originally the Greek name for the portion of the theatre between the stage and the auditorium in which the chorus performed, literally meaning 'a dancing place'. In its present usage, orchestra means either the place where the band is placed in a theatre or hall or the band itself. The use of orchestra in the latter sense is generally limited to those bands used for the performance of operatic, symphonic and similar music.

The size of the orchestra has grown considerably from the time when it first took the form established by Mozart and Haydn. From the first, the strings arranged in five groups (1st violins, 2nd violins, violas, violoncellos and double-basses) have formed the basis of the orchestra. The growth of the woodwind, brass and percussion sections has taken place mainly in that order. The basis of the woodwind became 2 flutes, 2 oboes, 2 clarinets and 2 bassoons; to these a piccolo, a double-bassoon, and less generally a cor anglais and bass clarinet have been added. The basis of the brass became first, 2 horns and 2 trumpets, and later 4 horns, 3 trumpets and 3 trombones and a bass tuba. The percussion began as a pair of kettledrums; later a third kettledrum under the same player and a bass drum, side drum and triangle under a second player were added. At first the strings were really in four parts, the double-bass simply doubling the violoncello part; now the double-bass has considerable independence and the other string parts (though basically in four parts) are often sub-divided. A harp has become a frequent addition.

Additions of brass, as by Wagner in *The Ring,* and of the organ, as by Elgar in *The Dream of Gerontius,* and various percussion instruments have been made in certain suitable instances. The regular addition of saxophones, cornets, bells and the like, however, does not appear to add materially to the resources and elegance of the orchestra, which seems to be organically complete without them.

The customary lay-out of the orchestra has changed from time to time. The present custom is for the strings to be placed nearest the conductor arranged in this order: first violins (on his left), second violins, violas and violoncellos (on his right), and the double basses behind the violoncellos. The wind are placed behind the strings, the woodwind to the left, the brass to the right. The percussion are placed at the back. The size and shape of the stage or orchestral pit obviously influence the lay-out, and conductors have their own personal fancies.

Orchestration, the art of using and combining the instruments of an orchestra. Orchestration as it is now understood had hardly begun to evolve before Mozart and Haydn. During their time the essential features of the orchestra became stabilized, and this led naturally to the enlargement of it in the hands of Beethoven.

Before the 18th century no general principles of instrumental grouping or treatment had been formulated. Handel wrote most of his instrumental music simply for strings, occasionally employing wind instruments, more often than not merely to double the string parts. Bach made use of a far greater range of instruments than Handel, but his practice was invariably to choose the particular instruments he required for each work. His choice of instruments from composition to composition varied greatly; apart from the basis of strings there was no apparent standard size or arrangement of his orchestra.

Haydn and Mozart wrote for about thirty-five players. About one-third were wind and percussion players, flutes, oboes, clarinets (sometimes), bassoons, horns, trumpets, trombones (sometimes, but not in symphonies), and drums; the rest were strings. The crudeness of the instruments and the lack of skill on the part of players were the main factors in limiting the instruments used and their treatment. Beethoven made more regular use of the clarinets, more use of the trombones, double bassoon and a larger percussion group. The enlarged wind and percussion demanded a greater number of instruments to each string part.

The vast improvement in the construction of wind instruments during the 19th century led to the general increase in the number of wind instruments employed by composers, and a development in their treatment of them. Modern composers commonly write for twenty to twenty-five wind and percussion players; to balance these, about three times the number of string players are wanted, making a total of about a hundred players.

Orchestrina di Camera, the name of a series of instruments, built on the harmonium principle, imitating the quality of certain orchestral wind instruments.

Organ, the largest and most complex musical instrument under the control of one performer. The organ is a keyboard wind instrument in which a large number of pipes are brought under the control of the player by elaborate mechanical, pneumatic or electrical engineering. Organs vary greatly in size and design.

The evolution of the organ may be traced from the syrinx. Though early writers indicate that the most important features of the primitive organ had been discovered before the Christian era, any attempt at a detailed history would be purely conjectural. The hydraulus is the earliest indication of a successful combination of the essential features. Organs appear to have been adopted for religious use by the Christian Church by the 5th century. From then on numerous references to, and descriptions of organs occur, giving, however, only uncertain indications of the details of the advances in mechanical construction.

The primitive organs of the long period from the 5th to the 11th century had a number of bellows which, by successive blasts, made an attempt to give a continuous and even supply of wind to the pipes. The crude keyboard consisted of slides which the player moved in and out. Each slide controlled several pipes which all sounded together when the slide was out. These organs appear to have been more primitive than the hydraulus which preceded them. The hydraulus had a means of keeping a steady wind supply by water pressure, possibly a lever key mechanism, and a stop action controlling the use of the several pipes which sounded from each key.

From the 11th century onwards, the improvement in organ construction was rapid. A primitive keyboard of clumsy levers replaced the slides used during the 11th century. The number of keys and ranks of pipes increased during the 12th and 13th centuries; the remaining four of the five chromatic semitones were added (B♭ was present a number of centuries earlier), a fifth and octave and possibly also a third and tenth were added to the unison to give the effect of harmonics, and to enrich the quality of the note.

By the 14th century the compass of the keyboard was sometimes two and a half octaves. Improvements in the mechanism allowed the pipes to be arranged in the manner used now, small ones in the middle; this enabled the compass to expand unhindered by all the large pipes being clustered at one end. During this century relief from the constant use of all the pipes appears to have been obtained by the first use of more than one keyboard.

The greatest advances in organ construction were made during the 15th century. The invention of pedals and a stop action date from the beginning of this century, and during the century improvements in the action made possible successive reduction in the size of the keyboard. The stops received individual names, though at first they all belonged to the same class of open metal cylindrical pipes of full scale. During the century, stopped pipes of wood or metal, reed pipes and open metal pipes narrow in scale

were introduced. By the beginning of the 16th century all the
features of the mature organ were present – manuals, pedals and
stops, and a manageable keyboard of about four octaves, with
an efficient mechanism and wind supply.

The lower limit of the organ compass became established,
during the 16th and 17th centuries, as the C two octaves below
middle C (*a*). The compass extended upwards for four octaves or
a little over (*b*). The pedal keyboard had the same lower limit but
a compass of only two and a half octaves (between *a* and *c*). It
was for an instrument of these dimensions that Bach wrote.

(*a*)   (*b*)   (*c*)

Later the manual compass became extended upwards to A and
finally to C, making five octaves.

Four important additions during the 18th, 19th and 20th
centuries have become regular features of the organ – the swell,
couplers and other accessories, composition pedals and lastly
composition pistons. The replacement of the mechanical tracker
action by tubular pneumatic and then electric action in the late
19th and the 20th centuries has revolutionised the engineering
of organ design, and has enabled an elaboration of the console
and a refinement of the player's control over the organ un-
imaginable with even the best purely mechanical action.

A modern organ has two, three or four manual keyboards and
a pedal keyboard. A fifth manual keyboard is sometimes added,
but it can hardly be considered as making a useful addition to
the resources of the instrument. Small instruments with one
keyboard are made, but the absence of even one other keyboard
is the loss of an essential feature of the organ. Each keyboard
controls primarily one section of the pipes of the instrument,
forming in themselves a complete department or organ of the
instrument. Both the keyboard and the organ are known by the
same name, the Choir manual, for instance, operating the Choir
Organ. In some large organs more than one organ may be
playable from the same keyboard, or an organ may be playable
from two or more manuals, not being specifically allotted to any

particular one. The four usual manuals from the lowest upwards control the Choir, Great, Swell, and Solo respectively and the fifth when added is placed at the top. Four is the maximum number of keyboards which an organ player can conveniently manage, and the control of additional departments from these four manuals presents no difficulty to the modern electrical engineering employed in organ design.

The stop controls are arranged on either side or above the manuals, and are grouped according to the departments they control. Balanced pedals controlling the swell boxes (in which are the Swell Organ and usually also the Choir or Solo Organs) are placed in the centre above the pedal keyboard. Composition pedals are placed on either side of the swell pedals, and composition pistons are placed under the manual to which they relate. The controls over coupler action and other accessories are placed as is convenient, either together or near the other controls associated with the manual or organ to which they relate.

The Pedal Organ is generally regarded as being pitched an

ORGAN PIPES

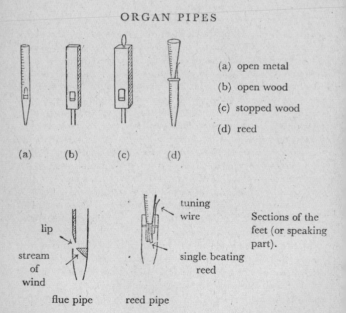

(a) open metal

(b) open wood

(c) stopped wood

(d) reed

(a)   (b)   (c)   (d)

tuning wire

lip

stream of wind

single beating reed

Sections of the feet (or speaking part).

flue pipe   reed pipe

octave below the manual organs. This is, however, rather misleading. The Pedal Organ does include stops pitched an octave below
written pitch, but their normal use is to double the proper bass
at the octave below (in much the same way as the double bass
doubles the violoncello an octave below), not to sound by themselves. The absence of an adequate number of Pedal Organ stops
at the unison pitch of the manual organs, making the use of
manual to pedal couplers obligatory, is only an expedient to
save expense.

The advances in the mechanism of the organ have made
possible the derivation of a number of stops from one rank of
pipes. This device originally met with considerable objection;
however, its judicious use is clearly preferable to the excessive
use of couplers to compensate for the lack of a larger number of
speaking stops. Stop controls are now made in three forms, the
draw stop handles, pivoted rocking tablets and press buttons.
The separation of the console from the rest of the organ (now
becoming common) is a most desirable feature which has been
made possible by electric action.

The great variety in the design of modern English organs
(quite apart from the differences between organs of various
countries) makes a description of a typical organ impossible.
Further, the specification of organs is needlessly complicated
by the use of fancy and foreign names for registers.

Organum, a term used in various senses during the early centuries
of polyphony. No ready distinction between organum and
descant is possible, both terms being used in different senses by
theorists of the time. In its most primitive form, organum
implied the art of adding parts in parallel octaves, fifths and
fourths to a given part. Though this may be the sense now
sometimes meant by organum, the term did not in fact keep
this limited meaning.

Ornament, a decoration, usually melodic, indicated by a sign or by
small notes and performed in an understood fashion, or inserted
arbitrarily by the performer. The practice of decorating the
main outline of a melody may be found in Gregorian music
and music of the Middle Ages. During the 16th, 17th and 18th
centuries ornaments played a prominent part in keyboard music,
and embellishments not indicated in the music were undoubtedly
added by signers, not necessarily to the improvement of the
music, though a certain amount of it was probably expected by
the composer. The ornaments employed in France were codified

during the 18th century, a process to which Lully made a considerable contribution. German, English and French ornaments differed from one another a good deal.

Ossia (It.), or else. Indicates that one of two parts is an alternative to the other, usually being simpler or more restricted in range.

Ostinato (It.), obstinate. Used loosely to describe a section in which a theme is repeated over and over again. 'Basso ostinato' is thus the Italian equivalent for 'ground bass'.

Ouseley, The Reverend Sir Frederick Arthur Gore (b. London 1825, d. Hereford 1889), achieved distinction as an organist and composer of church music. He was closely associated with St Michael's College, Tenbury, from its foundation in 1854, and became Professor of Music at Oxford in 1855.

Overblowing, the production of overtones by forcing the wind supply in a pipe. Overblowing may occur in the organ if the supply of wind from the bellows to the reservoir is not carefully regulated or controlled. It is necessary for the production of the notes of the upper octaves in the flute.

Overspun Strings, strings of the pianoforte, violin or other stringed instrument, wound round with fine wire to give them greater weight, so increasing their depth of pitch and richness of quality.

Overstringing, the arrangement of the strings of the pianoforte so that the lower bass overspun strings lead diagonally over the longest unspun strings.

Overtones, those tones, other than the fundamental, which give quality to a note. Individually, overtones pass unnoticed by the ear, though their presence may be readily demonstrated scientifically.

Overture, usually an instrumental prelude to an opera or a play, particularly a play for which incidental music has also been written; sometimes an instrumental composition intended solely for concert use. With the evolution of the sonata and symphony, 'first movement form' was commonly adopted for overtures. The form of operatic overtures has varied from time to time. Previously overtures had usually consisted of a short introduction followed by the main section in a lively fugal style, and one or two pieces in dance form were sometimes added. Concert performances of such overtures separated from their operas was one of the features of the evolution of symphonic music. Two rather different forms of extended overture became recognised – the French overture and the Italian overture. One of the operatic reforms of Gluck was the adoption of an overture which had relevance to the drama of the opera; this it had not before. Later the use in the

overture of subject-matter taken from or derived from the body
of the opera cemented the relationship between the two. However,
neither the use of particular forms nor the use of subject-matter
from the body of the opera has ever been a restriction essential
to an operatic overture.

Besides those symphonic movements intended solely for concert
use, many operatic overtures are remembered while the operas
to which they were written are forgotten.

P

Pachelbel, Johann (b. Nuremberg 1653, d. there 1706), was an organist
and composer important as a fore-runner of Bach. Elaborate
settings of chorals were one of the forms of composition in which
he specialized.

Pachmann, Vladimir de (b. Odessa 1848, d. Rome 1933), was an
eminent pianist admired particularly for his performances of the
works of Chopin.

Paderewski, Ignacy Jan (b. Kuylówka 1860, d. New York 1941), was
the son of a Polish patriot. He began his career as a pianist and
by his brilliant technique, musicianship and personality established
himself in the front rank of virtuosi. He worked for the freedom
of his native country and became its first Prime Minister in 1919.
As a composer he is known by a few small pieces.

Paganini, Niccolo (b. Genoa 1782, d. Nice 1840), came of humble
parents. From an early age he received instruction in violin
playing from his father, a musical enthusiast, and gave his first
public performance when he was nine. In 1797, accompanied by
his father, he made his first professional tour. A little later he left
home and began the chequered career which, though genuinely
full of strange adventures, has been grossly distorted. After
pawning his own violin he was first lent and then given a
Guarnerius; on another occasion he was given a Stradivarius.
From 1801 he lived for a few years in Tuscany with a lady of
rank, a retirement from public appearance which later gave rise
to the false rumours that he had been in prison. The story of
his career is a record of his amazing success.

Paganini has been described as first among virtuosi of the
violin. His brilliant technical feats employed effects previously
unknown. By his use of stopped harmonics he extended the

compass of the violin, added brilliance and made possible double notes in high passages previously considered impossible. He sometimes played with only one string, used unusual tunings, and made amazing use of combined pizzicato and arco runs. These, among other effects, astounded the audiences of his day and revolutionized the technique of violin playing, even though many of his effects now savour of charlatanism.

Pair, a word used in the term 'pair of organs' and 'pair of virginals' which were common in 16th-century writings and earlier. The derivation of these terms is not known. In all probability there is no difference in meaning between these terms, 'the organs' and 'the virginals' (forms also common in the 16th century) and the more modern usage, organ and virginal. The derivation of the term 'double organ' used in the 16th century is also unknown; it may have meant an organ with a compass downwards to double C two octaves below middle C.

Palestrina, Giovanni Pierluigi da (b. Palestrina 1525, d. Rome 1594), is commonly known by the name of his birth-place. Little is known with certainty of his youth. In 1544 he was appointed to the Cathedral of his native town as organist. In 1551 he was called to Rome to become choirmaster of the choir connected with St Peter's and in 1555 he became a member of the college of singers attached to the Papal Chapel, but was later dismissed because he was married. He subsequently held various appointments, the first being at St John Lateran. Following criticisms of the unsuitability of much of the church music of that time, Palestrina was re-appointed to St Peter's in 1591. In 1585 he was given the title of 'Composer to the Papal Chapel' and during the rest of his life remained closely associated with the music of St Peter's and of the Papal Chapel.

Among the most beautiful of Palestrina's 94 masses are that dedicated to Pope Marcellus II and that of the Assumption. These, with some three to four hundred motets and a large quantity of liturgical music, Magnificats, Lamentations, Hymns and the like, make up his sacred music. His madrigals, some 140, do not show any marked difference in style from his sacred music.

Palestrina summarized the achievements of Italian 16th-century polyphony and crystallized all that was good in Roman Catholic church music, setting a pattern and standard that has, so far at least, remained unchallenged.

Palmgren, Selim (b. Björneborg 1878), still living.

Pandean Pipe, probably the oldest of all wind instruments, made in many forms of many materials. Stopped tubes, which are bound together, are sounded by being blown across the open end. Modern forms of the instrument have gained temporary popularity.

Pandora, the Greek name of an ancient plucked stringed instrument with a long straight neck and a small body, in contrast to instruments of the lute pattern. Instruments of this form date from the ancient Babylonian and Egyptian civilisations, and were possibly known to the latter as the nefer. In Greece the pandora very probably preceded the lyre. Instruments of pandora pattern and with names having a similar first syllable were known in a great many ancient civilisations.

Pandore, an English instrument, a variety of cither, used for the bass of a consort during the 16th and early 17th century.

Paradisi, Pietro Domenico (b. Naples 1710, d. Venice 1792), commonly known as Paradies, was a teacher and composer. He lived in London for a number of years.

Parallel, a term used in the same sense as consecutive, but not having the same special application to the intervals of the octave and the fifth. While a succession of thirds, sixths, fifths or octaves may all equally well be referred to as parallel motion, only a succession of octaves or fifths are referred to as 'consecutives'.

Parlando (It.), speaking. Equivalent to 'parlante'.

Parlante (It.), speaking. Used in instrumental music in a similar sense to 'cantabile'. Used in vocal music to indicate a tone of voice approximating to speech.

Parratt, Sir Walter (b. Huddersfield 1841, d. Windsor 1924), achieved distinction as an organist. He was appointed Master of the Queen's Musick in 1893, and Professor of Music at the University of Oxford in 1908.

Parry, Sir Charles Hubert Hastings (b. Bournemouth 1848, d. Rustington 1918), achieved distinction as a composer and as a prominent figure in musical education. He was appointed Director of the Royal College of Music in 1894, was Professor of Music in the University of Oxford from 1900 to 1908, and held the presidencies of a great many musical societies.

Parry composed music of all kinds, but, as with Stanford, the greater bulk of his compositions has given place to that of his successors. The most successful of his works, and those which have achieved the most permanent place in the repertory, are among his sacred and secular vocal compositions. His *Blest*

Pair of Sirens and *Jerusalem* are fine examples of his command of massive choral effect and his ability to write a magnificent melody. Many of his smaller motets are among the best that have been produced during the last two centuries.

With Stanford and Mackenzie, Parry must be counted as one of the outstanding musical figures leading the revival of English music, and one of the great precursors of the flourishing school of English composers of the early 20th century.

Parsley, Osbert, (b. 1511, d. 1585), was an English musician. Sacred music by him is included in *Tudor Church Music*. He was buried in Norwich Cathedral, where he was a lay-clerk.

Parsons, Robert (b. Exeter, d. Newark 1570), became a gentleman of the Chapel Royal. Some church music and a little secular music by him is extant.

Part, the single line of vocal or instrumental music sung or played by the individual performer in concerted music, or, by an extension of meaning, a readily distinguishable melodic line in keyboard music. The whole text for a keyboard performer, in concerted music, may equally well be described as his part. So also may the separate portion of the text for the right hand, left hand and feet.

Parthenia, the first volume of music for the virginal printed in England. It contained compositions by Bull, Byrd and Gibbons.

Partials, the members of the harmonic series present in a musical note. The partials other than the fundamental are referred to as upper partials or more usually overtones.

Partimenti (It.), divisions. This name was given to bass parts, usually figured, used for exercises in counterpoint.

Partita (It.), a name apparently originating in the 17th century in Germany for a group of dance tunes played consecutively and so forming a suite. The term was used by Bach in this sense and also in the sense of variation.

Part Playing, the art of preserving the contrapuntal nature of music on the keyboard by keeping the phrasing and character of the parts distinct.

Part Song, a song for two or more voices. In English usage the part song is commonly distinguished from the madrigal by its harmonic style, and from the glee by being intended for choral use, but like them is commonly a composition of small dimensions intended for unaccompanied performance.

Part Writing, the disposition of the parts, particularly in a composition harmonic rather than contrapuntal in character.

Passacaglia, originally an Italian or Spanish dance similar to the chaconne. The original difference between the passacaglia and chaconne is no longer known. The passacaglia became divorced from its dance origins during the 17th and 18th century, surviving in France till then, and received considerable attention as a form for instrumental composition. The music of the passacaglia is constructed on a ground bass, but the theme may be transferred to an upper part and may be decorated.

Passage, a portion of music without any consideration of its size or relation to the remainder of the composition, particularly when the portion may be identified by some special feature of whatever kind. Passage is also used in a special sense to denote a portion of music with little or no artistic meaning, designed mainly for the display of the vocal or instrumental dexterity of the executant.

Passamezzo, an Italian dance, most likely a variety of pavan. A 'passamezzo pavana' and a 'galliard passamezzo' are to be found in *The Fitzwilliam Virginal Book.*

Passepied (Fr.), a dance said to have been originated by the sailor of Basse Bretagne. It was introduced into the suite and into the ballet. The passepied bears some similarity to the minuet but is quicker. The music is in three-four or three-eight time and usually begins in the third beat of the bar. In the suite, the passepied is in two or more parts, each repeated, the last part (or last two of four parts) being usually in the minor key, while the others are in the major.

Passing Note, a note moving by step between two notes which are part of the harmony. Passing notes are essentially discordant. They are described as diatonic or chromatic, unaccented or accented as the case may be.

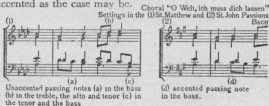

Choral "O Welt, ich muss dich lassen"
Settings in the (1) St. Matthew and (2) St. John Passions
BACH

Unaccented passing notes (a) in the bass
(b) in the treble, the alto and tenor (c) in the tenor and the bass

(d) accented passing note in the bass.

Nocturne No. 10, Op. 32, No. 2
CHOPIN

Unaccented passing notes
(e) chromatic (f) diatonic.

Passion Music, the musical settings of the passion story. The Matthew, Luke, Mark and John Gospel narratives are prescribed for Palm Sunday, the following Wednesday, Thursday and Good Friday respectively. The custom of reciting the passion stories during Holy Week has existed since the 4th century at least. By the 12th century it had become traditional for the story to be recited by three clergy, a narrator (tenor), one representing Christ (bass) and one representing the crowd (alto). Each of the three parts had its own traditional chant.

During the 16th century settings of the crowd portions for three or more voices became more and more common. Also during this period a distinct type, the motet passion, had a short vogue. In it the whole story was set in motet fashion, not even the words of Christ and other individual persons being sung by soloists. The traditional plainsong was often incorporated in one of the parts. The step of substituting the vulgar tongue for the Latin took place about 1520 at the instigation of Luther. Obrecht (motet passion), Byrd, Lassus and Victoria, among many others, contributed Latin passions. Johann Walther (1496–1570), Luther's musical helper, was the first to set the passion story in the vernacular.

In the 17th century the passions of Schütz form a link between the simple earlier styles and the large-scale passions of Bach, which are unrivalled by any other contemporary or later contribution to passion music. From the 18th century onwards works inspired by the passion story sometimes follow more or less closely the gospel texts, others are better described as oratorios based on the passion story.

Pasticcio (It.), a pie. A variety of musical drama in which the movements are taken from various operas, not necessarily all by the same composer, so as to present together as many favourite airs as possible. Hence pasticcio may be taken to include (a) a compound opera to which two or more composers have each contributed an act or scene, (b) an arrangement by one composer of the most successful airs of his various operas into one dramatic entertainment, and (c) the arrangements of the music from various operatic sources for an entertainment in which the music is incidental.

Pastoral, an instrumental or vocal composition characterised by its six-eight, nine-eight or twelve-eight time, the simple form of its melody, and commonly also by the use of a drone bass.

At one time the name was also used for an opera or dramatic

composition of a pastoral or legendary character usually giving considerable opportunity for ballet and pageantry.

Pastoral Oboe, another name for a shepherd's pipe.

Patter Song, a song characterised by the large number of words sung in the shortest possible time. Such songs are naturally found most often in comic opera or in operas in which a comic element is introduced.

Paumann, Conrad (b. Nuremberg, *c.* 1410, d. Munich 1473), was a distinguished organist, and is important as an early composer for the organ. He was born blind.

Pause, the sign ⌒ placed over a note or rest to indicate a lengthening of the time value of that note or rest by an amount at the discretion of the performer.

Pavan, a solemn dance, possibly of Italian origin, though commonly said to have come from Spain. It was very popular in the 16th and 17th centuries, and a large number of instrumental pavans have survived. It is commonly in two-two time, and is usually followed by a galliard.

Peal, a set of bells tuned to the major scale and hung for change ringing.

Pearsall, Robert Lucas (b. Clifton 1795, d. Wartensee 1856), was a composer who is remembered for several of his many part-songs and compositions in the madrigal style.

Pedal, an appliance on the organ, pianoforte and harp, worked by the feet. On the organ are the pedal-board, the composition pedals and swell pedals. On the pianoforte two pedals, the una corda pedal and the sustaining or damper pedal, are now usually found, though from time to time various modifications to the action have been brought under the control of pedals. On the harp the pitch of strings may be altered one or two semitones by means of a set of pedals.

Pedal Board, the keyboard played by the feet of a performer, now an essential feature of the organ.

Pedal Note (on a brass wind instrument), the fundamental or first harmonic regardless of the use of the valve or slide. The pedal notes on the trombone and deep-toned brass instruments are difficult to obtain; on the trumpet they are almost impossible.

Pedal Organ, the department of an organ properly, and nearly always exclusively, played from the pedal-board. On some modern organs the pedal organ may be coupled to (and therefore played from) one of the manuals.

Pedal Point, a sustained note round which the harmony and counter-point continues. This early harmonic device was derived from the drones found in certain musical instruments. Its use in the bass was soon established, and its particular effectiveness on the organ recognised.

The pedal point normally begins and ends by forming part of the harmony. The intermediate harmonic clashes, resulting from the independent movement of the harmony against the pedal point, are one of its most exciting features.

Symphony No.1
BRAHMS

and so on, concluding.

Pedal point for 8 bars

The principle of the pedal point was extended to notes sustained in an upper part (an inverted pedal) and later to notes sustained in two or more parts simultaneously. The tonic and the dominant were the first and most commonly used notes for pedal points.

Pedrell, Felipe (b. Tortosa 1841, d. Barcelona 1922), was given little formal musical training but came to be the leader of the revival of music as a serious study in Spain. His most important work was the publication of the complete works of Victoria and a great deal of the music of other early Spanish composers.

Peerson, Martin (b. *c*. 1580, d. 1650), was an English musician. He contributed to *The Teares or Lamentacions* compiled by Leighton, and several of his compositions are in *The Fitzwilliam Virginal Book*.

Pentatonic Scale, a scale of five notes reaching the octave on the sixth.

There is good evidence that the octave so divided represents the form of early scales.

Pepusch, John Christopher (b. Berlin 1667, d. London 1752), was a musician who is remembered mainly as the arranger of the music for Gay's *The Beggar's Opera* and its sequel *Polly*. He composed or arranged the music for a number of dramatic works, was a teacher, and published two treatises on composition. He came to England about 1700.

Percussion, instruments in which the sound, whether of definite or indefinite pitch, is produced by hitting a stretched membrane or metal, wood, or other material in any shape or form. Also a group of such instruments in an orchestra.

Perdendosi (It.), losing itself. Used in the sense of 'dying away'.

Pergolesi, Giovanni Battista (b. Jesi 1710, d. Pozzuoli 1736), was a composer of historical interest rather than of importance. His importance is considered to have been greatly exaggerated, possibly, it is suggested, as the result of his early death. His reputation rests mainly on his opera *La Serva Padrona* and his *Stabat Mater*.

Peri, Jacopo (b. Florence 1561, d. there 1633), was a composer closely connected with the rise of opera. The music he wrote for *Dafne* by Rinuccini has been lost, but *Euridice* by Rinuccini and Peri, produced in 1600, has survived complete.

Per Recte et Retro (Lat.), backwards and forwards. This term describes the imitation in 'cancrizans' and 'al rovescio'. A composition al rovescio need not incorporate any genuine canonic writing. However, if the parts are interchanged in the second half, a composition al rovescio will resemble a canon cancrizans. This has led to confusion in the use of the three terms.

Perti, Giacomo Antonio (b. Bologna 1661, d. there 1756), was a composer of opera and one of the most distinguished composers of church music of his period.

Pes (Lat.), foot. This name was used for the tenor part during the early centuries of polyphonic music. The reason for this curious use of pes is not known.

Pesante (It.), heavy. Indicates that a passage is to be played with great firmness.

Phagotus, a reed instrument evolved by Afranio. It was apparently a development of the bagpipe and had nothing in common with the bassoon.

Phantasy, another form of the name 'fancy'.

Philips, Peter (d. *c.* 1630 probably in Brussels), was an English musician who lived in the Netherlands. A number of compositions by him are in *The Fitzwilliam Virginal Book*, and a number of motets and madrigals by him have been reprinted.

Phrase, one of the smallest portions into which an extended composition may be marked off. The musical and literary uses of the word correspond.

Phrasing, the art of marking off in the text, or indicating in performance, the phrases into which a composition falls. During the
19th century an indication of the phrasing by the composer
became more common; previously, however, the phrasing was
left to the understanding of the performer. Phrasing implies not
only the broad divisions of a composition into phrases, but all
the subtleties which give meaning to each individual phrase.
By varying the phrasing a quite different meaning may be given
to a composition, apart from the differences resulting from
the use of varying expression.

Physharmonica, a precursor of the harmonium, invented by Anton
Häckel in 1818 in Vienna.

Piacere (It.), pleasure. Indicates at a cadenza that the style, speed
and expression are at the discretion of the performer.

Piacevole (It.), agreeable. Indicates a graceful style free from passion
or excessive expression.

Pianette, a low upright pianoforte.

Piangendo (It.), weeping. Properly used as an indication of style
or expression only in vocal music.

Pianissimo (It.), very softly. Usually expressed by *pp*.

Piano (It.), soft. Usually abbreviated to *p*.

Pianoforte, distinguished as a keyboard stringed instrument from
the clavichord and harpsichord by being sounded by hammers.
The credit for the invention of the pianoforte is given to Cristofori,
a harpsichord maker of Florence. His invention, however, was
probably not the first instrument to make use of a hammer
action. Cristofori made four instruments with a hammer action
in 1709, in Florence under the patronage of Prince Ferdinand
de Medici. Marius, a French harpsichord maker who submitted
instruments to the Paris Academy in 1716, and Schroeter, a
German musician who submitted pianoforte actions to the court
at Dresden, indicate that attempts to produce a hammer pianoforte action were widespread at the beginning of the 18th century.

After the invention of the hammer action, the earliest experiments were concerned with obtaining an efficient damper action
to work in conjunction with it, so that though the hammer
rebounds, leaving the string free to vibrate, the damper remains
raised until the key is released. One of the outstanding early
makers was the German maker Gottfried Silbermann, whose
instruments were seen by Bach in 1726, and were played by him
before Frederick the Great in 1747.

The earliest pianofortes were all tail-shaped like the harpsichords. Upright pianofortes, on the same principle as the upright harpsichords, were made from the middle of the 18th century. Small square pianofortes, of the shape commonly associated with the spinet, appear to have been made first by Johannes Zumpe, a German who worked under Shudi the harpsichord maker. The earliest reference to one of these instruments is in 1762, when Fétis began his studies. Upright pianofortes with strings passing below the keyboard appear to have been first made towards the beginning of the 19th century.

The popularity of the pianoforte in England dates from 1762, the year in which J. C. Bach came to the country. Towards the end of this century a fresh invention (or marked change and improvement) in the action was made by Americus Backers assisted by John Broadwood. This began the long series of inventions by which the modern grand pianoforte evolved. Frames strengthened with metal were designed from 1820 onwards, single cast metal frames appearing within the next twenty years. Shortly after 1850 the practice of overstringing became common.

In the earliest pianofortes, stops (as on the harpsichord) controlled certain alterations to the action, one stop commonly muting the strings with felt, two others raising the dampers from the bass and treble strings. Stop action gave place later to pedal control.

Two is now the usual number of pedals, though occasionally a third pedal is introduced between the other two. The left hand pedal is an una corda which shifts the keyboard slightly to the right; the right hand pedal raises the dampers. The middle pedal, when present, keeps the dampers of individual notes raised after the fingers have left the key until that pedal is released; the rest of the dampers stay under the control of the keys and right hand pedal. A pedal diminishing the range of the hammers has been tried instead of the una corda, but this and the mute pedal are now used only on certain cheap upright pianofortes.

The compass of early pianofortes was limited to about five octaves, two and a half above and below middle C. Modern pianofortes usually have seven octaves upwards from the A a little over three octaves below middle C. The compass upwards is often extended to C, and even further extensions of a few notes at both ends of the compass have been tried.

Various other experiments have been tried, such as the use of sympathetic strings and the use of two keyboards, as in the harpsichord. The purpose and effect of sympathetic strings is more efficiently gained from the damper pedal. Two keyboards would

make such a fundamental change in the character of the pianoforte that it is doubtful whether they are likely to become a
common feature.

Pibgorn, a small beating reed instrument, now obsolete, used by the
Celtic and Welsh peoples.

Pibroch, the English form of the Gaelic piobaireachd, a pipe tune.
This highest kind of bagpipe music takes the form of a theme,
the 'urlar', followed by some three or four variations.

Piccinni, Niccola (b. Bari 1728, d. Passy 1800), was a Neapolitan
composer who achieved considerable success with his light operas.
He is remembered as the figure pitted against Gluck by the
admirers of Rameau and the pro-Italian party. Piccinni was a
modest man and an admirer of Gluck. He knew no French, and
made no claims to be an exponent of opera on the grand scale.
His opera *Iphigénie en Tauride*, composed as a rival to Gluck's,
failed disastrously.

Piccolo, the highest wood-wind instrument of the orchestra. It is a
small flute which sounds an octave above the normal orchestral
flute. Its natural scale is D, like the flute, but it does not extend
below to C. Its compass upwards is at least two and a half octaves.
Music for the piccolo is written an octave lower than it sounds.

Piccolo, a metal or wooden organ stop of flute quality of 2 foot pitch
on the manuals.

Piece, a name used musically in a non-technical sense for any instrumental movement. The name is not generally used for vocal
compositions, nor for sonatas and symphonies. The musical use
dates from the 18th century, when it was first associated with the
term suite, a suite of pieces.

Pietoso (It.), pitiful. Indicates an expressive style.

Pilkington, Francis (d. 1638), was an English musician. His published
songs and madrigals are included in *The English Madrigal School*
and *The English School of Lutenist Songwriters*. He contributed
to *The Teares or Lamentacions* compiled by Leighton.

Pipe and Tabor, the traditional country combination of flute and
drum, the pipe in this case being of the recorder variety.

Piston (on an organ), a small press button operated by the thumb or
finger to control certain stops or groups of stops. The action of the
piston rearranges the stops it controls to a pre-set pattern regardless of which stops are already off or on.

Piston (of a valve brass instrument), the moving arm of the valve
action operated by the finger.

Pitch, one of the attributes of a note. The pitch of a note depends on the frequency of its fundamental, the pitch of the note rising as the frequency is increased.

Though pitch is largely a relative matter, the standard of pitch is of prime practical importance. During the 16th century different pitches were in use for different kinds of music, the highest and lowest differing by about a fourth. In England there appear to have been three pitches in use. In the 17th century an attempt was made to standardise pitch, and throughout the period from Purcell to Beethoven pitch was fairly stable at about A=420 vibrations per second, seldom varying from this by more than about half a semitone. During the 19th century the pitch of wind instruments was gradually raised as the greater brilliance so obtained was realised; strings and voices had to conform to this, to the detriment of music in general. Since the middle of the 19th century, a number of attempts have been made to standardize pitch. As the result of a Commission in 1859, the standard of A=435 was adopted generally in France; but well into the 20th century an unsatisfactory state of affairs continued to exist in England. In 1909 A=452.4 was made the official pitch for bands of the British Army and to this standard other wind bands generally conformed. Apart from these uses of the high pitch, the Continental standard was gradually accepted throughout the country. The high and the low pitches were commonly known as old and new Philharmonic pitches. In 1939 an international pitch was at last agreed of A=440, and to this the military bands of the British Army have conformed. Some wind bands still play at the old high pitch.

Più (It.), more.

Pizzetti, Ildebrando (b. Parma 1880), still living.

Pizzicato (It.), pinched. Indicates to string players that the strings are to be plucked instead of bowed.

Plagal Modes, those ecclesiastical modes derived from or related to the 'authentic modes'. Each plagal mode has the same final as the authentic mode to which it is related, but has a different dominant and range.

Plainsong, the name now given to the whole body of church music which developed before the rise of polyphony. In the first instance, what is now called plainsong enjoyed the more general titles of music or song. One of its features was the absence of any definite time in the music. The rise of polyphony made the adoption of a time system essential, and the two forms, the old plainsong and the new measured music, became distinct. Freedom from the time and key systems which became a necessary part of music embodying counterpoint and harmony are essential features of plainsong. Properly all early unison unmeasured music may be called plainsong, but the dominant importance of the Gregorian collection of Latin plainsong has resulted in the name plainsong usually referring to Gregorian music of Rome. The rival collection of Ambrosian music of Milan retained to a great extent its own distinctive features, but other rites were swamped at an early time by the Roman rites.

Playford, John (b. 1623, d. *c.* 1686), was a publisher of English music without rival during his career. His own *Introduction to the Skill of Music,* 1654, remained a standard text-book for a hundred years. His collection of airs for country dancing, the *Dancing Master,* 1651, is one of the most important sources of English national music. Other publications were *The Musical Companion* in 1672, a second edition which included what was originally Hilton's *Catch that catch can,* a Psalter with the tunes set in four parts in 1671, and another with the tunes set in three parts in 1677. His son, *Henry* (b. 1657, d. 1706), succeeded him in the business.

Plectrum, a quill, small piece of horn, wood, ivory or other material used in place of the fingers or finger-nails for playing various stringed instruments. The Greeks appear to have played the lyre with a plectrum, and to-day instruments of the mandoline family are played with plectra. The jacks on a harpsichord are also plectra.

Pleno (It.), full.

Pleyel, Ignaz Joseph (b. 1757, d. Paris 1831), was a prolific composer of instrumental music. He founded the distinguished firm of Pleyel, pianoforte makers, of Paris.

Plica, a particular note in medieval music, consisting of a breve or long with the addition of some grace note; its precise nature has been forgotten.

Pochette, the French counterpart of the English kit.

Poco (It.), a little.

Point, the original name of the dot placed after a note. It was first introduced in medieval music, where it was called a point of perfection or sometimes point of augmentation confirming or conferring perfection on a note, that is making its duration equal to three of the next shorter notes.

Point, a short phrase treated imitatively.

Pointing (in psalm singing), the manner in which the chant is to be fitted to the words. The pointing is indicated by signs and varying type.

Polka, a round dance said to be of Bohemian origin. It appears to have originated towards the middle of the 19th century and its popularity increased rapidly. The music is in two-four time and is rather slower than that of a march. Characteristic metrical figures of the polka are:

Polonaise, a stately Polish dance said to have developed in the late 16th century from the opening processional march on ceremonial occasions. It was readily adapted as an instrumental form during the 18th century, and interest in it as a dance was lost. The polonaise is written in three-four time and has the pace of a march. It should begin on the first beat of the bar and the last bar should have the figure:

The notes marked * are both leading notes.
The figure

is characteristic of the accompaniment.

Polska, a Swedish dance, of similar character to a Scotch reel. It is usually written in a minor key in three-four time.

Polyphony, the combination of two or more melodies in a harmonious manner. The complementary term is homophony, the harmonization of a melody which keeps its predominant importance over the added harmonies. The distinction between polyphonic and homophonic music is clearly one of degree. By the polyphonic period is meant the period lasting approximately from the 9th to the 16th century, during which the importance of the melodic line of the individual vocal parts was far greater than that of the relatively simple harmonic structure on which it was based.

Polytonality, having more than one tonality. This term has been used to describe certain recent systems of harmony. The characteristic feature of these systems is the simultaneous movement of harmonies of various tonalities superimposed on each other.

Pommer, the name given on the Continent to the large varieties of shawm.

Pomposo (It.), pompously.

Ponte, Lorenzo da (b. Ceneda 1749, d. New York 1838), was the author of the librettos of Mozart's *Figaro*, *Don Giovanni* and *Così fan tutte*.

Ponticello (It.), little bridge. The bridge of a stringed instrument.

Porpora, Niccola Antonio (b. Naples 1686, d. there 1767), was a composer and an outstanding teacher of singing. His compositions had little lasting value, but the success of his pupils and the testimony of his contemporaries go far to support the claim that he was the finest teacher of singing that there has been.

Port, a name at one time used in Scotland for certain compositions, mainly for the harp. Whether port meant a particular type of composition or merely a 'composition' (in the same sense as 'piece') is no longer known.

Portamento (It.), carried. Indicates that the voice is to glide from one note to the next.

Portative Organ, a small organ which could be carried in procession, commonly found as part of the musical equipment of a large church until the 16th century.

Position (on the trombone), the various amounts of extension of the slide. When the slide is closed it is said to be in first position. Each extension lowers the pitch one semitone.

Position (on instruments of the violin family), the place of the left hand on the finger-board of instruments of the violin family. In first position the four fingers are placed conveniently to obtain the four notes above that sounded by the unstopped string. In second position the hand is held a little nearer the bridge of the violin so that the fingers now play conveniently four notes one degree higher up the scale than they do in first position. Another similar shift of the hand produces third position, and so on for the seven positions used on the violin, viola or violoncello.

Positive Organ, originally a small stationary organ as opposed to a portative organ. Later the name became commonly used for an organ of chamber dimensions, and has in recent times been used for small organs suitable for country and mission churches.

Post Horn, a small straight brass or copper wind instrument played with a cupped mouthpiece, originally intended for use as a signal by mail coaches.

Postlude, the counterpart of 'prelude', especially a voluntary played after a church service.

Poulenc, Francis (b. Paris 1899), still living.

Power, Lionel (f. 15th century), was an English composer. Nothing is known of his life. A number of his compositions appear in the *Old Mall Manuscript* and he was the author of a musical treatise written in English.

Praetorius, Michael (b. Kreuzberg 1571, d. Wolfenbüttel 1621), was the most famous of a number of musicians, of more than one family, who adopted this surname in place of Schultz. Praetorius left a large number of compositions besides his treatise on music, *Syntagma Musicum,* a book of great historical interest and value. Four volumes are mentioned; the fourth volume was, however, either not completed or has been lost. The first three volumes treat the various aspects of music, styles of composition, musical instruments and the like, but not counterpoint, which was to have been treated in the fourth volume.

Pralltriller (Ger.), a melodic ornament, in effect an inverted mordent. It has no equivalent English name.

Precentor, the director of the choir in a cathedral or collegiate church. The precentor is often a dignitary of importance whose responsibility is by no means limited to the supervision of the musical portions of the service. However, the extent of the responsibility and importance of the office varies from place to place. Though the origin of the title is from the musical duties of the office, the appointment is now often filled more for ecclesiastical than for musical considerations.

Prelude, strictly any composition used as an introduction to another or to a group of compositions. It is sometimes used in the same sense as overture; but it is more often used as the name for the first movement, not in a dance form, of a suite, or as the first of two or more movements, as for instance a prelude and fugue, or as the name of an independent composition of no prescribed form.

Preparation, the sounding of a note as part of a concord before it is suspended to form a discord.

Presa (It.), taken. The sign indicating in a canon where the various voices are to enter.

Prestissimo (It.), very quickly.

Presto (It.), fast. Used as an indication of speed, quicker than 'allegro', and also as the name of a movement.

Pricksong, the old English name for written counterpoint as distinct from extemporized counterpoint. Pricksong is described by Morley and the term is used by Shakespeare.

Primo (It.), first. Used to distinguish the first player from the second (secondo), and also to distinguish a portion of the music to be played the first time but not the second.

Principal, an organ stop an octave higher than the metal open diapason, but otherwise similar to it.

Printing of music. The first authentic record of printed music is of a Missal printed in Rome in 1476. On the Continent, music printing was frequent from the beginning of the 16th century. The earliest real example of printed music in England is a song book printed by Wynken de Worde in 1530, though crude examples of musical illustrations in the text of books date from about the beginning of the century. Printing of music in England was well established by the beginning of the 17th century. John Day, Thomas East and John Playford are among the important early English printers of music.

Programme music, music which purports to describe, or be inspired by a particular story or mood. The complementary term is absolute music. In its crudest form programme music is purely imitative; many sounds, bird song, thunder and the like, are readily imitated. More subtly, the programme is no more than a suggestion to help in appreciating the composition. The distinction between programme music and absolute music is not well defined. Music originally with a programme may well be as enjoyable without it, and a programme undoubtedly assists many listeners to enjoy more fully a composition with no intended programme.

Progression, the movement from one note or chord to another, or a chain of such steps.

Prokofiev, Sergei Sergeievitch (b. Solnzevo 1891), still living.

Prolation, the relation between semibreve and minim in medieval music. In major prolation the semibreve equalled three minims; in minor prolation, two minims.

Proportion, a term used in musical terminology during the evolution of notation, and described in detail by Morley. The musical use of this term corresponded to the arithmetical ratio rather than to proportion. It was used mainly of the ratios between the frequencies of notes, and to a lesser extent of the ratios of various times.

Proprietas (Lat.), propriety. This term was used in medieval music to describe those ligatures which began with a note sung as a breve.

Prout, Ebenezer (b. Oundle 1835, d. Hackney 1909), gained a reputation as a teacher and musical theorist. His series of text-books on the various aspects of composition achieved success as standard text-books. He edited and provided additional accompaniments for Handel's *Messiah.*

Psalmody, a term used in various senses for the singing of the psalms. Three plainsong types of psalmody have been used, antiphonal psalmody, responsorial psalmody and direct psalmody. In the Anglican and other Protestant churches metrical versions of the psalms became widely used. In the Anglican church the now accepted method of singing the psalms is to Anglican chants.

Psalter, properly the Book of Psalms. Commonly, however, an English psalter includes not only the psalms, but also other canticles which are sung in a similar manner to the psalms. Three distinct kinds of psalters have been in use in the English church; the metrical psalter, containing the psalms paraphrased into verse and set to metrical tunes; the prayer book form of the psalms, pointed and set to Anglican chants; and the same set to the Gregorian psalm tones.

Psaltery, an ancient plucked stringed instrument similar in pattern to the dulcimer but played with the fingers or a plectrum. The psaltery survived in use into the 17th century.

Puccini, Giacomo Antonio Domenico Michele Secondo Maria (b. Lucca 1858, d. Brussels 1924), was the most famous of a distinguished family of musicians. He studied at the Conservatorium in Milan. His first success was in 1884, with an opera; in 1896 *La Bohème* placed him in the forefront of Italian composers of his time. *Tosca* was produced in 1900. *Madame Butterfly*, perhaps the best known and finally most successful of his operas, was a failure when first produced in 1904, and was subsequently revised.

Purcell, Henry (b. 1659, d. Westminster 1695), was the son of a musician. Both his father, also Henry, and his uncle, Thomas, were appointed Gentlemen of the Chapel Royal on its re-establishment in 1660; both held appointments at Westminster Abbey and various other appointments at Court. On his father's death in 1664 Purcell was adopted by his uncle and later became a chorister in the Chapel Royal. In 1673 he was appointed assistant to the keeper of the King's instruments and became keeper himself ten years later. In 1674 he became organ tuner at Westminster Abbey and five years later replaced Blow as organist; he held this last appointment till his death, when Blow was re-appointed. He was appointed to the Court on a number of occasions and enjoyed Royal patronage throughout his life.

Purcell was a prolific composer, contributing with equal success to the theatre and to the church, and writing equally well both instrumental and vocal chamber music. Of his dramatic works, *Dido and Aeneas*, written for a girls' school in Chelsea, can alone be considered a genuine opera. Besides *King Arthur,* *The Fairy Queen* and *The Tempest,* which are perhaps the best known of his five operas with dialogue, he wrote incidental music and songs for some forty plays. His Odes and Welcome Songs were written mostly as occasional music for his Royal patrons. A little liturgical music, some hymns, psalms, and a number of sacred songs survive, but anthems form the greater part of his sacred music. Some hundred secular songs, apart from those in his dramatic works, are extant. Sonatas and fantasias for strings, with and without continuo, and a variety of pieces for the harpsichord form the main part of his instrumental music. The numerous catches, rounds and canons which he wrote, though giving an interesting sidelight on contemporary culture, are of less musical worth.

Until recent years, while Byrd and his contemporaries remained forgotten, Purcell was claimed as unquestionably the greatest English composer. His work is less well known than it should be, *Dido and Aeneas,* the music for strings, many of the songs and much of the church music being well worth a great deal more attention than they receive at present.

Purfling, the line of three slips of wood, the outer left white, the middle stained black, following the outline of stringed instruments of the violin and guitar families.

Q

Quadrille, a dance for an equal number of couples arranged in a square. It originated from the introduction of contredanses into the ballet in the middle of the 18th century. The name was originally 'quadrille de contredanses'. The present form of the quadrille was settled by the beginning of the 19th century. It consists of five dances: 'Le Pantalon', in six-eight time, 'L'Éte' in two-four time, 'La Poule' in six-eight time, either 'La Trénise' or 'La Pastourelle' in two-four time, and 'Finale' consisting of three repeated sections. Except for the finale, the dances are of thirty-two bars and begin after eight bars of music which are repeated at the end.

Quality, one of the attributes of a note. By their quality, notes of the same pitch and volume may be distinguished. Quality depends on the extent to which overtones are present with the fundamental.

Quartet, a composition for four voices or instruments. The string quartet for two violins, viola and violoncello has taken first place in the repertory of chamber music since the time of Mozart and Haydn. Quartets for pianoforte, violin, viola and violoncello and for other instrumental combinations are distinctly fewer than quartets for strings. The form of instrumental quartets has followed that of the sonata. Vocal quartets are not associated with any particular form, and may be either with or without accompaniment. Apart from incidental occurrence in opera and oratorio, and excepting madrigals, part songs, motets and the like which may incidentally be for four voices, vocal quartets are few. Brahms alone in such works as his *Zigeuner Lieder* has made any considerable contribution to music for a quartet of solo voices.

Quasi (It.), as if. Used in terms of style and expression in the senses of 'in the style of' and 'between'.

Quaver, an eighth of a semibreve. It is written ♪ and its corresponding rest ♪ .

Quilter, Roger (b. Brighton 1877), still living.

Quint, an organ stop sounding a fifth above the unison.

Quintaton, an organ stop of stopped pipes, usually of metal of 16-foot pitch on the manuals or pedals. The quintaton is voiced so that the third harmonic (the twelfth above the fundamental) is slightly prominent.

Quintet, a composition for five instrumentalists or singers. The usual combination of instruments for which quintets have been written is the usual quartet of strings with the addition of a second viola or a pianoforte. The use of a second violoncello, or more rarely a double bass, rather than a second viola, is generally considered less satisfactory. Quintets for one clarinet or more rarely a horn, an oboe or a harp with a string quartet, or for five wind instruments are less common than the purely string quintet or the pianoforte quintet. The form of instrumental quintets usually follows that of the sonata and symphony.

The addition of a fifth voice to the vocal quartet has proved particularly effective. Vocal quintets are not associated with any particular form. Most examples occur incidentally in opera and among madrigals and motets.

Quodlibet (Lat.), as you please. A form of composition popular in the 16th and early 17th centuries as a musical joke. The characteristic feature of the quodlibet was the juxtaposition of two or more melodies which, by their nature or their words, were incongruous.

R

Rachmaninov, Sergei Vassilièvich (b. Novgorod 1873, d. California 1943), was a distinguished pianist and an able composer. He began his musical studies at the St Petersburg Conservatory when he was nine, and three years later moved to that at Moscow. As a composer he achieved his greatest success with his pianoforte works; his *Prelude in C♯ minor* has gained remarkable popularity. Of his four pianoforte concertos, the second in C minor is the best known.

Racket, a double reed wood-wind instrument, a precursor of the bassoon.

Raff, Joseph Joachim (b. Lachen 1822, d. Frankfort 1882), was a composer mainly of pianoforte music. At one time he enjoyed an astonishingly wide popularity in Germany and England.

Rallentando (It.), slowing gradually. Indicates a gradual reduction in speed.

Rameau, Jean Philippe (b. Dijon 1683, d. Paris 1764), was the son of an able organist. His father intended him to become a magistrate but Rameau became absorbed with music from an early age. He subsequently had a distinguished career as an organist, composer and musical theorist, and has been claimed with much justification as the greatest musician France has had. He achieved great success with his operas. His treatise on the science of harmony displays profound research and a wealth of invention. The variety of his harmony, orchestration and treatment of the voices was far superior to that of his contemporaries and the freshness of his ballet music set a standard soon copied in Italy and Germany.

Rank (of organ pipes), a complete set of pipes of the same quality. Formerly each rank of pipes would be under the control of one stop only. Now, however, ranks of pipes are commonly extended giving rise to registers of varying pitch (including mixture stops) on both manuals and pedals.

Ravel, Maurice (b. Ciboure 1875, d. Paris 1937), was the son of a French Swiss father and Basque mother. He entered the Paris Conservatoire in 1889. He is said to have shown a marked individuality of style in composition from the first. At the beginning of the century there was hostility to Ravel's style, and in 1905 he was declared ineligible in the preliminary competition for the Grand Prix de Rome, a criticism of his technique which could hardly be justified and which caused indignation even among the critics hostile to him. From that time his compositions were published regularly.

A delicacy of touch and preference for small-scale work are a characteristic of all Ravel's compositions, of which songs and music for the pianoforte form the larger part. He wrote little for the orchestra and much of what he wrote consists of arrangements from piano versions, as is the case with *Pavane pour une infante défunte, Ma Mére l'oye* and *Le Tombeau de Couperin*. The ballet *Daphnis et Chloé* and the *Bolero* are examples of his original orchestral work. He has also made several notable contributions to chamber music.

Ravenscroft, Thomas (b. *c.* 1590, d. *c.* 1633), was an English composer and the editor of various collections of music. *Pammelia,* 1609, *Deuteromelia,* 1609, and *Melismata,* 1611, are collections of rounds and vocal pieces, mostly of the madrigal variety. His other publications were *A Brief Discourse,* 1614, and *The Whole Booke of Psalmes,* 1621. Portions only of a number of anthems by him are extant.

Ray, the second note of the scale in Tonic Sol-fa.

Re, the second note of the scale in solmization.

Rebec, the old French name for a bowed string instrument preceding the viol.

Recapitulation, a restatement of the subject matter of a composition. This term is particularly used for the third section of a movement in first movement form; it is not used for the restatements of the principal subject of a movement in rondo form.

Recitative, the declamatory portions of an opera, oratorio or cantata. Broadly speaking, the narrative of the opera, oratorio or cantata is set in recitative while the choruses, arias and the like are reserved for special dramatic effects and for comment and reflection on the narrative. In its most primitive forms, the voice part of a recitative has little melodic interest, and the accompaniment is simply a series of chords indicated by a figured bass and intended to be played on the harpsichord or organ. Where the accompaniment is of this form, the interest lying entirely in the declamation of the words, a considerable freedom in the time is possible, the rhythm following the sense of the words. This freedom, however, becomes less as the recitative is more elaborately accompanied.

Recitativo Secco (It.), dry recitative. The more primitive kind of recitative. The accompaniment consists of a few chords only and so allows the singer to follow freely the rhythm of the words.

Recitativo Stromentato (It.), instrumented recitative. The more elaborate kind of recitative. It has a fuller accompaniment than 'recitativo secco' and therefore gives the singer less freedom to vary the time.

Reciting Note, the note in both the Gregorian psalm tones and Anglican chants on which the greater proportion of each verse of the psalms or canticles is sung. In the Gregorian psalm tones the reciting note is invariably the dominant of the mode; the two terms are therefore often used in place of each other.

Recorder, the chief representative of those flutes, played with a whistle head, which held an important place for some centuries before the general adoption of the sideways-held flute. The recorder had six finger-holes for the first three fingers on each hand, one thumb-hole and an extra hole for the little finger, notes outside the natural scale being obtained by cross-fingering. Recorders were made in various sizes, a set of four being common, each instrument having a compass of a little over two octaves. A revival of recorder making and playing has taken place during the last few years.

Redford, John (b. *c.* 1485, d. *c.* 1545), was an English organist, composer and dramatist. He held appointments at St Paul's Cathedral. A large number of compositions by him for the organ based on plainsong melodies are extant. The anthem *Rejoice in the Lord always*, by which he is generally remembered, is almost certainly not by him.

Reed, the speaking part of many instruments, often also forming the mouthpiece. The name is taken from the kind of plant from which the part is frequently made. Reeds are described as free or beating, and the latter as single or double, making three distinct varieties. A free reed has one tongue which vibrates through a slot as wind is sucked or blown through the slot. A single beating reed has one tongue which overlaps the edges of the slot leading to the resonating tube, and which vibrates when wind is forced between the almost touching edges. A double reed has two tongues which are almost touching, and which vibrate when wind is forced between them.

Reed Stop (on an organ), any register composed of reed pipes.

Reel, a dance of obscure and ancient origin. In various forms the reel is popular in Scotland, Ireland and Denmark. The music is usually in four-four, sometimes in six-four time. The Irish reel is much faster than the Scottish reel. In Yorkshire, the reel is associated with the sword dance, and a hornpipe tune is used for the dance.

Regal, a small organ originally composed of reed pipes only, probably invented in the later half of the 15th century. In later instruments flue pipes were added, the reed pipes forming the regal stop. With the incorporation of reed pipes in the positive organ, the distinction between the regal and positive was lost.

REEDS

(a) and (b) Clarinet mouthpieces
(a) without the reed
(b) with the reed, held in place
by a metal clip

(a)   (b)

(c) single free reed as
in the harmonium.

(c)

(d) bassoon reed
(e) oboe reed

(d)   (e)

Reger, Max (b. Brand 1873, d. Leipzig 1916), was the son of a teacher. The early part of his life was varied but not remarkable. From 1901, when he moved to Munich, he began to take a prominent place in musical life, chiefly as a result of his pianoforte playing. With the support of the organist Straube he rapidly gained a reputation for his organ music, and from that time his life was successful. In 1907 he became musical director at the University of Leipzig, and in 1911 Director of the Court Orchestra at Meiningen. He soon relinquished the first of these appointments, and the second ended after two years on the death of the Duke. He held a few teaching appointments, undertook concert tours with great success, and was given a number of academic honours. But the wide recognition of his compositions during his lifetime appears to have been to him the most gratifying aspect of his success. The most important of his compositions are his valuable contributions to organ music.

Register (of an organ), a characteristic sound produced over the compass of the manuals or pedals by a rank or ranks of pipes and controlled by a stop.

Apart from some two or three dozen registers whose names have become fairly standardized, a good deal of variation in the choice of names for registers now exists. Archaic and foreign names are often used. The most important registers and the names under which they are commonly met are:

Acoustic Bass	Flute	Quintaton
Bassoon	Gamba	Salicional (and Salicet)
Bourdon	Gedact	Suabe Flute
Claribel Flute	Geigen	Trombone
Clarinet	Hautboy	Trumpet
Clarion	Mixture	Tuba
Diapason	Piccolo	Twelfth
Dulciana (and Dulcet)	Principal	Voix Céleste
Fifteenth	Quint	Vox Humana

They are described separately. The prefixes

Double	Open
Harmonic	Stopped
Lieblich	Sub

are also described separately.

The sounding pitch of a register is invariably indicated by a number against its name. A note two octaves below middle C is sounded by an open flue pipe of about eight feet long. Since the bottom note on the manual and pedal keyboards of an organ are

taken as being two octaves below middle C, a register sounding
the notes played is said to be of 8-foot pitch. Hence registers
labelled

  2 sound two octaves above the unison,

  4 sound one octave above the unison,

  8 sound at the unison,

 16 sound one octave below the unison,

 32 sound two octaves below the unison.

Register (of the voice), a portion of the compass of a voice produced by
the vocal chords in a particular manner.

Registration, the art of using and combining the registers on an organ.
The very great variation in the design of organs makes registration largely a matter in the hands of the performer.

Related Keys and *Remote Keys,* keys more or less closely associated with
one another from the harmonic and melodic point of view.

Keys having more sharps or fewer flats than a given key are
said to be on the sharp side, those with fewer sharps or more flats
on the flat side. The closest relation between keys is that between the major and minor keys having the same signature.
Each of the seven degrees of the scale and each of the seven triads
formed on them may be treated as belonging to either key. Keys
one step on either the sharp or flat side of a given key have six
degrees of the scale and four triads in common with the given key.
The keys one step on the sharp side are the dominant key and its
relative, and on the flat side the sub-dominant and its relative.
All these keys, the relative of the tonic key, the dominant and subdominant keys and their relatives are considered to be closely
related to the tonic key. During the 17th and 18th centuries modulation within the cycle of closely related keys dominated the structure of both short and extended musical forms.

Relative Keys, two keys, one major and the other minor, which have
the same key signature. One is said to be the relative major or
relative minor of the other.

Repeat, the sign ≣≣ used to indicate that the music is to be played
again from the previous reversed form of the sign ≣≣ or from
the beginning.

Repetition (on the pianoforte), the rapid reiteration of a note. A good
repetition is one of the features of pianoforte action to which the
inventions of Erard contributed most.

Reports, an old English and Scottish term for points of imitation. It
was used specifically for settings of the tunes of the Metrical
Psalms in which each line was treated as a point of imitation.

Reprise (Fr.), repetition. Though used in the general sense of repetition, reprise is conveniently used for the recurrence after the development of the first group of subjects in first movement form.

Requiem, the Mass for the dead. The portions taken for a musical setting are:

Introit ('Requiem aeternam'),
Kyrie,
Gradual and Tract ('Requiem aeternam' and 'Absolve Domine'),
Sequence or Prose ('Dies irae'),
Offertory ('Domine Jesu Christe'),
Sanctus,
Benedictus,
Agnus Dei,
Communion ('Lux Aeterna').

To these are sometimes added 'Libera me' and 'Taedet animam meam'.

Resin, another spelling of rosin.

Resolution, the relief of the emotional stress of a discord by its movement into the subsequent harmony. Traditionally a discord resolved by moving to a satisfying concord, but developments in harmony, even before the styles now classed as modern, made chains of discords resolving on one another a common feature and so made the original definition too limited.

Resonance, a phenomenon of acoustics which plays an important part in the construction and effectiveness of musical instruments generally. Any body, such as a stretched string or cavity, which will produce sound, will itself respond by sounding if certain notes (particularly that which corresponds to its own natural frequency of vibration) are sounded in its neighbourhood. The sympathetic strings on such instruments as the viola d'amore sound when the notes to which they are tuned are played on the other strings, and the effectiveness of both pedals on the modern pianoforte is due to this phenomenon.

Respighi, Ottorino (b. Bologna 1879, d. Rome 1936), studied music in St Petersburg with Rimsky-Korsakov. He later became head of the St Cecilia Conservatorium in Rome, and achieved distinction as a composer. His compositions include several operas and a number of descriptive orchestral compositions.

Respond, a form of plainsong chant which evolved from responsorial psalmody.

Response (in its widest use in the English church), any sentence sung following something sung by the priest. The 'Versicles and Responses' of Morning and Evening Prayer, the Litany, the Amens, the Doxology to the Gospel and the Responses to the Commandments all come under this heading.

Responsorial Psalmody, the earliest method of psalm singing used in the Christian church. In its simplest form Responsorial Psalmody was probably adopted direct from the synagogue. In Responsorial Psalmody, the psalms were sung by a soloist and the choir. The soloist sang the greater portion of each psalm, while the congregation sang a short response at the close of each verse. Though in the first instance the soloist's part was little more than a monotone, this method of psalm singing led to very considerable elaborations which survive in the 'respond' and 'gradual'.

Rest, the sign indicating a silence, of shape appropriate to its duration and named after its corresponding note.

Resultant tone, a further tone produced when two tones are sounded together. Thus if

be heard. In this case the resultant tone is called a differential tone, since its frequency is the difference between the frequencies of the original tones. It has also been considered that summational tones exist. Thus if

be heard. Resultant tones may also arise from the combination of any of the partials of one note with those of the other. However, only the difference tones between fundamentals are sufficiently loud to be of noticeable importance.

Retardation, a term sometimes used of a suspension which resolves upwards instead of downwards.

Rhapsody, a title used for a musical composition, instrumental or vocal, adapted from the Greek name for a professional reciter of epic poetry, and the poems which, when recited as a series, constituted an epic poem. Liszt and Brahms were among the first to use the title, which has subsequently become popular. Some of their rhapsodies are by analogy appropriately so called, but the title has become loosely used for a composition of imaginative and melodious character of no specific form.

Rheinberger, Josef Gabriel (b. Vaduz 1839, d. Munich 1901), was an organist, teacher and prolific composer. Though he contributed to most types of music, only his organ music is commonly known. In his organ music Rheinberger, unlike so many German composers of his time, does not follow the style of Bach, except in his breadth of style and lack of dependence on registration. He left twenty sonatas, all in different keys, which suggests that he had twenty-four in mind.

Rhythm, the nice flow of accents and certain other subtleties of expression which give life to a composition. As with metre, an analogy may be drawn between literature and music. As literature may be rhythmical or unrhythmical, whether or not it is metrical, so in music rhythm may be considered to be something above metre. Rhythm is often inappropriately used for time and even speed. There are many instances in which rhythm is used where metre might be more apt. The so-called 'rhythmic modes', for instance, might more aptly be called 'metrical modes'.

Rhythmic Mode, a metrical pattern (of which there were six) to which writers of the early polyphonic period made their melodies conform. The modes (or moods) were:

No.	Foot	Poetical scansion	Musical time-values
1.	Trochee	– ∪	
2.	Iambus	∪ –	
3.	Dactyl	– ∪ ∪	
4.	Anapaest	∪ ∪ –	
5.	Molossus	– – –	
6.	Tribrach	∪ ∪ ∪	

Ribible, a bowed stringed instrument mentioned by writers of the Middle Ages, probably either any rebec or some particular form of it.

Ribs, the sides of string instruments of the violin type.

Ricercare (It.), to search out. A title used in the 17th and early 18th centuries for a fugue particularly full of devices of strict imitation. An earlier use of the title appears to have been for a fantasia on a familiar theme such as a street cry or popular song.

Richardson, Ferdinand (b. *c.* 1558, d. Tottenham 1618), was an English musician. Eight compositions by him are in *The Fitzwilliam Virginal Book.*

Ricochet (Fr.), bounding. Indicates in violin music a type of staccato obtained by making the bow rebound from the strings.

Riemann, Karl Wilhelm Julius Hugo (b. Grossmehlra 1849, d. Leipzig 1919), was one of the most eminent German historians of music in the 19th century. His *Dictionary of Music*, published in 1882, was a work of first importance.

Rigadoon, a lively dance, characterized by a jumping step, probably originating in Provence or Languedoc. It became popular in England in the 17th century. The music was in two-four or four-four time, in three or four repeated sections of unequal length, the third being short, and beginning on the third or fourth beat.

Rigore (It.), rigour. Applied to time and pace.

Rimbault, Edward Francis (b. London 1816, d. there 1876), was an organist, writer on musical matters and an editor of early English music.

Rimsky-Korsakov, Nicholas Andreievich (b. Tikhvin 1844, d. St Petersburg 1908), came of an aristocratic family. Though he showed a marked aptitude for music he was trained for the Navy. Towards the end of his time at the Naval College in St Petersburg he made the acquaintance of Balakirev and his followers; this resulted in Rimsky-Korsakov turning his attention to music in earnest. He did not leave the Navy until 1873, though he had joined the teaching staff of the St Petersburg Conservatory two years earlier and had achieved, even earlier, success with his compositions. During the remainder of his life he was eminent as both composer and teacher.

Best known of his orchestral works are the symphonic suite *Scheherezade* and the symphonic poem *Sadko;* of his operas *The Snow Maiden* has met with success in England. Vocal and instrumental chamber music are among the rest of his compositions. His brilliant orchestration is a feature of his orchestral writing; his treatise *The Foundations of Instrumentation* is a work of importance. He orchestrated a number of compositions by other composers, such as Moussorgsky's *Boris Godounov*.

Ripieno (It.), supplementary. This term distinguishes the accompanying from the solo instruments, particularly when the two do not have independent parts in tutti passages. Like 'concertante', its complementary term, ripieno belongs to old instrumental music.

Ritardando (It.), holding back. Similar in sense to 'rallentando'.

Ritenuto (It.), holding back. Indicates, properly, a brief reduction of speed. Often used in the same sense as 'rallentando'.

Ritornello (It.), a little return. A term used generally for a short instrumental section played between the scenes of an opera or during the action for dramatic effect, or between the phrases of a song or anthem. It was also the name given to an old variety of Italian verse, and is still used in some parts for folk-songs with the same characteristics.

Rogers, Benjamin (b. Windsor 1614, d. Oxford 1698), composed a certain amount of vocal church music and some vocal and instrumental secular music. He became organist of Magdalen College, Oxford, and was the composer of the *Hymnus Eucharisticus*, sung every May Day from Magdalen Tower.

Roll, the rapid regular beating of a drum. The roll is written in music as a trill.

Romance, a title used by Mozart, Schumann and others with no apparent specific significance. As in poetry the name appears to imply a composition of an expressive, personal character, regardless of its form.

Romantic, a term adopted from literature. It describes the outlook and style of those composers who (like their literary counterparts) were concerned with expression of their personal feelings. They were not concerned, as were the classical composers, with composing music which was beautiful for its own sake – that is, absolute music – but with programme music, with their own feelings as the programme. This change from the classical outlook involved making new forms to replace those which were established. It even created a tendency towards the abolition of form.

Bach, Haydn, Mozart and Brahms were among those whose outlook and style was classical. Weber, Chopin, Schumann and Wagner were romantic. Beethoven is usually classed as belonging to the classical period, but in so far as he was expressing what he himself felt and thought he was one of the first romantics.

The terms romantic and classical are closely related to the terms programme and absolute. Broadly speaking, the classical composers wrote absolute music, the romantic composers programme music. However, absolute and programme are far less clearly defined than classical and romantic.

Ronald, Sir Landon (b. London 1873, d. there 1938), achieved distinction particularly as a conductor. He was appointed Principal of the Guildhall School of Music in 1910. A few of his songs have achieved a wide popularity.

Rondo (in its early undeveloped form), one of the primitive types of musical structure. The elementary type of rondo had one principal subject to which a return was made after the introduction of other material.

The mature extended form of the rondo of Beethoven began with the principal subject followed by a second subject in the dominant (or relative major in the case of a rondo in a minor key). The principal subject was then repeated and followed by a third subject. The principal subject was repeated a third time, followed by the second subject in the tonic key, and the whole movement concluded with a coda. The practice of varying the recurrences of the principal subject was adopted by Beethoven. There is clearly much in common between rondo and first movement form; the deliberate recurrence of the principal subject, complete or otherwise, is the characteristic feature of the rondo.

Root (of a chord), the bass note of the triad from which the chord is derived. The conception of the root of a chord was applicable only so long as the chords in general use could be considered as derived from triads.

Rootham, Cyril Bradley (b. Bristol 1875, d. Cambridge 1938), achieved distinction as an organist and musical scholar. He was appointed organist of St John's College, Cambridge in 1901, and from then till his death was an important influence in the musical life of the University. His setting of *Brown Earth* by Thomas Moult, published in the Carnegie Collection, is among the best of his compositions.

Rosalia (It.), the exact repetition of a phrase a tone higher. The name is taken from an old popular air *Rosalia, mia cara* which embodies this feature.

Roseingrave, Daniel (d. Dublin 1727), and his son, *Thomas* (b. Winchester 1690, d. Dun Laoghaire 1766), were both organists and composers of church music. Little of Daniel's music is extant. Among the music published by Thomas were compositions for the organ and for the harpsichord.

Rosin, a preparation of the residual gum from the distillation of turpentine. It is used on the bows of stringed instruments to give them 'bite' on the strings.

Rosseter, Philip (b. c. 1575, d. London 1623), was an English musician. His published songs are included in *The English School of Lutenist Songwriters*.

Rossini, Gioacchino Antonio (b. Pesaro 1792, d. Passy 1868), was the son of a slaughter-house inspector who was also town trumpeter. He received musical instruction from his youth. His parents both became connected with the theatre, his mother as a singer and his father as a horn player; by the age of thirteen Rossini was sufficiently good as a singer, horn player and accompanist to join

his parents and assist in earning the family living. He received
formal teaching in composition at Bologna. From 1810 onwards
his operas were produced regularly and his reputation grew steadily; the next twelve years are a record of his successes in Venice,
Milan, Rome and Naples. At the beginning of 1822 Rossini
married an opera singer, Isabella Colbran, shortly after paying a
four months' visit to Vienna. By this time, his reputation had
spread throughout Europe, and already some twenty of his operas
were being performed. The next year, he accepted an invitation to London, visiting Paris on the way. During the next six
years, the production of his operas continued regularly, culminating with *William Tell,* his masterpiece. For reasons still a matter of
speculation, he did not write another opera.

The remainder of his life is of little interest. By 1841 he
completed the *Stabat Mater* begun nine years earlier. He began
to suffer from ill-health which for many years became progres-
sively worse. However, he gained a measure of relief during
his old age. In 1845, a year after Isabella's death, he married
again. During his last years he wrote little but pianoforte music.
Rossini's reputation now rests on the two most famous of his
operas, *The Barber of Seville* and *William Tell.*

Rota, the name commonly given to the famous canon 'Sumer is
icumen in'.

Rotte, a variety of lyre found in Northern Europe from ancient times
until the end of the Middle Ages.

Round, a form of canon particularly associated with England which
had great popularity during the 17th and 18th centuries. In
the round, the canon is at the unison, the entries are at regular
intervals and at the end of the melody a return is made to the
beginning, so that the music passes round the performers. A canon
at the unison, in which the interval between the entry of the last
voice and the next entry of the first voice is the same as the interval
between the initial entries, may be written so that the entries and
the harmonies are shown at once.

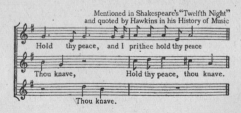

Mentioned in Shakespeare's "Twelfth Night"
and quoted by Hawkins in his History of Music

Each voice enters as the previous voice begins the next line of music. It would be logical and convenient if the possibility of arrangement in this form were considered the distinguishing feature of a round. More extended canons at the unisons, in which there is a lapse after the initial entries before the return, are sometimes called rounds; this makes the distinction between a perpetual canon and a round somewhat artificial. Clearly, a round, in the limited sense described, does not require the same ingenuity in construction as the more extended canon, even though the latter is at the unison and has its initial entries at equal intervals.

Rounds, in bell ringing, the sounding of the descending major scale.

Rubato (It.), robbed. This term describes the slight variation of notes from their strict value which passes unnoticed as an essential part of expression. It is used to draw attention in expressive passages to the necessity for this integral part of shading and expression.

Rubebe, a bowed stringed instrument preceding the viol and larger than the rebec.

Rubinstein, Anton Gregor (b. Wechwotynetz 1830, d. Peterhof 1894), was of Jewish parentage. He was one of the finest pianists of all time. As a composer he had much technical skill, but the success he achieved was not lasting.

Ruckers, Hans (b. *c.* 1555, d. *c.* 1625), was the first of a famous family of harpsichord makers of Antwerp. He is credited with many improvements in keyboard instruments. The instruments of the Ruckers family are considered to have been unsurpassed in tone, and they remained in use in England, France and the Netherlands until the end of the 18th century, when the harpsichord was superseded by the pianoforte.

Rumba, a Cuban dance which became popular in America and Europe from about 1930.

S

Sachs, Hans (b. 1494, d. 1576), was a cobbler of Nuremberg and greatest of the Meistersinger. Some thousands of his songs are extant.

Sackbut, the immediate ancestor of the trombone.

Saint Cecilia, considered as the patron saint of music at least from the early 16th century. The reasons are obscure.

Saint-Saëns, Charles Camille (b. Paris 1835, d. Algiers 1921), came of humble parents. He showed marked musical ability and enjoyed a sound musical education from an early age, He entered the Paris Conservatoire in 1848, and obtained his first appointment as an organist in 1853. During the next few years he established his reputation as a composer, and from then onwards his career was an almost uninterrupted series of successes. He contributed to nearly every branch of music. Though his technical ability, orchestration, and sense of form were remarkably high, only a few of his large number of compositions survive. His musical importance was as one of the leaders of the revival of French music.

Salicet, an organ stop similar to the salicional, but of 4-foot pitch.

Salicional, a soft open metal organ stop, very small in scale, of reedy quality and of 8-foot pitch.

Saltarello, an Italian dance found as the second section of many old dances. The saltarello was commonly founded on the theme of the first section, from which the dance as a whole took its name.

Saraband, a dance form frequently used in the suite as a slow movement. It is in two sections, each repeated. It is written in three-four or three-two time, has a strong accent on the second beat, and ends on the second or third beat rather than the first.

Suite No.11
HANDEL

As a stately dance, the saraband was known in Europe at the beginning of the 16th century. It became particularly popular in Spain, England and France. Though commonly considered a Spanish dance, it was possibly of oriental origin. In England it was grouped with country dances; Playford included examples of it in his *Dancing Master.*

Sarrusophone, a wind instrument of conical bore made of brass and played with a double reed. It was designed in 1863 by a French army bandmaster. A complete family of the instruments was designed. The lowest members of the family have been used in the orchestra on rare occasions.

Sautillé (Fr.), jumped. In violin playing refers to a skipping movement of the bow.

Sax, Charles Joseph (b. Dinant 1791, d. Paris 1865), and his eldest son, *Antoine Joseph* (b. Dinant 1814, d. Paris 1894), were Belgian musical instrument makers of outstanding ability. The younger

Sax, usually known as Adolphe, designed the instruments named after him, the saxophone, saxhorn and saxotromba.

Saxhorn, a brass wind instrument with valves, played with a cupped mouthpiece, related to the trumpet and horn, designed by Adolphe Sax. The saxhorn is built in some seven pitches, so giving a range of about five octaves with more or less the same tone colour. The upper group speak from the second harmonic and have a range of about two octaves, while the lower speak from the fundamental and have a range of about three octaves. All the members of the family are written for as transposing instruments, the second harmonic being written as middle C on the treble clef.

(a)	(b)	(c)	(d)	(e)	(f)	(g)
upper group				lower group		

(a) E♭ Soprano	} flügel horns	(e) B♭ (Euphonium)
(b) B♭ Alto		(f) E♭ (Bombardon)
(c) E♭ Tenor	} alt horns	(g) B♭ (Contrabass)
(d) B♭ Baritone		

For convenience of use in the orchestra, these instruments are sometimes built in F and C instead of E♭ and B♭. The acoustical designs of Sax were far sounder than that of the horns and trumpets of his time. However, the use of the lower harmonics gives power and facility at the expense of quality. Though saxhorns have not added in any way to the orchestra (apart from their influence on the tuba), their adoption has completely re-organised military and wind bands.

Saxophone, a wind instrument made of brass, but keyed and played with a single reed. It was designed by Adolphe Sax about 1840 and introduced into French army bands five years later. The brass tube is conical, has six finger plates for the first three fingers of each hand, and about twenty other holes operated by keys. The mouthpiece is similar to the clarinet mouthpiece. A whole family of saxophones has been designed, from soprano to bass, but the alto and tenor instruments are the most popular. The saxophone bridges the gap between the usual orchestral wood wind and the brass; it is consequently of special value in the military band. The instrument has proved a remarkably popular member of the dance band, but has seldom been introduced into the orchestra.

Saxotromba, a brass wind instrument with valves designed by Adolphe Sax. It is no longer in use.

Scale, an orderly succession of the notes employed in music. The diatonic scales (major, minor and modal), the chromatic scale, the whole-tone scale and the pentatonic scale are the principal scales which have been used in European music.

Scarlatti, Alessandro (b. Palermo 1660, d. Naples 1725), and his eldest son, *Giuseppe Domenico* (b. Naples 1685, d. there 1757), are the most famous members of a family of musicians. Little is known of Alessandro's early life. The family left Sicily in 1672 for Rome.

Alessandro married in 1678. The next year, with his opera *Mistaken Identity,* he gained the patronage of Queen Christina of Sweden, who had settled in Rome, and was appointed maestro di cappella to her. Some few years later (possibly in 1682 or 1684) he moved to Naples where in 1684, with another opera, he gained the appointment of maestro di cappella to the Viceroy of Naples. In 1702 he returned to Rome to escape from the political troubles in Naples; however, his leaning towards dramatic music can have had little better opportunity in Rome, where the popes had attempted to suppress opera completely. In 1706 he was admitted to the Arcadian Academy, his reputation in Rome and Naples became considerable, and the remainder of his life was shared between the two cities. Though the music of Alessandro is now little known, he is one of the most important figures in musical history, particularly in the history of opera. He was one of the last to write chamber cantatas extensively and probably the first to write a real string quartet.

Domenico learned primarily from his father. In 1708 he met Handel and accompanied him to Rome, where he wrote a number of operas for the Queen of Poland's private theatre, and was appointed to St Peter's in 1715 as maestro di cappella. In 1719 he visited London, and two years later Lisbon. In 1729 he was invited to the Spanish court and appointed music master to the Princess of Asturias. Little is known of the next years of his life. He appears to have visited Dublin in 1769 and London the next year. Domenico's important contribution to music was his development of keyboard technique, such as the use of crossing the hands. He left some hundreds of pieces for the keyboard, the best known being perhaps *The Cat's Fugue.*

Scena, (It.), scene. Apart from its many meanings not specifically

musical, scena is used in the limited sense of an operatic movement of a dramatic rather than reflective nature.

Scheidt, Samuel (b. Halle 1587, d. there 1654), was the best organist
in Germany of his time, and one of the three celebrated composers of his time whose names began with S, the others being
Schein and Schütz. Though Scheidt owed his position among
his contemporaries to his vocal music, he is now remembered
for the important part he played in founding a noble tradition of
organ playing and composition.

Schein, Johann Hermann (b. Grunhain 1586, d. Leipzig 1630), was
perhaps less distinguished than Scheidt and Schütz. As a composer
Schein played an important part in the new musical movement
which started in Italy at the beginning of the 17th century.

Scherzando (It.), lively.

Scherzo (It.), a jest. Though it is a name appropriately applied to a
composition on account of its character without regard to its
form, it generally means a movement in a sonata or, more
especially, a symphony. The scherzo of the symphony evolved
out of the minuet, and certain features of the minuet may be
recognized in the scherzo. In the symphonies of Beethoven the
scherzo lost the form and character of the older minuet which it
superseded. The scherzo is almost always in three-four time. Its
form is sometimes identical with the straightforward form of the
minuet and trio, but is more often in a first movement, or a rondo
form, though disguised by the persistence of some rhythmic or
other feature. It commonly has a trio, a feature inherited from
the minuet. The lightness and humour and the quick pace of the
scherzo are the essential characters which give the scherzo its
importance in the structure of the symphony. Needless to say,
examples exist (such as the four scherzos for pianoforte by Chopin)
which do not conform to the general pattern either in form or in
character.

Schlick, Arnolt (b. Bohemia *c.* 1460, d. after 1517), was one of the
most important early organists. He was blind. Two books by him,
one on organs and organists, the other containing organ and
lute music in tablature, are extant.

Schneller (Ger.), an ornament apparently no different from the
pralltriller, though a distinction was said to exist between them.

Schönberg, Arnold (b. Vienna, 1874), still living.

Schottische (Ger.), a Scottish dance. The Schottische is a round
dance similar to the Polka, and also known as the German Polka;

it differed from the Écossaise. It was first danced in England in
1848.

Schubert, Franz Peter (b. Vienna 1797, d. there 1828), was the son of a
schoolmaster who had some ability as a musician. Schubert
showed his gift for music from his early youth; he soon learnt all
that his father, brother and the local organist could teach him,
and was readily accepted as a chorister at the Court Chapel when
he was eleven. His appointment as chorister gave him a general
education as well as an opportunity for increasing his knowledge
of music; during the next five years, though he received little
help in writing music, his progress in composition was rapid. In
1814, soon after leaving the court, Schubert joined the staff of his
father's school, so avoiding seven years' conscription in the army.
He left his father's school after three years and held no further
regular appointment.

The conditions of his living were precarious. In 1818 he was
engaged by Count Esterhazy as music master to his children, and
in 1821 he first gained publication of some of his songs. From
time to time his operas were produced and his orchestral and
chamber music was performed. On such irregular earnings his
livelihood depended. Apart from spending the summers of 1818
and 1824 in Hungary at the country seat of Count Esterhazy and
touring Upper Austria in 1825 with his friend Vogl, Schubert
spent his life in Vienna. The publications of his compositions is
evidence of the demand for his music, but though the merit of
his songs was praised by Beethoven in 1827, Schubert's real
genius was hardly recognized during his life. His carefree existence
and the small sums for which he sold his compositions kept him
near poverty. His irresponsible way of life and his exertions of
writing were no doubt largely responsible for the steady deterioration
of his health and for his early death. Schubert did not marry; the
importance of his love affairs has been very greatly exaggerated.

Although the quantity and variety of his compositions is
considerable, it is only fair to think of them as an indication of
what he might have achieved if his formal musical training had
been better, and his life longer. Schubert wrote over six hundred
songs, and it is as a song-writer that he is outstanding. Many of
his songs enjoy popularity; *Erlkönig, Gretchen am Spinnrade, Der
Doppelgänger, Du bist die Ruh* and his settings of Shakespeare's
songs *Who is Sylvia?* and *Hark, hark the lark* can but meagrely
represent the variety of his invention. Of his symphonies, No. 8
in B minor (*The Unfinished*) and No. 9 in C major are deservedly

the best known. Of the important contributions he made to instrumental chamber music, the string quintet in C major, written
shortly before he died, is among the best of its kind. His writings
for piano, alone or with other instruments, and his church music
are, as a whole, less successful. Such works as the incidental music
to *Rosamund*, the *Military March*, the *Ave Maria* and the *Serenade*
have a popularity which is a tribute to the melodiousness and
simple beauty of his music.

Schumann, Robert Alexander (b. Zwickau 1810, d. Endenich 1856),
was the son of a bookseller. Though his interest in the arts
generally was encouraged by his father, music formed no part
of his home background. He learned the piano from the local
church organist, and from an early age showed a remarkable
aptitude for music. However, though his father tried to get
lessons for him from Weber, Schumann spent the first eighteen
years of his life at Zwickau without receiving any special musical
training. In 1828 he matriculated at Leipzig University as a
law student, moving to Heidelberg in 1829. Two years were
spent nominally studying law, but during this time pianoforte
playing alone appears to have engaged him seriously. In 1830
he renounced law and returned to Leipzig to study music vigor-
ously under Wieck. His intention to become a virtuoso pianist
was frustrated by the damage done to a finger by a contrivance
of his own invention for developing the dexterity of the hand, and
he gave his full attention to composition, studying under Dorn,
conductor of the opera at Leipzig. In 1835 he produced a Symphony in G minor, but it proved a failure; and in the same year he
became sole editor of a musical journal which he had been a
party to starting the previous year. His work in writing of the
distinguished musicians of his time and of the new musical movement, in which many of them were to be important figures, was
most valuable to the musical development taking place.

After he had mastered the routine of his editoral duties, he
turned his attention again to composition, and in the next few
years many of the pianoforte works on which his fame largely
rests were written.

During the years following 1835, Schumann became closely
associated with Mendelssohn, and also with Clara Wieck, the
daughter of his old teacher. Clara was one of the most accomplished pianists of her day; she and Schumann were married in
1840, after a long struggle to overcome the objection of her
father. Earlier in that same year he had obtained the degree of

Doctor of Philosophy from the University of Jena for his work as critic and composer.

From writing for the pianoforte he turned to writing for the voice. Over a hundred songs were composed during 1840. His invention apparently exhausted in this direction, he next turned his attention to the orchestra and smaller instrumental groups, and in the period from 1841 to 1845 almost all his best works in the larger forms appeared. In 1844 the Schumanns moved from Leipzig to Dresden, where they stayed till 1850; during the later part of which period he was active with choral conducting. In 1850 Schumann succeeded Miller as director of music at Düsseldorf, but as a conductor proved inefficient. In 1853 he gave encouragement to Brahms, who stayed in Düsseldorf for a while. As a master of music generally and as a composer in particular – his inability as a conductor was recognised – Schumann enjoyed the admiration and respect of all.

At various times, in 1837 and again in 1844, Schumann suffered seriously from mental strain. In 1854 he attempted to drown himself in the Rhine, and though having periods of mental clearness, he was obliged to spend the last two years of his life in a private asylum.

A piano quintet and piano quartet are considered his outstanding contribution to concerted chamber music. In his pianoforte music, besides such larger works as the F minor Sonata and *Faschingsschwank,* are the slighter, though perhaps better known and in many ways more attractive, *Fantasiestücke* and his delightful contributions to music for the young. Of his largest-scale compositions, the pianoforte concerto stands well above the few other compositions he left in this form. He also left four symphonies and a quantity of sacred and secular choral music.

Schütz, Heinrich (b. Köstritz 1585, d. Dresden 1672), was the most eminent of the three celebrated S's, the others being Schein and Scheidt. He received a good general as well as musical education. In 1616 he was appointed organist to the Elector of Saxony at Dresden; from 1631 the wars in Saxony disturbed his musical life at Dresden, and between 1633 and 1641 he spent his time at various courts. He returned to Dresden in 1641, but for some five years was unsuccessful in his attempts to reorganise the music. The most important of his compositions are his contributions to oratorio; perhaps the best known are his four settings of the passion story, which are the last of his works to be preserved. In these he was the predecessor of Bach.

Sciolto (It.), freely. Used in a similar sense to 'ad libitum', but applied to longer passages.

Scordatura (It.), mistuning. The principle of tuning stringed instruments in other than the normal manner originated with the various tunings adopted for the lute and viol to suit the key of certain compositions. This device of varying the tuning was frequently employed by the earliest violinists, and is still used by Scottish reel players but rarely otherwise. The raising of the fourth string a tone to A is the most commonly used. The use of scordatura will simplify the fingering in certain keys and enable passages otherwise impossible to be performed. The practice is to write the music so that the player may ignore the unusual tuning, and play from his part as though his instrument were tuned in the usual way.

Score, all the individual parts in a composition written together one above the other so that the whole nature of the composition may be seen. Scores are described as full, vocal or short.

A full score, the score proper, gives each part on its own line.

A vocal score gives the voice parts in full, each on its own line, but gives the accompaniment reduced to an arrangement on two staves.

A short score gives either vocal or instrumental parts on two lines for convenient reading.

Although the essential features of a score were realized as early as the 13th century, and though composers of the polyphonic period must have written in some form of score, the great majority of both written and printed vocal music of that period has had to be re-scored from part books. The first orchestral scores date from the late 16th century. The arrangement of the parts has varied from time to time. Scores for a number of instruments or voices now conform in the main to the same overall plan; woodwind (at the top), brass, percussion, harps and keyboard instruments and (at the bottom) strings. If there are voices, they are placed immediately above the violoncellos and double basses. (See Table VI, pp. 246-7.)

Scoring, the art of orchestration.

Scotch Snap or *Scotch Catch*, the figure ♫. which is a feature of the slow strathspey and certain other examples of Scottish music. It became a vulgarism in pseudo-Scottish music of the 18th century.

Scott, Cyril (b. Oxton 1879), still living.

Scriabin, Alexander Nicholaevich (b. Moscow 1872, d. there 1915), achieved distinction as a composer and pianist. His musical ideals became closely woven with his religious and philosophic

TABLE VI

The common English, French, German and Italian names for the instruments of the orchestra

In the order in which they are usually arranged in a score

English	French	German	Italian
Woodwind			
Flute	Flûte	Flöte	Flauto
Piccolo	Piccolo, Petite Flûte	Piccolo	Piccolo
Oboe	Hautbois	Oboe	Oboe
Cor Anglais	Cor Anglais	Englisches Horn	Corno Inglese
Clarinet	Clarinette	Klarinette	Clarinetto
Bass Clarinet	Clarinette Basse	Bass-Klarinette	Clarinetto Basso
Bassoon	Basson	Fagott	Fagotto
Double Bassoon	Contre-basson	Doppel-Fagott	Contra Fagotto
Brass			
Horn	Cor	Horn	Corno
Trumpet	Trompette	Trompete	Tromba
Trombone	Trombone	Posaune	Trombone
Tuba			
(there is not uniformity in the use of instruments of this class)			
Percussion			
Kettledrums	Timbales	Pauken	Timpani
Side Drum	Tambour Militaire	Kleine Trommel	Tamburo Militaire
Triangle	Triangle	Triangel	Triangolo
Bass Drum	Grosse Casse	Grosse Trommel	Gran Cassa
Cymbals	Cymbales	Becken	Piatti
Xylophone	Xylophone, Claquebois	Xylophon	Zilafone, Organo Di Legno
Glockenspiel	Glockenspiel, Carillon	Glockenspiel	Campanetta
Gong	Tam-Tam	Tam-Tam	Tam-Tam

English	French	German	Italian
Harp	Harpe	Harfe	Arpa
Strings Violin Viola Violoncello Double Bass	 Violon Alto Violoncelle Contrebasse	 Violine Bratsche, Viola Violoncell, Cello Kontrabass	 Violino Viola Violoncello Contrabasso

In general, French forms the plural by adding the suffix s, German by adding the suffix en or er, and Italian by changing the final o into i or the final a into e.

English	French	German	Italian
Harpsichord Organ Pianoforte	Clavecin Orgue Piano	Cembalo Orgel Klavier, Pianoforte	Clavicembalo Organo Pianoforte
Chorus, Choir Orchestra	Choeur Orchestre	Chor Orchester	Coro Orchestra

beliefs. He devised a harmonic system based on the higher members of the harmonic series (Nos 8 to 14), which, omitting the 12th, were usually arranged in fourths.

arranged

The majority of his works were for piano, a few for orchestra.

Second, the interval covering two degrees of the scale, three forms of which commonly occur:

(a)   (b)   (c)

(a) the major second, (b) the minor second and (c) the augmented second.

Secondo (It.), second. Used to distinguish a second player from the first (primo). Also used to distinguish a portion of the music to be played the second time but not the first.

Segno (It.), the sign 𝄋 referred to in the term 'dal segno'.

Segue (It.), follows. Used in the same sense as 'attacca'.

Seguidilla, a Spanish national dance. The origin of the name, as of the dance itself, is uncertain. There are three varieties of seguidilla, the lively Seguidillas Manchegas, the stately Seguidillas Boleras and the slow, sentimental Seguidillas Gitanas.

Sellinger's Round, an English round dance which, with its 16th-century tune, became particularly popular during the 17th century.

Semibreve, the longest note now usually used. It is written 𝅝 and its corresponding rest ▬.

Semichorus, half or part of the full chorus.

Semiquaver, a sixteenth of a semibreve. It is written ♬ or in groups ♬ , and its corresponding rest 𝄿.

Semitone, half a tone. Theoretically a semitone may be of various sizes according to the system of tuning adopted for the diatonic scale. However, in practice all semitones have been identical on the piano since the adoption of equal temperament, in which the octave is divided into twelve equal semitones.

Semplice (It.), simple. Indicates that no unessential expression should be added.

Sempre (It.), always.

Senza (It.), without.

Septet, a composition for seven singers or instrumentalists. Both varieties are rare.

Sequence, the repetition of a melodic or harmonic phrase or figure at different positions in the scale. It is a device which in various

Pianoforte Sonata No. 30, Op. 109
BEETHOVEN
Vivace ma non troppo

forms may readily be found throughout music. The sequence may be either diatonic or chromatic, fall regularly with the accent, or at each repetition fall with the accent in a different place.

Seraphine, a keyboard free reed wind instrument, a predecessor of the harmonium.

Serenade, an evening song. The title has been used indiscriminately, not only for various kinds of music intended to be played in the evening or reminiscent of that time of day. The title is commonly associated with a song to be sung to a lady by her admirer standing in the street below her window.

Serenata (It.), a title used for various kinds of composition. Though simply the Italian word from which serenade has been taken, serenata has more precise meanings. It has been used as the title for certain vocal compositions in the form of a secular cantata, and also for certain instrumental compositions, popular during the second half of the 18th century, having some of the characteristics of both the suite and the symphony. The serenta commonly began or ended with a march, and included one or more minuets; the other movements were of no prescribed form, but the gavotte and bourrée of the older suites did not appear in it.

Serinette, a miniature barrel organ much used in France to teach birds to whistle popular tunes.

Serpent, a wind instrument, part brass, part wood, with finger holes or keys and played from a cupped mouthpiece. It was probably invented towards the end of the 16th century as a double-length great cornett, and went out of use during the 19th century. It was an important member of the crude bands in churches in England, and was commonly used in churches in France. Mendelssohn wrote for it in a number of his overtures.

Service (in its limited musical sense), a setting of certain portions of the English rite. These settings are grouped under the title of Morning Service, Evening Service and Communion Service.

(a) Morning Service.

Venite (Psalm 95).

Te Deum.

Benedictus.

and

Benedicite, alternative to Te Deum.

Jubilate (Psalm 100), alternative to Benedictus.

(b) Evening Service.

Magnificat.

Nunc Dimittis.

and

Cantate Domino (Psalm 98), alternative to Magnificat.

Deus Misereatur (Ps. 67), alternative to Nunc Dimittis.

(c) Communion Service.

       Lord have mercy (Kyrie)
       I believe   (Credo)
       Holy, holy, holy   (Sanctus)
       Blessed is He   (Benedictus)
       O Lamb of God   (Agnus Dei)
       Glory be   (Gloria in excelsis)

The inclusion or omission of some of these portions has of course followed variations in the English Prayer Book and in popular usage. The late Tudor and early Stuart composers usually wrote music for the Venite as for the other canticles, but the practice of singing the Venite to chants has now superseded the use of a setting. The Benedicite has been rarely set. The Cantate Domino and Deus Misereatur did not become popular until the Restoration. Following the usage of the time, the late Tudor and early Stuart composers set only the Kyrie and Credo. The Sanctus was commonly set from the Restoration onwards. After the rise of the Oxford Movement, the Gloria in Excelsis was also set and later the Benedictus and Agnus Dei as they came into general use, though they had no place in the Prayer Book. The Greek 'Kyrie' and the English 'Lord have mercy' have continued side by side as alternatives.

Seventh, an interval covering seven degrees of the scale. Three forms commonly occur:

(a) the major seventh,   (b) the minor seventh,
(c) the diminished seventh.

The chords formed from the triads by adding to them the sevenths above their roots are known as chords of the seventh. Since a triad may be major, minor, diminished or augmented, and a seventh may be major, minor or diminished, there are several different kinds of chords of the seventh.

(a), (b), (c) and (d) all occur diatonically in the major keys; (e) occurs on the sharpened leading note in minor keys. (b) was the first chord of the seventh to play an important part in harmony.

It occurs on the dominant in both major and minor keys (in the case of a minor key the leading note being sharpened), and it is known as the chord of the dominant seventh. (e) may be used for enharmonic modulation. It occurs on the sharpened leading note in minor keys, and it is known as the chord of the diminished seventh.

| (a) | (b) | (c) | (d) |
| Key, B♭ minor | C♯ minor | E minor | G minor |

(a), (b), (c), and (d) are in root position, first, second and third inversions respectively, in the keys named. These four chords are identical on the keyboard, and differ only in notation.

Sextet, a composition for six singers or instrumentalists. Instrumental sextets are not numerous, though Brahms has left two notable sextets for two violins, two violas and two violoncellos. Vocal sextets are sometimes to be found incidentally in operas.

Sextolet, a group of six notes of equal length, played in the time of four, and distinguished by a 6 placed over or under the group. The sextolet should be distinguished from a double triplet. The distinction may be made clear by the notation:

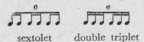

sextolet   double triplet

Sfogato (It.), airy. A term used by Chopin to indicate the delicacy required in little cadenzas and ornaments.

Sforzando (It.), forcing. Indicates that a note or a group of notes is to be specially emphasised. It is usually abbreviated to *sf* or *sfz*.

Sgambati, Giovanni (b. Rome 1841, d. there 1914), was one of the most important Italian musicians of his time. He was an able pianist and composer and was responsible for introducing to Rome many of the most famous works of Beethoven and Brahms and others. He was particularly successful in writing for the pianoforte; his quartet in D flat is one of his best known works.

Shake or *Trill*, one of the earliest, and now the most important ornament in music, and one to which a great many ornaments common in music of the 16th, 17th and 18th centuries are related. The trill consists of the rapid alternation of the main note with the one above it. It is now indicated by *tr.* placed over or under a note. If the trill is prolonged it is indicated by **tr** 〰〰〰〰

The precise number of alternations depends on the skill and taste of the performer. The difference in effect of (a) and (b) is considerable, in one case the accent being on the principal note, in the other on the subsidiary note. Various schools of thought on the nature of the trill have preferred one or the other. From Bach to Beethoven (b) appears to have been the accepted form, though later and in modern times (a) has become preferred. Where (a) is the usual form (b) may be indicated by a grace note:

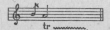

though at one time this might have led to confusion. Examples exist, from the period when (b) was the accepted form, of (a) being indicated by

The interpretation of trills of the period when ornaments were an important feature of instrumental music is usually indicated in the score.

Shanty, a song used mostly by sailors when pulling on a rope, and therefore, in its natural form and use, now obsolete. The shanty is simply an instance of the valuable way in which a song can give cohesion to team work. The name may have been transferred to the song from the similarly named log huts in which the lumber men of North America and Canada lived; they also made use of songs when pulling. It is unlikely that it was derived from the French 'chant'.

Sharp, the sign ♯ which raises a note one semitone from its natural pitch either as an accidental or as part of the key signature.

Sharp, Cecil James (b. London 1859, d. there 1924), was one of the leaders of the revival of English folk music. His researches have preserved a vast amount of folk song and dance which would probably otherwise have been lost. Important among his publications are *The Country Dance Book* and *Country Dance Tunes* (which have made available those dances with their tunes to be found in Playford's *Dancing Master*) and *English Folk Songs from the Southern Appalachians*.

Shawm, a double-reed wood-wind instrument with a conical bore from which the oboe evolved. In England, shawm included all sizes of these instruments, whereas on the Continent the larger instruments were known as pommers or bombards.

Shepherd's Pipe, a pastoral oboe, a double-reed wind instrument similar to the chanter of the bagpipe. It was sometimes combined with a wind-bag.

Shield, William (b. Durham 1748, d. London 1829), became Master of the King's Musick in 1817. He composed a number of musical dramatic works of various kinds − opera, pantomime and the like.

Shofar, a Jewish wind instrument of ram's horn.

Short Octave, a feature of some early keyboard instruments. So long as the sharps (or flats) were not used in the lowest part of the range, economy in pipes or strings and keys could be effected. The strings or pipes of the unwanted notes were omitted; the lowest wanted strings or pipes were attached to the keys of the unwanted notes instead of to their proper keys, which were then also omitted.

Short Score, the arrangement of a vocal or instrumental score on two staves for convenience in reading or playing.

Shudi, Burkat (b. Schwanden 1702, d. London 1773), was a famous harpsichord maker. He learnt harpsichord making in London from Tabel, a Fleming, who had the tradition of Ruckers, and in turn passed it on to the house of Broadwood, of which he was the founder.

Si, the seventh note of the scale in solmization, added to the original six names for the notes of the hexachord.

Sibelius, Jean (b. Tavastehus 1865), still living.

Siciliana, a name used for movements having a certain characteristic dance rhythm. The siciliana is usually in six-eight time with the figure $\frac{6}{8}$ ♫ ♩ ♪ | as a feature. It is usually in a minor key and is intended to be played fairly quickly and smoothly. The name is derived from a dance song popular in Sicily.

Signature, either the key signature or the time signature.

Simile (It.), like. Indicates that a phrase or passage is to be played in the same way at each repetition, or that it is to be continued in the same manner as before.

Sinding, Christian (b. Königsberg 1856, d. Oslo 1941), was an able pianist and a pleasing composer. A few of his compositions have achieved popularity.

Single Tonguing, the normal method of tonguing in playing wind instruments.

Sink-a-pace (a corruption of the French cinque pas), the name by which the galliard was sometimes known.

Siren, a device for producing sound, which, though hardly a musical instrument, has played an important part in acoustical research. In principle it consists of a circular disc, with equally-spaced holes round the edge, which by revolving on its centre alternately permits and prevents the escape of wind directed against it. As the frequency of the puffs comes within the range of audio frequencies a note is heard. By attaching a counter to the revolving disc or to the shaft the frequency of the note may be accurately adjusted and measured. The siren has been made in various more or less complicated forms for the purposes of research.

THE SIREN

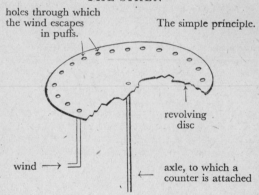

holes through which the wind escapes in puffs.

The simple principle.

revolving disc

wind ⟶

axle, to which a counter is attached

Sir Roger de Coverley, an English dance already considered old by the beginning of the 18th century, and the only one to have kept its popularity until the present time. Various claims for the origin of the name have been given. It is danced by any desired number of couples arranged in two lines, and was popularly adopted as the last dance of a ball.

Sixth, the interval covering six degrees of the scale. Three forms commonly occur:

(a) minor sixth, (b) major sixth, (c) augmented sixth.

Three chords incorporating the augmented sixth, and two incorporating the major sixth have special names:

(d) Italian sixth, (e) French sixth and (f) German sixth; (g) in the key of A minor, 'or its equivalent in any other minor key, a Neapolitan sixth and (h) the added sixth.

Slide, a device on brass wind instruments. Slides are of two kinds, those for tuning and those for completing the chromatic scale between the natural harmonies. The tuning slides consist of small U-shaped portions of tubing by which the length of the vibrating column of air may be altered. Beside the main tuning slides, slides are also fitted in valve instruments to each valve. The slide of the trombone works in the same way, but on a larger scale, and slides freely under the control of the player.

Slow Movement, the generic name for all movements of a slow character, particularly those occurring in a sonata, symphony or similar extended composition.

Slur, a curved line over or under a group of notes. Slurs are needed for various related purposes, all indicating that the notes they cover are in some way to be grouped together. Slurs may mark the phrases of an extended legato passage, showing where the legato should be broken. In string music slurs are used to indicate the bowing; in vocal music slurs may be used to show the breathing, though this generally follows from the sense of the words. A slur over two notes indicates that the second is to be shortened and weakened.

Smart, Sir George Thomas (b. 1776, d. London 1867), was the most important member of a musical family. He became distinguished as a conductor and organist. His nephew, *Henry Thomas* (b. London 1813, d. there 1879), achieved distinction as an organist and composer of organ music.

Smetana, Bedřich (b. Litomyšl 1824, d. Prague 1884), was the son of a brewer employed on the estate of Count Waldstein. His father was an amateur musician and from an early age he enjoyed a musical life. After a period of hardship while studying in Prague, he was appointed to the family of Count Leopold Thun as resident music master. The general unrest in Bohemia at this time made success impossible and he accepted an appointment at Gothenburg in 1856. With the improvement in the political situation he returned to Prague in 1861 and was instrumental in establishing a

National Theatre. He may be credited with founding the modern Czech National School of composers. His music is primarily programme music. Best known of his compositions are the opera *The Bartered Bride,* which justifiably achieved great success, and *Vltava,* the second of his cycle of symphonic poems with the general title *My Country.*

Smith, 'Father' (b. Germany, *c.* 1630, d. London 1708), was óne of the most celebrated organ builders in England in the later part of the 17th century. He came to England in 1660. His real name was Bernard Schmidt.

Smith, John Stafford (b. Gloucester 1750, d. London 1836), was distinguished as a singer, organist, composer and musical antiquary. It is now generally agreed that the tune to which the American national song *The Star-spangled Banner* is sung was composed by him, and was sung originally to a poem by Ralph Tomlinson *To Anacreon in Heaven.*

Smorzando (It.), fading away. Used in a sense similar to 'morendo', but not restricted in use to the end of a movement.

Smyth, Dame Ethel Mary (b. London 1858, d. Woking 1944), was the daughter of a general. She studied composition at Leipzig for a short time, and established a reputation as a composer and as a supporter of the campaign for women's suffrage. A mass and an opera, *The Wreckers,* are among her more important compositions.

Snare, a piece of catgut stretched over the head of certain drums. By jarring against the vellum, the snare produces a peculiar effect when the drum is struck. A group of four to ten snares is usually used.

Soggetto (It.), a fugue subject of orthodox length as distinct from an 'andamento' or an 'attacco'.

Soh, the fifth note of the scale in the Tonic Sol-fa.

Sol, the fifth note of the scale in solmization.

Solfeggio (It.), a vocal exercise usually sung to the syllables of the sol-fa notation.

Solmization, the method of illustrating the mutual relation of the notes of the musical scale by associating certain syllables with them. The principles of solmization were used by the Greeks, who gave names to notes of their tetrachord dependent upon their position in the tetrachord and regardless of the position of the tetrachord. The Tonic Sol-fa names used for the notes of the diatonic scale, regardless of any change in its position by transposition, are with slight changes those adopted in the early 11th century by Guido d'Arezzo. He noticed that the melody of a late 8th-century hymn began successively on the six notes of the hexachord.

The completion of the scale with Si (taken from the last line of the above) appears to have occurred about the end of the 16th century. Two changes bring the scale to the form in which it is now commonly known; do replaced ut, as a more convenient syllable for singing, and has been generally recognised for two hundred years; and, in Curwen's Tonic Sol-fa, te replaced si, so as to avoid two notes having the same initial letter.

Solo (It.), alone. Any composition for one singer or instrumentalist, or a passage in which the interest is centred on one singer or instrumentalist.

Also a part sung or played by a single performer.

Solo Organ, the fourth manual organ of a modern English church organ, played from the highest manual of four. It is composed of stops, loud and soft, intended for solo use.

Solo Stop, (on an organ), any stop on the solo organ, or any stop especially suitable for solo use.

Somervell, Sir Arthur (b. Windermere 1863, d. London 1937), became Principal Inspector of Music to the Board of Education and the Scottish Education Department. Besides his work in the sphere of education, he has made a number of notable contributions to vocal and instrumental composition. His setting of Tennyson's *Maud* is among the best of English song cycles.

Sonata, an extended instrumental composition. The name appears to have been adopted in the first instance in the sense of a composition for instruments as opposed to a cantata, a composition for voices, but later became generally reserved for composition for one or two solo instruments. Trio, quartet, quintet, or more rarely a composition for some larger specified chamber group of instruments invariably implies a composition of precisely the same structure as would be expected in a sonata of the same period. The mature symphony and concerto differ from each other, and from the sonata, in their treatment of the forms common to all three (differences demanded by the larger resources of the orchestra and the combination of orchestra and solo instrument) rather than in any radical difference in the forms used.

The development of the structure of the movements of a sonata rather than the addition of more movements of simple structure is one of the main features commonly distinguishing the sonata from the suite. The sonata should not therefore be identified merely with the 19th-century compositions of this name. The sonatas of A. and D. Scarlatti, J. S. and C. P. E. Bach and those of modern writers are (with perhaps a few exceptions) appropriately so named, though differing both in the number and form of their movements from the sonatas of Haydn, Mozart and Beethoven. There are sonatas of two movements by A. Scarlatti, of one movement by D. Scarlatti; the *Golden Sonata* for two violins and continuo of Purcell has five movements. Further, the name sonata was used for compositions apparently differing in no way from suites by the same composer.

The sonata of Haydn and Mozart usually had three movements – the first quick in first movement form, the second slow and the last a rondo or another movement in first movement form; a minuet occasionally replaced the middle or the last movement. Beethoven began by making the minuet or a scherzo an additional middle movement coming either before or after the slow movement. Though this four movement plan is commonly recognized as the standard form of the mature sonata conformity to it was by no means the rule. Later sonatas have shown a good deal of variation.

Sonata Form, the name misleadingly though commonly given to the form in which the first movement of sonatas, trios, quartets and so on, and symphonies and concertos of the 19th century were usually written. The name 'first movement form' is more appropriate.

Sonatina, a sonata of short and simple design.

Song, an art form belonging equally to poetry and music. It may be described as a short metrical composition in which the meaning is conveyed equally by words and melody.

Vocal rather than instrumental music is most likely the older branch of music. It seems likely, however, that vocal music was first developed as an accessory to the dance. The wealth of sacred vocal music which accumulated during the early centuries of the Christian era, and was preserved by the teaching orders and by the careful oral tradition of the church until an exact musical notation had been evolved, cannot be paralleled by an equally carefully preserved body of secular vocal music. There was undoubtedly a close connection between folk song and the non-liturgical music of the church; numerous parallels between popular songs and late Latin hymns have been noted. It is with difficulty and uncertainty that the oldest songs in written notation of the 12th century can be transcribed. From then onwards the Troubadours, Trouvères, Minnesinger and Meistersinger developed the art of song, and left copious records of their art, undoubtedly inheriting much from the past.

Through the close association of words and music, the songs of various countries have developed distinctive characteristics of style even more than have other forms of musical art.

France must be credited with the oldest extant song in notation, and with being the home of the Troubadours and their Jongleurs, the Trouvères and their Minstrels, and of the Metrical Psalter in which the art of secular song was made to minister to the congregational needs of the church. Of the many French composers who have contributed to the literature of song, Fauré is the most outstanding.

Germany begins its history of song rather later than France, first with the Minnesinger, then with their successors, the Meistersinger, who, though influencing the development and spread of song, did not reach a high level in their compositions, which were stamped by pedantry. At the same time, in Germany folk song grew independently and gained at least as high a place as in other countries. With the rise of the Lutheran Choral, secular song melody was incorporated into the congregational music of the church to an even greater extent than it had been in France. Schubert stands at the head of German song writers, but Schumann and Brahms are eminent among those who turned their attention to song, and lastly, Wolf, primarily a song writer, has made a notable contribution to German song.

Italy, though responsible for so much in the development of vocal music, has contributed little to the song proper. Her most important contribution was in the opera and in particular in its off-shoot the aria, which quickly became a markedly stereotyped form.

England produced one incomparable school of song-writers, the composers of the ayres with lute accompaniment, of whom Dowland was the leading figure.

Needless to say, the folk music of all countries contributes to the repertory of song, and contributions have been made by a great many composers not primarily song-writers. Further, operas, particularly those of the stereotyped Italian style, are a rich source of song, and numerous arias survive from operas now dead and unlikely to be revived.

Song Without Words, the English name for the short pianoforte compositions by Mendelssohn which were in simple form and melodious style.

Soprano, a woman's voice with a high range. The name is commonly used synonymously with treble.

Soprano Clef, the C clef placed on the bottom line to show that that line corresponds with middle C.

middle C

Sordino (It.), used in the same sense as 'mute'. The root of the Italian term, however, is deafness, not dumbness. Sordo (It.), muffled.

Sostenuto (It.), sustained. Similar in sense to 'tenuto'.

Sostinente Pianoforte, a name given to various pianofortes incorporating some contrivance enabling them to produce a sustained note, as on the organ. The hurdy-gurdy may be considered an ancestor of the many-keyed sustaining instruments, other than the organ. Since the 16th century several attempts have been made to overcome the inability of keyed stringed instruments to sustain the sounds they produce; none has proved successful.

Sotto Voce (It.), under the voice. Indicates that the voice must be toneless.

Sound, a series of disturbances or vibrations in matter to which the ear is sensitive. It may be represented and analyzed as a wave motion. Sound will not travel through a vacuum; it travels through the atmosphere at about 1,100 ft. per second, regardless of the kind of sound. Sounds may be described as musical or noisy. There is no fixed boundary between the two; regular vibrations will sound musical and constitute a note, irregular vibrations sound a noise. The ear hears as sounds vibrations which occur with a frequency of between about 30 and 30,000 vibrations a second.

Sound Board (in an organ), the upper part of the wind chest on which the pipes stand.

Sound Board, the belly of a pianoforte.

Sound Holes, the two holes, each in the form of an *f*, facing each other on the belly of each member of the violin family, and in crude forms in earlier stringed instruments. The sound holes regulate the vibrations of the various parts of the instrument; their precise shape has an important influence on the tone of the instrument.

Sound Post, the small piece of wood standing in the body between the belly and back of each member of the violin family. The sound post helps to co-ordinate the vibrations of the belly and back of the instrument. Its precise position and the material of which it is made have an important influence on the tone of the instrument.

Sousa, John Philip (b. Washington 1854, d. there 1932), was an American bandmaster. His numerous marches have achieved a well-deserved popularity.

Speaker Key, a key on reed wind instruments which opens small holes, so facilitating the production of the higher notes sounding as harmonics.

Speaking Length, the length of an organ pipe above the mouth, on which the pitch of the sound produced largely depends.

Speaking Stop (on an organ), a stop controlling a register as distinct from a coupler or other accessory.

Spianato (It.), level. A term used by Chopin to indicate a smooth style of performance.

Spiccato (It.), separated. Indicates to string players a type of staccato bowing used mainly in quick passages.

Spinet, a keyboard stringed instrument in which the strings are set in vibration by jacks or quills. Both the origin and early use of the name spinet are confused. The name may have been derived either from spina (It.), a thorn (in which case the quill pointing of the jacks are an essential characteristic of the true spinet), or from *Spinetti* (f. 1503), who adapted the early harpsichord to the oblong shape since commonly associated with the name spinet. However, the name spinet has been applied to instruments of the harpsichord variety, whether in an oblong case or not, and also to the early pianoforte built in an oblong case.

Spiritoso (It.), spiritedly. An indication of style rather than speed.

Spitta, Julius August Philipp (b. Wechold 1841, d. Berlin 1894), was a writer on music. He is remembered chiefly for his book on Bach. He edited the complete works of Schütz and the organ works of Buxtehude.

Spohr, Louis (b. Brunswick 1784, d. Cassel 1859), was one of the greatest violinists of his day. The great reputation he gained as a composer has failed to last. His violin concertos were perhaps the most important of his compositions; his oratorios, such as *The Last Judgement,* still enjoy a small popularity in England, but his nine symphonies are almost forgotten.

Spontini, Gasparo Luigi Pacifico (b. Majolati 1774, d. there 1851), was a composer mainly of opera. He achieved remarkable success during his lifetime. He enjoyed the patronage of King Frederick William III, and his appointments at court gave him an unrivalled opportunity for the production of opera on the grandest and most brilliant scale. The first performance of *Olympia* in Berlin in 1821 was a complete triumph for him; however, his success was steadily eclipsed by Weber's *Der Freischütz* produced also in Berlin five weeks later. His opera *La Vestale* has occasionally been produced until fairly recent times. Generally speaking, Spontini is now remembered merely as a historical figure.

Squire, William Barclay (b. London 1855, d. there 1927), was one of the most distinguished musical scholars of his day. With Fuller Maitland he prepared a scholarly edition of *The Fitzwilliam Virginal Book*, a production that is a notable example of his contributions to musical antiquarian research.

Stabat Mater, a hymn on the Crucifixion sung during Passion Week.

Staccato (It.), detached. Indicates that the notes of a phrase are to be shortened, leaving a space between each. It is usually expressed by a dot over each note or chord.

Staff, an alternative name for the stave.

Stainer, Sir John (b. London 1840, d. Verona 1901), achieved distinction as an organist, teacher and composer. In 1872 he became organist of St Paul's Cathedral and Professor of Music in the University of Oxford. He is remembered mainly for his widely popular oratorio *The Crucifixion*. His research work represented by *Dufay and his Contemporaries* is, however, far more indicative of his real merit as a musician.

Stanford, Sir Charles Villiers (b. Dublin 1852, d. London 1924), achieved distinction as a teacher, composer and conductor. He became organist of Trinity College, Cambridge in 1873 and Professor of Music in the University in 1887. He taught composition and conducted the orchestra and operatic class at the Royal College of Music from its opening in 1882. Besides these appointments from time to time he held various others, such as that of Conductor to the Bach Choir. He taught a great many of the English composers who have since produced distinguished work.

As a composer he made many notable contributions to the repertory of English music. Among his operas, *Shamus O'Brien* was a great success, and his *Irish Symphony* at one time enjoyed popularity. But his larger works, in particular, have tended to give place to the works of his successors which show greater originality of thought. A number of his smaller sacred and secular choral works, such as his Service in B♭ and his *Songs of the Sea*, and some of his organ music, have taken a more permanent place in the repertory.

Stave, the parallel horizontal lines, now invariably five in number, upon which music is written.

Steffani, Agostino (b. Castlefrance 1654, d. Frankfurt 1728), was in his youth a poor choir boy; nothing is known of his parents. He became one of the most remarkable men of his age. He was not only one of the most able musicians of the time, but also a diplomat who enjoyed the confidence of the highest religious and political leaders. Some of his compositions, such as a *Stabat Mater* for six-part choir, organ and strings, are among the best works of their period.

Stein, Johann Andreas (b. Herdesheim 1728, d. Augsburg 1792), was the founder of German pianoforte-making, and the head of a family of pianoforte-makers and pianists.

Sticcado-Pastrole, an early name for a kind of wooden dulcimer.

Stockhorn, a small beating reed instrument, now obsolete, used by Scottish peasants. It was probably identical with the pibgorn.

Stop (on a harpsichord), simply an adaptation of this feature on the organ. A small lateral movement of the stop handles brings the appropriate rack of strings into play.

Stop (on an organ), either a register or the handle, tab or other implement by which a register, coupler or other accessory is controlled.

Stopped Pipe, an organ pipe stopped at the upper end with a wooden plug or metal cap. A stopped pipe gives a note approximately an octave lower than an open pipe of the same length.

Stopping (on any stringed instrument), the action of shortening the portion of the string which vibrates, so raising the pitch of the note obtained from the string. The string is usually pressed against the fingerboard by a finger of the left hand, as is the case with members of the violin family.

Stradivari, Antonio (b. probably 1644, d. Cremona 1737), brought the violin to perfection. Little is known of his early years; a violin labelled as made by him refers to Nicole Amati as his master and is dated Cremona 1666. The probable date of Stradivari's birth is known from his habit of adding his age to his labels. He married twice; only two of his sons, *Francesco* (b. Cremona 1671, d. there 1743) and *Omobono* (b. Cremona 1679, d. there 1742), of his first marriage, followed their father's profession. Working from the design of Amati, Stradivari experimented with a number of variations in the proportions of his instruments; his success in these experiments, combined with the precision and beauty of his work, resulted in the quality of his instruments which has remained unsurpassed. It has been estimated that between the years 1666 and 1737 Stradivari made about 1,100 instruments, of which 540 violins, 12 violas and 50 violoncellos are known to-day.

Strauss, Johann (b. Vienna 1804, d. there 1849), and the eldest of his five children, also *Johann* (b. Vienna 1825, d. there 1899), both achieved world-wide fame as performers and composers of dance music, particularly of the waltz.

Johann the elder was apprenticed to a bookbinder, but by 1826 he had formed a band of fourteen players and gained remarkable success with his early waltzes. With an enlarged band his services became in constant demand, and his music established the fame of the 'Sperl', a favourite amusement place. From 1833 onwards he made tours of Germany, France and England. He married Anna Streim, daughter of an innkeeper, in 1824; they separated after eighteen years.

Johann the younger became a clerk in a savings bank, but by 1844 he appeared as a conductor with his own band, playing his own waltzes as well as those written by his father. He held appointments at St Petersburg, visited London, Paris and New York, as well as many lesser centres, continuing the fashion set by his father. From the first he was a prolific writer of waltzes, later turning his attention to operetta. He was married twice, on each occasion to a singer.

To Johann the elder is the credit for establishing the popularity of the waltz, and setting the particularly high standard of music associated with it. To Johann the younger is the credit of furthering his father's work, and writing waltzes such as *The Blue Danube* and *Tales of the Vienna Forest* and the operetta *Die Fledermaus*.

Strauss, Richard Georg (b. Munich 1864, d. Garmisch-Partenkirchen 1949), was the son of a horn player in the opera orchestra. Strauss' musical education was in the classical tradition; he began composing songs and chamber music, and some of his compositions had already attracted attention when in 1885, with the help of Bülow, he began his musical career as a conductor at Meiningen. In 1903 he was given an honorary doctorate by Heidelberg University with a diploma which declared that he was first among living German composers. Within a few years he had justified this claim beyond all doubt.

Strauss produced symphonic poems and operas which all but place him in the front rank, and made some notable contributions to song and chamber music. In his symphonic poems he enlarged the descriptive scope of music far beyond that reached by Liszt; *Don Juan*, written when he was twenty-four, *Till Eulenspiegel*, and *Don Quixote* are well known, and give Strauss a pre-eminent place amongst German composers of programme music. In his operas *Salomé* and *Elektra* he made extreme use of motives in the Wagnerian fashion, and produced music dramas savage and sordid, and magnificent in design; these were followed by the tremendously successful baroque comedy *Der Rosenkavalier*, quite different in style.

Strauss continued to conduct and compose until the end of his life. He conducted a concert in London in 1947 and showed that his ability had not deteriorated. Though his last compositions may lack the force of his earlier works, they still showed supreme craftsmanship and masterly orchestration. Some consider Strauss greatest in his lighter works, such as *Till Eulenspiegel* and *Der Rosenkavalier*, considering *Salomé* and *Elektra* outrageous morally and musically. However, he proved himself the most important of Wagner's successors, and the last of the great line of German composers.

Stravinsky, Igor (b. Oranienbaum 1882), still living.

Stretto (It.), narrow. Usually refers to a characteristic device of fugue in which a second entry of the subject, or its answer, occurs before the first has been completed.

String, a stretched length of gut, silk or wire free to vibrate between supports. The string alone gives only a faint sound, and a sound-board of some kind is an essential adjunct. The musical properties of a stretched string were known from ancient times. From the 6th century B.C. the single, stretched string, the monochord, was one of the main pieces of apparatus in the scientific study of sound. Gut was used by the ancient Egyptians, Greeks and Romans. Silk was used in the East. Wire strings were not known until the mid-14th century. Gut strings, commonly called cat gut, are made from the intestines of sheep and goats, the best being those of lambs of a certain age. Both wire and gut are used in modern stringed instruments.

Stringendo (It.), pressing. Indicates a progressive increase in speed and excitement.

String Plate (on a pianoforte), the iron plate to which the further ends of the strings are attached. The string plate is now generally cast in one piece with the metal frame.

Strings, instruments of the violin family are so called when forming an orchestra, either alone or with other instruments, or when needed in small groups for chamber music.

Suabe Flute, an open wooden flue organ stop, of 4-foot pitch on the manuals.

Sub, a term used on organ stops in the sense of 'under' or 'an octave below'.

Subdominant, the fourth note of any scale in the modern key system.

Subito (It.), suddenly.

Subject, the name given to any musical idea important by reason of its own nature or by the treatment it receives during the course of a movement. The name is equally applicable to a small group of notes forming the subject of a fugue, and to a relatively lengthy theme containing melodic, harmonic and rhythmic ideas upon which a set of variations is written. The two subjects upon which a composition in first movement form is constructed may often be more properly considered as two groups of subjects.

Submediant, the sixth note of any scale in the modern key system.

Succentor (in a cathedral), the deputy to the precentor.

Suite, an extended instrumental composition for one or more solo instruments or for orchestra, consisting of a number of movements in dance form. The distinction between the sonata and the suite was not fully established until the time of Mozart. Many earlier compositions having either title would now be definitely recognised as the other, while examples having some of the features of both are plentiful. The suite acquired several distinctive features. Each movement was simple in design and all the movements were in the same key. Each movement of the suite dwelt on some few metrical figures characteristic of it to the exclusion of the complexity and variety characteristic of the mature forms of the movements of a sonata.

The wealth of forms based on dances is a characteristic of the music of the late 16th, 17th and early 18th centuries, and the artistic advantage of grouping contrasted movements was soon recognised. The practice of grouping dance forms had existed for some time before the title of suite came into use. Lesson in England, partita in Germany, ordre in France and sonata in Italy were all used for what may be recognised as suites. After the title suite had been adopted in its now accepted sense, it was still sometimes used for compositions having little if any of the commonly recognised features of a suite. Such is the case, for instance, with some of the suites of Handel.

The standard form of the mature suite as exemplified by Bach, among others, consisted of Allemand, Courante, Saraband and Gigue, in that order. The most important movement commonly added to this standard nucleus was the Prelude (placed first). A great variety of movements have been interpolated, particularly between the Saraband and Gigue, among them Gavottes, Bourrées, Minuets, Musettes and Passepieds.

In modern times the title of suite has been used for any extended composition consisting of a number of movements, often following a prescribed programme but not conforming to the accepted idea of a sonata or symphony; for arrangements for concert performance of ballet music, incidental music and the like; for selections and arrangements for concert performance of music by old composers whose music might otherwise not be revived; and for compositions which may rightly be said to conform to the older concept of suite.

Suk, Josef (b. Krecovice 1874, d. Prague 1935), achieved distinction as a violinist and composer. He studied composition under Dvořák, whose daughter he married. He was one of the founders of the Bohemian String Quartet.

Su (It.), on. *Sul* or *Sulla*, on the.

Sullivan, Sir Arthur Seymour (b. London 1842, d. there 1900), was the son of an Irish soldier-bandsman. Sullivan had a sound instrumental training. He became a chorister in the Chapel Royal and in 1856 became the first holder of the Mendelssohn Scholarship at the Royal Academy of Music and with it studied at Leipzig two years later. He received the degree of Mus.D. from both Cambridge and Oxford and was knighted in 1883.

Sullivan enjoyed great success during his lifetime as a composer of instrumental and choral music of all kinds. Though his large-scale serious compositions are almost forgotten, many of his small essays, such as his setting for the hymn *Onward, Christian Soldiers!* and the song *The Lost Chord*, still enjoy popularity. The continued success of the operas he wrote in collaboration with W. S. Gilbert is a tribute to the good taste of both words and music, and to the simple tunefulness and good workmanship of the vocal and instrumental writing. *H.M.S. Pinafore, The Pirates of Penzance, Patience, Iolanthe, Princess Ida, The Mikado, Ruddigore, The Yeomen of the Guard* and *The Gondoliers* followed one another between 1878 and 1889.

Sul Ponticello (It.), on the bridge. Indicates to string players that the bow is to play near the bridge.

Summation Tone, the less important of the two kinds of 'resultant tone'.

Superdominant, an alternative name for the submediant.

Supertonic, the second note of any scale in the modern key system.

Suppé, von (b. Spalato 1819, d. Vienna 1895), whose full name was *Francesco Ezechiele Ermenegildo Cavaliere Suppé Demelli,* came of Belgian stock, though his family had lived in Cremona for two generations. He was a prolific composer of the light varieties of opera and stage music. His overtures *Poet and Peasant* and *Light Cavalry* have achieved wide popularity.

Suspension, the delay of one or more notes of a chord in changing to the next chord. The delayed notes commonly form a discord with those notes of the new chord which are sounded at the expected time. The discord is usually resolved by the part containing the delayed note falling one degree to a note of the new chord.

Madrigal "Straccia me pur"
MONTEVERDI

(a simple chain of suspensions)

Choral "Herzlich thut mich verlangen"
Setting in Cantata No. 161
BACH

(a more elaborate use of suspensions)

Süssmayer, Franz Xavier (b. Steyer 1766, d. 1803), was a pupil and close friend of Mozart. He is remembered for his work in completing the *Requiem,* for which Mozart gave him instructions from his deathbed.

Svendsen, Johan Severin (b. Christiana 1840, d. Copenhagen 1911), was a composer. His work was of a high character, but he has failed to achieve eminence.

Sweelinck, Jan Pieterszoon (b. 1562, d. Amsterdam 1621), was one of the greatest of early organists. He was a composer of vocal and organ music, though only the former was published in his lifetime.

His organ music presents the earliest known example of an independent pedal part in what is one of the earliest examples of a fully developed organ fugue.

Swell (on a harpsichord), the device introduced, after the fashion of the organ swell, towards the middle of the 18th century. In 1769 Shudi patented the Venetian swell and the advantages of his invention were adapted for the organ.

Swell Box (on an organ), the box with shutters on one or more sides in which are the pipes forming the swell organ or any other enclosed organ on a modern organ. The shutters on swell boxes are now invariably of the Venetian pattern.

Swell Organ, the second most important organ on a modern English church organ. The name was first given in 1712 when Jordan obtained a crescendo by raising a large sliding shutter forming one side of a box in which the pipes were enclosed. Early Swell Organs had a limited compass, sometimes from middle C upwards, more often from the G below middle C, and even much later only from the C an octave below middle C. The Swell Organ has often been more generously supplied with reed and mixture stops than the Great Organ, though its chief flue stops are on a slighter scale than those of the latter.

Swell Pedal (on an organ or harpsichord), a pedal controlling the shutters of a swell box. Originally swell pedals were simple levers which left the swell box either closed or fully open; later, however, the lever pattern gave place to a balanced pedal which could be left in any position.

Sympathetic Tone, a sound produced by the phenomenon of resonance.

Symphonic Poem, a title first used by Liszt. The title has been generally adopted to describe large-scale orchestral compositions which are not in any one of the generally recognised musical forms, and which follow or illustrate a prescribed programme.

Symphony, an extended orchestral composition. The name appears to have been first used for purely instrumental passages occurring in the course of compositions in which the main interest centred round a voice or voices. During the 17th century all instrumental passages, from an extended overture to short introductions in an opera, oratorio or the like, were called symphonies. The development of the distinct type of overture which became known as the Italian overture is the most obvious forerunner in form of the independent orchestral symphony of Haydn. The concerto and concerto grosso of the first part of the 18th century clearly contributed to the development of extended forms for orchestral

compositions. However, many forms influenced the evolution of
the symphony.

During the second half of the 18th century the progress of
the overture followed the development of the instrumental sonata.
As important as the evolution of the outline of the structure of
these various forms was the development in the treatment of the
instruments used, and a standardisation in the choice of instruments. Most important in this respect was the establishment of the
strings as the basis of the orchestra, and their independent treatment. The violas playing with the basses, the strings playing all
the time, the wind merely reinforcing the strings in certain passages
– these were common features of the mid 18th-century treatment
of the orchestra.

The place of the symphony as the prime form for extended
orchestral music, and the distinction between symphony and
concerto were established by Haydn and Mozart. Four movements
became the standard form, as with the sonata – the first in first-
movement form, the second a slow movement, the third a minuet
and trio, and the last a rondo. Of these the greatest variety in
form is found with the second movement. The third evolved into
the scherzo, and a movement similar in scale and design to the
first movement began to be used in place of the rondo for the last
movement. Symphonies have, broadly speaking, kept to this four-
movement pattern. Haydn, Mozart, and Beethoven, in his early
symphonies, severely limited the choice of keys for the four movements; the second movement in a closely-related key was usually
the only movement in other than the key of the symphony as a
whole. Beethoven, in his later symphonies, made a far wider choice;
so did Brahms. The evolution and development of the symphony
transformed it from the early slender essays of Haydn and Mozart,
each lasting but a quarter of an hour or so, to the massive essays
of Beethoven and Brahms, relatively few in number, but each
taking nearly an hour or more to perform.

The latter part of the 19th century, and the 20th century
have seen the structure of the symphony varied in many ways,
though the four-movement structure had remained remarkably
stable as the standard form in which large-scale extended orchestral
compositions are most effectively cast. But apart from this, it
would be wrong to associate the symphony in a dogmatic fashion
with any particular outline or internal structure of its movements.
Disregard for precedent is no less a feature of modern symphonies
than of other modern compositions.

Syncopation, a disturbance in the normal flow of the time accents. The effect of a syncopation depends on the conflict between the normal and syncopated accents. A syncopation can be felt only if the normal flow of accents has been established (and so continues in the mind of the listener), or is clearly present in one part while another has the syncopation. These two requirements are fulfilled in examples (a) and (b) and the syncopations are clearly felt. Example (c) is only a syncopation on paper.

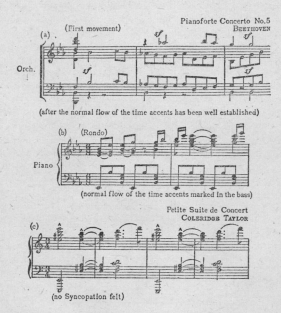

Syrinx, The Greek name for the so-called Pandean pipe.

T

Tablature, a system of musical notation. Various tablatures were used for certain instruments between the 15th and 18th centuries. Generally speaking, in tablatures pitch and duration are indicated by different signs. The tablature may indicate the exact pitch (as in most tablature for keyboard instruments), or merely the manner of producing the note (as in all tablatures for plucked and bowed stringed instruments); in some cases the duration of each note is indicated, in others only the instant at which the note is to be sounded.

The lute tablatures are the most important of all. The French and Italian lute tablatures were in use from the early 16th to the early 19th century; they were similar in principle but differed a good deal in detail. Italian tablature was confined mostly to Italy and Spain; French tablature prevailed elsewhere in Europe. The English lutenists of the late 16th and early 17th century generally followed the French variety. These tablatures in principle were simple. Each line on the tablature corresponds to one of the main strings on the lute. Numbers or letters on the lines indicated whether the strings were to be left open or stopped to raise the pitch one, two, three, or more semitones. The intervals of time at which the strings were to be plucked were indicated at first by signs (similar to the tails of the crotchet, quaver and so on) and later by ordinary notes.

"And would you see my mistress' face"

From Rosseter's Book of Airs 1601
Music by ROSSETER

(transcription of the lute tablature)

Table, a name sometimes used for the belly of a violin.

Tabor, a long narrow drum with a single snare on the vellum head on which the strokes are made. It is rarely used in the orchestra. The combination of pipe and tabor played by one performer was popular in England for several centuries.

Tabret, the Biblical drum.

Tacet (Lat.), it is silent. Indicates that the voice or instrument is not to play.

Tallis, Thomas (b. *c.* 1505, d. Greenwich 1585), was an English musician. Little is known with certainty of the facts of the early part of his life. He was holding some appointment, probably that of organist or master of the choristers, at Waltham Abbey on its dissolution in 1540. He was appointed gentleman of the Chapel Royal, probably at about this time, and from then onwards fuller details of his life are known. In 1575 Tallis with Byrd was granted a monopoly for printing music paper and music. In the same year he published, jointly with Byrd, a set of motets, *Cantiones Sacrae,* describing himself and Byrd as joint organists of the Chapel Royal. Tallis was married in 1552, but had no children. The later years of his life were spent at Greenwich. He was buried in St Alphege parish church.

Tallis' Latin church music, reproduced in *Tudor Church Music,* includes two masses, a setting of the Lamentations and a large number of motets, one of them, *Spem in alium,* being for eight five-part choirs, 40 parts in all. His English church music includes settings of the Preces and Responses, two services, nine tunes for Archbishop Parker's Psalter of 1567, and a number of anthems. A very small quantity of secular music by him is also extant.

Tambourin, an old Provençal dance, originally accompanied on a flute and by a kind of drum — hence the derivation of its name.

Tambourine, an instrument, strictly a member of the drum family, consisting of a skin head stretched over a wood ring and played by being struck by the fingers. The old English name for it, timbrell, is derived from tabor. The tambourine was known to most ancient peoples. In many forms of the instrument, jingles of bells or metal discs are attached.

Tampon, a two-headed drumstick used for rolls on the bass drum.

Tangent (of a clavichord), the thick pin, flattened at the top, which acts both as a bridge and as a hammer, marking off the length of string to vibrate and at the same time causing it to vibrate.

Tango, a dance of Mexican origin, particularly popular in Spain, which imitates the movements of Negroes, and in its uncultured form is far more suggestive and far less presentable than the habanera. The rhythm of the tango is similar to that of the habanera, but the tango is much faster.

Tanto (It.), so much. A term used by Beethoven in the same sense as 'troppo'.

Tarantella, a South Italian dance. The music is in six-eight time, is played faster and faster and changes irregularly from major to minor. It is generally danced by a man and a girl, or by two women, women often playing castanets and a tambourine.

The tarantella has been ignorantly believed to cure a form of insanity, hysteria or St Vitus dance, sometimes known as tarantism, which was thought to be caused by the bite of the largest of European spiders, the Lycosa Tarantula.

Tarrega, Francisco (b. Villareal 1852, d. Barcelona 1909), was a masterly player on the guitar. He advanced greatly the technique of guitar-playing, and proved that the guitar was worthy of the attention of serious musicians.

Tartini, Giuseppe (b. Pirano 1692, d. Padua 1770), achieved fame as a violinist and as the founder of a school of violin-playing at Padua. He composed extensively, particularly for the violin, and made numerous contributions to the literature of music. In spite of the colourful and exaggerated form in which certain facts of his personal history have survived, Tartini was an important figure in the early development of the violin and its music. His marriage, to one of his pupils, incurred the wrath of a cardinal. Tartini was obliged to leave his wife in Padua and wander the country until he found asylum in the monastery at Assisi. While at Assisi he wrote the sonata by which he is best known, *The Devil's Trill*, said to have been written after he had heard the devil play to him in a dream. Also at this time he is said to have discovered the third sound resulting from two sounds, the differential tone, though not knowing its scientific explanation.

His violin-playing in the monastery chapel, even though he was hidden from the sight of visitors, led to his being discovered and allowed to return to Padua and rejoin his wife. In Padua in 1728 he established a school of violin-playing. Many tempting offers failed to induce him to visit London and Paris, and, apart from rare tours in his own country, he remained in Padua for the rest of his life.

Tattoo, the name of a British army signal. The German equivalent of this name has been used by Beethoven, and by others since, for a kind of short march.

Tauber, Richard (b. Linz 1892, d. London 1948), achieved fame as a tenor, particularly for his singing in operettas by Mozart and Lehar.

Tausig, Carl (b. Warsaw 1841, d. Leipzig 1871), was the most remarkable pianoforte virtuoso of his day. The brilliance and infallibility of his technique and his powers of endurance were considered astonishing. He was an accomplished musician and has left a number of clever transcriptions for the pianoforte of organ and orchestral compositions.

Taverner, John (b. *c.* 1495, d. 1545), was an English musician. He was appointed to the newly-founded Cardinals' College at Oxford in 1526, where his duties included teaching the children and playing the organ. He was subsequently involved in religious controversies and so remained at Oxford for only three and a half years. He spent the rest of his life at Boston. Taverner is one of the most important early composers of sacred music. His church music has been published in the Carnegie edition of *Tudor Church Music*; it includes eight masses (one of them, the most commonly known, based on the folk song *The Western Wynde*) and a number of Latin motets. Three small secular pieces written for Wynken de Worde's Song-book in 1530 are also extant.

Tchaikovsky, Peter Ilich (b. Kamsko-Votinsk 1840, d. St Petersburg 1893), was the son of an inspector of Government mines. His family was in no way musically distinguished, and his early love of music was discouraged. The family moved to St Petersburg in 1850. He began a career in the Ministry of Justice, but resigned from his position of clerk in 1863 to study music in earnest, working under Anton Rubinstein at the Conservatorium in St Petersburg. In 1866 he joined the staff of the Conservatorium in Moscow, which Nicholas Rubinstein (Anton's younger brother) had organized. He married in 1877, but the marriage was a disaster and lasted only nine weeks. He left Russia and for the next thirteen years received the patronage of a wealthy widow, Nadejda von Meck, and was enabled to compose untroubled by financial considerations. After a short stay in Italy he returned to his duties at the Conservatorium in 1878, but very soon resigned. The remainder of his life was spent partly touring (he visited both England and America) and partly living in the country. Tchaikovsky suffered greatly from nervous disorders which more than once came near to madness and certainly coloured his music. His last symphony, No 6 in B minor (*The Pathetic*), is tragic in the extreme and a masterpiece of personal expression; he died of cholera ten days after the first performance of the symphony.

Among his most popular compositions are the delightful ballets *The Sleeping Beauty* and *The Swan Lake*, the suite arranged from the ballet *Casse-Noisette* and the first of his three piano concertos, that in B♭ minor. His orchestral fantasias *The Tempest* and *Francesca da Rimini*, and the overture *Romeo and Juliet* rank with his fifth and sixth symphonies. The overture *The Year 1812* has a popularity it hardly deserves. Two only of his eight operas, *Eugen Onegin* and *Pique-Dame*, have achieved more than initial success. Only a small proportion of his many songs are really good, and neither they nor a number of compositions for the piano have become as popular as his orchestral music. Of his chamber music, the piano trio and the three string quartets merit attention. His *Serenade in C* is a useful contribution to the repertory of music for strings.

Tchaikovsky was uncompromising in his judgement of other composers. He profoundly admired Mozart but could not endure Brahms. His own music is unequal in quality, but his works are full of beautiful melody and his orchestration is delightful. On his own admission he did not master form, yet many of his longest essays are amongst the finest of their kind.

Te, the later name used in place of 'si' for the seventh note of the scale in solmization.

Te, the seventh note of the scale in tonic sol-fa.

Telemann, Georg Philipp (b. Magdeburg 1681, d. Hamburg 1767), was one of the most prolific composers of all time, and is said to have composed with a remarkable facility. In his day he was considered a composer of first rank, but time has shown his work to be without invention or imagination. He was a master of counterpoint and of the accepted forms of his day. The superficiality of his work is particularly apparent in his sacred music which combines melodies of the Italian opera style with conventional counterpoint.

Tell-tale, a simple mechanical device invariably found on hand-blown organs to indicate to an organ blower, and sometimes also to the organist, the amount of wind in the bellows. A weight, connected by string over a pulley with the bellows, moves up and down according as there is more or less air in the bellows.

Temperament, an aspect of certain types of tuning in which some intervals, particularly the third and fifth, are slightly varied from their natural values. The scale tuned to just intonation was of little practical use except for purely melodic music limited to the particular key in which the scale was tuned.

The present tuning is properly called equal temperament,

since in all twelve keys the scale differs from a just intonation
by the same amount. In theory, the twelve semitones of the
octave are equal; in practice, tuners obtain a very good approxi-
mation to strictly equal temperament. If a method of obtaining
this tuning fails, so that the degree of difference from just intonation varies from key to key, the resulting temperament may be
described as unequal. The meantone system of tuning is sometimes inappropriately called an unequal temperament.

Tempo (It., plural tempi), time. Used in the sense of pace or speed.
The pace of music may be indicated in general terms verbally or
fixed exactly by a metronome mark. Neither method is entirely
satisfactory. Pace is relative, and what may be right in one set of
circumstances may be quite wrong in another. The number of
performers, the kind of building and other circumstances affect
the apparent pace; sense of pace seems to vary from one century
to another and from one nation to another. To indicate tempo
verbally, it has been customary to use the Italian terms Adagio,
Grave, Largo, Lento, Andante, Allegro, Vivace and Presto, and
their derivatives; Molto Adagio (very slowly) and Prestissimo
(very quickly) being the customary extremes. However, there is
no rigid agreement as to the order or value of the tempos and
many of the terms have been used ambiguously. To indicate
tempo exactly the number of time units to take place in a minute
is given: thus ♩= 80 indicates that eighty crochets should occupy
one minute on the average. It would be quite wrong to follow the
metronome beat in any rigid fashion.

Tempo Giusto (It.), exact time. Used in a similar sense to 'a tempo'.
Also used in the sense of 'at an appropriate speed'.

Tempo Ordinario (It.), common time. Used in the sense of four
crochets to a bar, also as an indication of a speed in the same
sense as 'moderato'.

Teneramente (It.), tenderly. Indicates a style similar to but more
gentle than 'dolce'.

Tenor, the largest and lowest-sounding bell of a peal.

Tenor, the vocal part sung by men with a high range. The normal
compass of tenor parts is about an octave and a half upwards
to the G above middle C. The tenor was originally the part
containing the plainsong melody.

Tenor Clef, the C clef placed on the fourth line to show that that note
is middle C.

middle C

Tenor Cor, a brass valve instrument. It was designed as a compromise between the tenor saxhorn and the French horn by a Henry Distin about 1860.

Tenor Drum, a drum similar in design to, and midway in size between the side drum and bass drum. It is used mainly in military bands and has been used only rarely in the orchestra.

Tenor Horn, the name sometimes given to the E♭ and B♭ middle members of the saxhorn family.

Tenuto (It.), held. Indicates that a note is to be given its full time value.

Ternary Form, form in which balance is obtained by repeating the first phrase (or section) or a considerable part of it after a second phrase of about equal importance.

A great many compositions of greater or lesser length have a ternary appearance. Many of the older Italian arias and the minuet and trio, for instance, are clearly in this form.

Many simple four-phase melodies have identical first, second and last phrases (*All through the night* is an example) and the theme for variations of Mozart's pianoforte sonata in A major (K 331) has a similar form. These are often quoted as examples of ternary form, but it is better to consider them as examples of one of the ways in which four phrases (not three or two) may be made to balance one another. The second phrase is not a casual repetition of the first. More often than not, there is a sense of rest after the second phrase and the third leads on to the last; the whole tune then falls into two sections which balance each other, and could well be called binary. For example, the musette in D (in *The Anna Magdalena Notebook*) by Bach:

is quoted by one authority (as an example of ternary form) in this manner

Fine   Da Capo

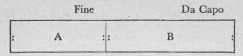

In full, this takes the form

A A , B B , A   or   A A , B B , A A

In several editions this musette is printed in the form

which, in full, takes the form

A A , B+A B+A

Without the repeats (but observing the Da Capo) both versions take the form

A , B , A

But, clearly, with repeats there is a considerable difference between them. The first still gives a ternary appearance, the second does not. In considering the form of a composition the repeats must not be overlooked.

It seems wise to use 'ternary form' to describe only those compositions which have, quite clearly, three parts of which the first and third are the same. The simple concepts of 'binary form' and 'ternary form' are inadequate as a basis for explaining the evolution of the simple extended forms which lead to the mature 'first movement form'. Using these terms for this purpose invariably leads to difficulties. Perhaps both terms are best avoided.

Terpsichore, the patroness of dancing among the nine muses of Greek mythology.

Terry, Charles Sanford (b. Newport-Pagnell 1864, d. Aberdeen 1936), became Professor of History in the University of Aberdeen in 1933. He has made valuable contributions to the literature on Bach, and has prepared a number of scholarly editions of Bach's chorals and cantatas.

Terry, Sir Richard Runciman (b. Ellington 1865, d. London 1938), became organist of Westminster Cathedral. He made a notable contribution to the revival of 16th-century church music, both by his research and by the high standard of the musical tradition he established at Westminster.

Terzet, a composition for three voices. The term has rarely been applied to instrumental music, and vocal compositions for three voices are now commonly called 'trios'.

Tessitura (It.), texture. This term is used to describe the lie of a composition, the predominant pitch regardless of extremes. It is used especially with regard to the lie of a vocal part.

Tetrachord, a group of four sounds forming a scale. Formed from the division of the smallest perfect concord, the fourth, to form the simplest of scales, the tetrachord was the basis of the Greek scale systems.

Theme, used with the same sense as subject, particularly where the subject is a self-contained section as it is in a 'theme with variations'.

Theorbo, a large lute, standing about 4 feet high and having two peg boxes, the lower for the strings tuned in normal lute fashion, the upper for open bass strings. The theorbo was commonly used with the bass viol for the lowest part of instrumental compositions during the 17th century. The theorbo may have had single bass strings while the lute had double bass strings. Further, the theorbo may have been regarded as an accompanying or concert instrument, while the lute was a solo instrument. The distinction, if any, between the theorbo and the arch lute is confused.

Third, the interval covering three degrees of the scale. Three forms commonly occur:

(a) the major third, (b) the minor third and (c) the diminished third, these being the inversions respectively of the minor, major, and augmented sixths. In the modern key system the two forms of scale are named major or minor according as the interval of a third from tonic to mediant is major or minor. Similarly the major and minor triads are distinguished by the nature of the third between the root and the middle note of the chord. Hence the special importance of this interval in harmony.

Thomas, Charles Louis Ambroise (b. Metz 1811, d. Paris 1896), was the son of a musician. He studied at the Paris Conservatoire, winning the Grand Prix de Rome in 1832. The production of *Mignon* in 1866 and *Hamlet* in 1868 marked the peak of his career as a composer of opera. In 1871 he became director of the Conservatoire and composed little more. Two years before his death he received the Grand Cross of the Legion of Honour on the occasion of the thousandth performance of *Mignon*.

Thorough Bass or *Through Bass,* another name for what is commonly known as 'continuo'.

Tibia (Lat.), flute. The flute of the ancient Romans.

Tie, a curved line joining two notes of the same pitch, indicating that they are to be played as one, with the time value of the two added.

Tierce de Picardie, the name given, for no known reason, to the use of a major third in the final chord of a composition in a minor key.

Timbrel, the old English name for the tambourine.

Time, the arrangement of the beats within the bar. The time of a composition is inherent in the texture of the music, and is invariably apparent from it. Rather confusingly the time of a composition is described from its notation, not from its aural effect, and it is ostensibly indicated by the time signature. However, the notation of time is inadequate, and gives rise to many inconsistencies in both usage and definition.

Times are called duple, triple or quadruple according to whether the number of beats in each bar is two, three or four. Time is called (rather misleadingly) simple or compound according to whether the beat is normally divided into two or into three. Taking the crotchet or dotted crotchet as the beat:

	Simple	Compound
Duple	$\frac{2}{4}$ ♩ ♩ ♫ ♫	$\frac{6}{8}$ ♩. ♩. ♫♫ ♫♫
Triple	$\frac{3}{4}$ ♩ ♩ ♩ ♫ ♫ ♫	$\frac{9}{8}$ ♩. ♩. ♩. ♫♫ ♫♫ ♫♫
Quadruple	$\frac{4}{4}$ ♩ ♩ ♩ ♩ ♫ ♫ ♫ ♫	$\frac{12}{8}$ ♩. ♩. ♩. ♩. ♫♫ ♫♫ ♫♫ ♫♫

The minim or dotted minim, quaver or dotted quaver, and so on, may similarly be taken as the beat. There is no difference in meaning between

A tune set by Purcell
under the title "A new Irish tune"
and now known as "Lilliburlero"

and

Both are in simple triple time and at the same speed, the difference is merely one of notation.

For convenience the crotchet or dotted crotchet, quaver or dotted quaver is most often chosen for the beat. This usually allows a duration of one whole bar to be represented by one note or rest no longer than a semibreve, and an adequate subdivision of beats without demanding notes or rests of less than a demisemiquaver duration.

The modern use of simple and compound in connection with time is identical with the medieval use of imperfect and perfect. Generally the distinction between simple and compound may be both seen from the notation and heard; occasionally, however, a passage may be written as though in a simple time while sounding in a compound time, or the reverse.

Choral "Jesu, joy of man's desiring"
Cantata No. 147
BACH

for instance, is, in effect, in compound triple time.

The time of a composition is described regardless of pace. According to the notation:

Serenade "Eine Kleine Nachtmusik", K. 525
(a) Menuetto *Allegretto*   MOZART

Vla octave higher

D.B. octave lower

(b) *Adagio*   Pianoforte Sonata No. 1
                                                  BEETHOVEN

dolce

(c) *Molto vivace* (♩=116)   Symphony No. 9
                                                  BEETHOVEN
                                                        etc.

Vl 2
pp   Vla

etc.

Vc

are all in simple triple time. (a) does, in fact, sound like three beats in a bar; (b), however, sounds like three groups of two beats in a bar, and (c) like one beat in a bar, or even more like compound quadruple time, four bars being grouped together and the beat being a dotted minim. On the other hand, though the Bourrée is written in duple time (with the minim as the beat) and the Gavotte in quadruple time (with the crotchet as the beat) the distinction between them with regard to the flow of the crotchets is very slight, if not negligible.

Since in effect one bar of quadruple time is little different from two bars of duple, some writers prefer to regard quadruple time as a variety of duple time, and it is frequently referred to as common.

A quadruple time of four beats accepted by the ear as a whole indivisible group (without a subsidiary strong accent on the third beat) does not occur in practice. The ear has too strong a tendency to divide four into two groups of two. Five (quintuple) and higher numbers of beats in a bar are less readily recognised as a whole by the ear, and are rarely used. Five-beat bars are, more often than not, an addition of two and three beats rather than a genuine group of five beats.

Time Signature, the fraction or sign placed after the key signature or, if there is no key signature, immediately after the clef. The time signature rather inadequately indicates the time; it may be considered as a fraction of a semibreve corresponding to the length of the bar. Simple and compound times are readily distinguished by a convention, as may be seen from the Table of Time Signatures.

In simple times, it will be noticed, the numerator of the fraction indicates the number of beats in a bar, and the denominator what kind of beats they are.

The time signatures of $\frac{4}{4}$ and $\frac{2}{2}$ are often written C and ₵, signs handed on from an older system of notation. (See Table VII, p. 284.)

Timpani, the commonly used Italian name for the kettledrums.

Toccata (It.), a title used from the beginning of the 17th century for keyboard compositions of certain styles but no particular form. The name appears to imply a composition to display the touch of the performer and a quick flowing movement, often of a brilliant nature, is characteristic of many toccatas.

Tomkins, Thomas (b. St David's *c.* 1573, d. Martin Hussingtree 1656), was the most notable of a family of English musicians flourishing during the 16th and 17th centuries. Some of his sacred music and his published madrigals are included in *Tudor Church Music* and *The English Madrigal School*, and he contributed to *The Triumphes of Oriana*.

Tonality, the sense of character of a melody by reason of the mutual relation of the notes of the scale in which it is written, and also the feeling for key which developed as the harmonies evolved from modal polyphony were organized in the major and minor key system. It depends on the balance of tonic harmonies with related harmonies, particularly dominant harmonies, and to a lesser extent subdominant harmonies. The balance gives a sense

TABLE VII
A Table of Time Signatures

Quadruple		Triple		Duple	
Compound	Simple	Compound	Simple	Compound	Simple
$\frac{12}{4}$	$\frac{4}{2}$	$\frac{9}{4}$	$\frac{3}{2}$	$\frac{6}{4}$	$\frac{2}{2}$
$\frac{12}{8}$	$\frac{4}{4}$	$\frac{9}{8}$	$\frac{3}{4}$	$\frac{6}{8}$	$\frac{2}{4}$
$\frac{12}{16}$	$\frac{4}{8}$	$\frac{9}{16}$	$\frac{3}{8}$	$\frac{6}{16}$	$\frac{2}{8}$

of satisfaction and finality to a close in the tonic key. Tonality became defined first by the general acceptance of the recognised forms of cadence, and later by the organisation of the keys in extended movements.

Tone, the larger of the two intervals in the diatonic scale, the smaller being the semitone. According to physical theory there are major and minor tones, corresponding to the ratios 9 : 8 and 10 : 9 respectively, and the tone is only approximately equal to two semitones. However, on the modern keyboard, where the octave is divided into twelve equal semitones, all tones are equal and the tone is precisely two semitones; further, the tone is identical with the major second and these two terms are commonly treated as synonymous. Two tones are treated as equivalent to a major third, and three tones (the tritone) as an augmented fourth or a diminished fifth. Similarly, one semitone is treated as equivalent to a minor second, one and a half tones as a minor third, and two and a half tones as a perfect fourth.

Tone, a Gregorian psalm chant.

Tone, quality of sound.

Tone, a musical sound without overtones. Individually overtones are themselves tones, as distinct from a note, which is a pleasant combination of tones in which the pitch of one predominates.

Tonic, the key note in the major and minor key system, corresponding to the final of the ecclesiastical modes.

Tonic Accent (or pitch accent), the importance given to a note by relatively higher pitch, particularly in vocal music.

Tonic Sol-fa, a method of musical notation and teaching. By Tonic Sol-fa is generally meant, in England, the system promoted by Curwen; this is in fact a revision, development and refinement of a principle used for many centuries. The names used for the notes of the scale were essentially those associated with solmization since the 12th century.

The relation between the staff and tonic sol-fa notation is seen from the following:

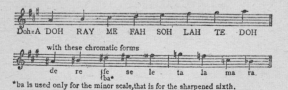

Doh=A DOH   RAY   ME   FAH   SOH   LAH   TE   DOH

with these chromatic forms

de   re   fe   se   le   ta   la   ma   ra.
          (ba*)

*ba is used only for the minor scale, that is for the sharpened sixth.

The Tonic Sol-fa notation follows the course of any modulations, the tonic of each new key becoming doh at a convenient and appropriate moment, so that the names for the chromatic notes will seldom be used, though they are occasionally useful to avoid frequent changes of the position of doh. Minor keys are treated as variants of their relative major – thus the tonic of a minor key is always lah. The duration of each note is shown by dashes and dots. The dash indicates a note prolonged, a blank indicates a rest. Bars, colons, full stops and commas are used to indicate divisions in the time.

TABLE VIII

A Tonic Sol-fa Modulator

		f^1		t
t		m^1		l
l		r^1		s
s		DOH^1		f
		TE		m
f	ta		le	
m		LAH		r
	la	se		
r		SOH		d
		ba	fe	t_1
d		FAH		
t_1		ME		l_1
	ma		re	
l_1		RAY		s_1
	ra		de	
s_1		DOH		f_1
		t_1		m_1
f_1				
m_1		l_1		r_1
r_1		s_1		d_1

The many advantages of Tonic Sol-fa, particularly in teaching singing and in impressing the mutual relation of the individual notes of the scale, may be readily recognized. However, the system begins to break down with certain modern idioms not readily associated with the traditional key system. The rule that doh indicates the tonic cannot apply if the tonic no longer exists. A system of fixing doh and naming all notes with reference to it, regardless of modulation, though preferred in France and Belgium, defeats one of the prime objects of Tonic Sol-fa, and has been rejected in England.

Tonguing, the movement of the tongue in playing wind instruments. The normal method is single tonguing. On some instruments, particularly the flute, double and even triple tonguing is possible. In ordinary tonguing the tongue moves as in repeating the letter T.

Touch, the weight and movement required to operate the keys of a keyboard instrument; also the skill and artistry of a performer in controlling the keys.

Tourdion, an old French dance, apparently the equivalent of the Italian saltarello, described by Arbeau.

Tourte, François (b. Paris 1747, d. there 1835), was the most prominent member of a family pre-eminent in the making of violin bows. Before Tourte the state of bow-making was chaotic; he may be credited with having invented the modern bow and reduced the art of bow-making to a science.

Tovey, Donald Francis (b. Eton 1875, d. Edinburgh 1940), was Reid Professor of Music in the University of Edinburgh from 1914 until his death. He is better known by his writings on music, such as his *Essays in Musical Analysis,* than by his compositions. Both his writings and his compositions show that he was among the most learned of musical scholars.

Tracker (in an organ), a flat thin strip of wood used to transfer movement from the keys or stops to the inside of the organ. Tracker action is now more or less out of date, being used only on small instruments or where an inadequate wind supply or lack of electricity makes pneumatic or electric action impossible.

Tranquillo (It), calmly.

Transcription, a term commonly used in a sense similar to arrangement. It would be convenient to limit the use of transcription to faithful reproductions in modern notation of older music originally in tablature, or with obsolete clefs, and the like.

Transition, a term used either in the same general sense as modulation or in some more specialised sense associated with modulation.

Transition has been used for the precise moment of changing key in a modulation, and also for brief changes of key not having the structural importance of a deliberate modulation.

Transposing Instruments, those instruments whose music is written, for convenience, in one key while sounding in another. Instruments made in different sizes, or with which crooks are used, have been commonly treated as transposing instruments. This convention enables a player to change from one instrument to a similar instrument pitched in another key without changing the fingering in relation to the written notes. In the orchestra, the clarinet, cor anglais, horn and trumpet are written for as transposing instruments.

At one time this convention was of greater value, and was used more extensively, than it is now. When wind instruments were effective only in their natural keys and keys closely related to them, they were often built in a number of sizes or with a number of crooks. As improvements in mechanism enable these instruments to be treated as complete chromatic instruments playable with equal facility in any key, even the present limited treatment of instruments as transposing instruments may completely disappear.

Those instruments sounding an octave above or below the written part (the double bass, double bassoon and piccolo) are not considered to be transposing instruments. Brass bands treat nearly all their instruments as transposing instruments, regardless of their treatment elsewhere.

Transposing Keyboard, an arrangement whereby the keyboard and the strings or pipes of an instrument could be moved relative to one another, so effecting a transposition. Transposing keyboards are now rarely found. The arrangement was first applied to organs in the 16th century, and various attempts to devise a satisfactory transposing keyboard have been made until recent times.

Transposition, a reproduction of a passage in another key.

are transposed forms of each other. Every note in (b) is at precisely the same interval, in this case a fourth, from the corresponding note in (a). In the course of a movement, a theme or passage may actually be transposed, as in the above example, though there is no change in the key signature. Whole compositions may be transposed, as is commonly the case with songs; in which case the key signature would be appropriately changed.

Travers, John (b. *c.* 1703, d. 1758), became organist of the Chapel Royal in 1737. Some of his church music is still sung.

Treble, the smallest and highest-sounding bell of a peal.

Treble, the vocal part sung by women or boys with a high range. The normal compass of treble parts is about an octave-and-a-half upwards from middle C. The name is held to be a corruption of triplum, the third part in early polyphonic music added above the altus and bassus.

Treble Clef, the G clef begun on the second line to show that that line corresponds with the G above middle C.

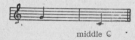

middle C

Tre Corde (Fr.), three strings. This term indicates the discontinuance of the use of the una corda pedal on the pianoforte.

Tremolo (It.), the rapid reiteration of a note. The tremolo is an important effect on all bowed stringed instruments. Written

it is played with a rapid alternation of up and down movements of the bow. The drum roll is strictly a tremolo. Wind instruments and keyboard instruments cannot properly or effectively produce a tremolo in the same fashion as the strings and drums, but something of the same effect is obtained by the rapid alternation of notes of the same chord.

played in one
breath or bow

(a) as it might be found for the pianoforte; (b) for wind instruments, particularly in arrangements of orchestral music for the pianoforte or wind band. The form (b) in string music is called a fingered tremolo.

The tremolo proper is a difficult technical feat for singers. In referring to singing, however, there is often confusion between the use of the terms tremolo and vibrato.

Tremulant, a device to be found on organs by which a rapid fluctuation in the wind pressure supplied to the pipe causes a corresponding pulsation in the notes produced.

Trenchmore, an old English dance popular during the 16th and 17th centuries.

Triad, a chord of three notes, the extreme notes being a fifth apart and each forming a third with the middle note; four forms commonly occur:

(a) the major triad, (b) the minor triad, (c) the diminished triad, and (d) the augmented triad.

The triad is the basis of the chords of the seventh, ninth, eleventh and thirteenth which are formed from it by the addition of thirds one above the other. This procedure is especially applicable to the triad on the dominant.

(a) a triad; (b), (c), (d) and (e) chords of the seventh, ninth, eleventh and thirteenth respectively.

Triangle, a percussion instrument commonly used in the modern orchestra. It is a steel rod of about seven-tenths of an inch diameter and 21 inches long, bent in the form of a triangle open at one angle, and is beaten with a steel rod about 6 inches long.

Trihoris, an old Breton dance, described by Arbeau.

Trill, another name for the 'shake'.

Trio, a composition for three instrumentalists or singers. The most common combination of instruments for which trios have been written is that of violin, violoncello and pianoforte. The form of instrumental trios usually follows that of the sonata and symphony. Vocal trios are not associated with any particular form, most examples occur incidentally in opera and among madrigals.

Trio, the second minuet, scherzo, waltz, march or other movement after which the first is repeated.

Triplet, three notes grouped together under a curved line and usually with a small 3 over the middle note, indicating that the three triplet notes have a total duration equal to that of two normal notes. Groups of any number of notes to be treated in a similar manner are now often met.

Tritone, an interval of three whole tones, that is an augmented fourth.

Triumphes of Oriana, a collection of madrigals made by Morley in honour of Queen Elizabeth and containing compositions by Bennet, Carlton, Cavendish, Cobbold, East, Ellis, Farmer, Gibbons, Hilton, Holmes, Hunt, Johnson, Jones, Kirbye, Lisley, Marson, Milton, Morley himself, Mundy, Nicholson, Norcome, Tomkins, Weelkes, and Wilbye. It has been republished in *The English Madrigal School*.

Trombone, a brass wind instrument with a slide, played with a cupped mouthpiece. It took its place in the orchestra rather more slowly than the trumpet, to which it is closely related. The trombone had its distinctive characteristic, the slide, from the first, having as its immediate ancestor the sackbut rather than the trumpet. It has been made in every register and key. The instruments now generally used are the tenor trombone in B♭ and the bass trombone in G or F. The series of notes obtained without using the slide is the harmonic series, as for the trumpet and horn. The fundamental notes of the tenor and bass trombone are:

Seven positions of the slide are recognised. Thus, if the octave of the fundamental is sounded on the tenor trombone, the following notes may be obtained by altering the position of the slide:

The complete chromatic compass may be considered as:

The fundamentals, known as pedal notes, are difficult to produce. In fact only those of the first three positions are possible.

Music for the trombone is generally written with the bass clef, but the tenor clef may be used for the higher notes of the tenor trombone. In either case the sounds are as written.

Trombone, a reed organ stop of 16-foot pitch, generally on the Pedal Organ.

Trope, a musical interpolation in the liturgical plainsong. Troping began in the 8th and 9th centuries and was practised until the 16th century. The elaborate tropes added to the original simple liturgical melodies called for words; consequently words were added to existing tropes and new tropes were composed with words of their own. Some tropes have survived as independent compositions. The sequence in the Mass, for instance, began as a trope to the Gradual and Alleluia, and the poem *O filii et filiae* as a trope to the Sanctus.

Troppo (It.), too much.

Troubadour, the name of the poet-musicians of noble birth who flourished in Southern France from the end of the 11th to the end of the 13th century. A great number of their lyrics have survived, though the melodies in many cases have been lost.

Troutbeck, The Reverend John (b. Blencowe 1832, d. Westminster 1899), translated many oratorio and opera librettos into English.

Trouvère, the counterpart in Northern France of the Troubadour of Southern France. The Trouvères flourished from the middle of the 11th to the end of the 13th century. A great number of their lyrics have survived, and in many cases the melodies with them.

Trumpet, as distinct from horn and tuba, may be taken to include all those wind instruments generally made of brass, which have a bore mainly cylindrical and which are played with a cupped mouthpiece hemispherical in shape. Further, the trumpet may be distinguished from the horn by its brilliant tone. With these distinctions, the ancestor of the trumpet is the Roman lituus, rather than the Roman tuba and cornu from which the modern tuba and horn may be considered as being derived.

The characteristic brilliance of the trumpet can be obtained only from a tube of adequate length, and is at its best in a trumpet pitched in D with

as its fundamental. During the 16th and 17th centuries such trumpets were used in groups, various members of the groups differing slightly in bore and mouthpiece so as to produce different portions of the harmonic series more readily. According to Praetorius, trumpets with the higher range should produce harmonics up to the 21st, which is considerably higher than the upper limit of the modern instrument. Further, the high and florid trumpet parts written by Bach and Handel in the 18th century cannot be played on the modern trumpet.

The orchestral trumpet was originally without valves, and like the horn was used in several keys. Attempts to bridge the gaps in the harmonic series by stopping (as with the horn) or by holes in the tube were unsuccessful, and the use of the slide (as with the trombone) did not prove generally acceptable and passed out of use. As with the horn, the trumpet with valves superseded that without valves during the 19th century. In the first instance the valve trumpet was made in F, but recently a smaller instrument in C (with a crook in B♭, and sometimes also A) has tended to take its place. The smaller instrument is more flexible than the larger, but not so noble in tone.

The notes obtained from the trumpet in F without the use of the valves are:

that is, the notes of the harmonic series. Apart from the fundamental, which is almost impossible, and the octave, which is very difficult to obtain, and the two notes marked *, these are the harmonics normally used.

The notes obtained from the trumpet in C without the use of the valves are:

Apart from the fundamental and the note marked *, these are the harmonics normally used. The notes obtained from the trumpet in B♭ or A are simply one tone, or a tone and a half, below those obtained from that in C. The effective compass of all three instruments is about the same, a little over two octaves with the C two octaves above middle C as the upper limit. It will be noticed that with the trumpets in C and B♭, lower notes of the harmonic series, less close together, are used; the instrument is therefore more dependent upon the use of the valves.

The trumpet is treated as a transposing instrument and music for it is written on the treble clef. The trumpet in F sounds a fourth higher than written. The trumpet in B♭ sounds a tone lower, and the trumpet in A one and a half tones lower than written.

Trumpet, a reed organ stop of 8-foot pitch on the manuals.

Tuba, a deep-toned brass wind instrument with valves, played with a cupped mouthpiece, related to the trumpet and horn. It is otherwise known as the euphonium (tenor tuba) or bombardon (bass tuba and contrabass tuba). The bore of the tuba is mainly conical like that of the horn, while its mouthpiece is hemispherical like that of the trumpet. The bass tuba (usually built in F), when used in the orchestra, is grouped with one bass and two tenor trombones. Its fundamental is

8va

and a complete chromatic compass upwards of three octaves is possible by the use of four valves. Several notes below the natural fundamental are also possible by use of the valves. Music for the tuba, as used in the orchestra, is now generally written as sounded.

Four of the five tubas specified by Wagner in *The Ring* were modified forms of horn. Only the largest of the five was a genuine tuba, being a contrabass tuba built in C.

Tuba, a reed organ stop of 8-foot pitch on the manuals. The tuba is generally on a high pressure and the loudest stop on the organ. It is usually on the solo organ.

Tubuphone, an instrument similar to the Glockenspiel, but having tubes of metal instead of steel bars.

Tucket, or *Tuck,* a trumpet sound often mentioned by Elizabethan dramatists.

Tudor Church Music, a scholarly edition of the church music of important English composers of the 16th century, prepared for the Carnegie Trust. The series of ten volumes includes music by Aston, Byrd, Gibbons, Merbecke, Parsley, Tallis, Taverner, Tomkins and White.

Tudway, Thomas (d. 1726), was an English musician who became organist of King's College, Cambridge, in 1670 and Professor of Music in the University in 1705. He is remembered by the important collection of cathedral music which he made.

Tune, a melody of simple obvious design, particularly one which predominates over its accompaniment. Originally the word appears to have been the same as tone.

Tuning, the adjustment of an instrument to the recognised scale. The requirements of various groups of instruments with regard to tuning vary considerably. Keyboard instruments (organ, harmonium, pianoforte and harpsichord) are tuned periodically by professional tuners. Stringed instruments generally (the violin family, harp and guitar) are tuned by the player before, and even during the course of an extended performance. Wind instruments are generally not tuned in the same sense as are keyboard and stringed instruments. The pitch of a wind instrument may be regulated as occasion demands, but the tuning of the individual notes is inherent in the construction of the instrument.

The tuning of keyboard instruments is therefore the most prominent as an acquired art. The main feature of any system of obtaining the required tuning is 'laying the bearings', that is obtaining one complete octave tuned in the required fashion. The adjustment of the rest of the instrument follows by tuning the octaves. Though the practices of piano and organ tuners differ in detail, the principle on which they work is the same. A chain of fourths and fifths starting and ending on the pitch note (in the case of the organ, middle C on the Principal) is tuned. The fifths are tuned slightly narrower and the fourths slightly wider than true.

Tuning Fork, the well-known pitch-carrier invented in 1711 by John Shore, a trumpeter. Tuning forks have great permanency of pitch; they may be tuned by filing the ends of the prongs to sharpen and the base between them to flatten. The quality of sound from a tuning fork approaches a pure tone.

Tuning Slide (of an organ pipe), a metal flap or cylinder at the upper end of a flue pipe by which the length of the pipe may be easily altered and the pipe tuned.

Turina, Joaquin (b. Seville 1882, d. Madrid 1949), achieved distinction as a pianist and as a composer of the genuine Spanish school. Though his main contributions have been to chamber music, he is best known by his brilliant orchestral study *Procesión del Rocío*.

Turn, a melodic ornament of four notes. The turn takes two forms, being either on a note or between two notes.

The upper grace note is invariably the next higher degree of the diatonic scale; the lower note, however, is generally more pleasing if only a semitone below the principal note regardless of scale.

Tutti (It.), all. Indicates those portions of a composition which are to be played by all the forces, particularly where the forces are divided into two groups, 'concertante' and 'ripieno', as is often the case in pre-19th-century orchestral music.

Twelfth, an organ stop of diapason quality sounding a twelfth above the unison.

Twelve Note Music (from the German Zwölftonmusik), a name given to music in certain idioms based on the twelve notes of the chromatic scale rather than on the seven notes of the diatonic scale. Twelve note technique evolved after the early attempts to reject the major and minor key system. The absence of key gave rise to the term atonal, which (if it can have any meaning in music) is misused in this connexion, a misuse which Schönberg has strongly opposed.

The most convincing demonstrations of the logical and artistic value of twelve note technique have been given by Schönberg and his pupils, Berg and Webern. In their technique, the twelve chromatic notes are arranged in some specific order which is then used as the basis or point of reference for a particular composition. The group may be inverted, reversed and its inversion reversed, so making the four mutually related forms.

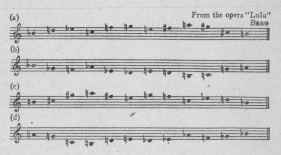

These may be represented diagrammatically:

(c)   (a)

(d)   (b)

These four forms and the twelve possible transpositions of each of them (forty-eight forms in all) are considered as equally valid forms of the twelve note group. Every phrase in a composition must be related (both melodically and harmonically) to the group on which the composition is based.

The twelve note group may have links with traditional scale forms, and may have special features of its own.

(p) and (r), minor triads   (q) and (s), major triads   (t), the whole tone scale

Example (e), for instance, contains two major and two minor triads and the whole tone scale, while example (f) contains all the intervals possible within an octave.

There are several impressive aspects of twelve note technique. Closer study shows that it is not so arbitrary as it at first appears. It has a close connection with mathematical principles (as have the older techniques). It becomes part of the music, and it is not necessary as an explanation before the music can be appreciated. Its use has not been limited to its first exponents. And, most impressive of all, it has been used as the basis of some of the most effective and successful music of recent years.

Tye, Christopher (b. *c.* 1500, d. 1573), was an English musician closely connected with Ely and Cambridge. He took the degree of Mus.B. at Cambridge in 1536 and Mus.D. in 1545; he was a lay clerk at King's College and in 1542, or the year before, was appointed Magister Choristorum at Ely. He was ordained in 1560, resigned from Ely the next year, and subsequently held a number of livings in the Ely area. Tye is one of the more important early composers of sacred music, writing both Latin masses and motets, and English services and anthems. His settings of *The Acts of the Apostles* are typical early examples of the simple domestic sacred music which was becoming popular during the middle of the 16th century. Much of his string music has not yet received the attention it probably deserves.

Tyrolienne, a kind of Ländler, a name adopted first for ballet music and later for trivial compositions purporting to represent the simple dances of Austria and Bavaria.

U

Uilleann Pipes, the proper name of the Irish domestic bagpipes blown by bellows. By a curious corruption the name became Union pipes and was thought to be associated with the union between England and Ireland of 1800.

Ukelele, a small variety of guitar.

Una Corda (It.), one string. Indicates in pianoforte music that the left pedal on the modern pianoforte is to be used. The una corda pedal shifts the keyboard and action slightly to the right so that one of the two or three strings to each note is not struck by the hammer. The unstruck string vibrates as a sympathetic string, thus slightly changing the quality of the sound produced. The reduction of volume resulting from the use of the una corda pedal should be considered as a subsidiary and not the main effect.

Unequal Voices, a term used in the same sense as 'mixed voices'.

Unessential Note, a note not forming part of the basic harmony, being in the nature of a melodic embellishment, such as a passing note, auxiliary note, changing note or appoggiatura.

Unison, identity in the pitch of two notes.

Up Beat, the upward movement of a conductor's arm or stick. The up beat invariably corresponds to the last beat in the bar; hence the term is often used as meaning the last beat in the bar, without any reference to a conductor.

Up Bow, the movement of the bow across the strings of a member of the violin family from the player's right to his left. In the case of the violin and viola this is generally more or less upwards. An up bow is indicated by the ∨ placed above a note.

Upper Partial, one of the partial tones of a note other than the first. Upper partial is therefore synonymous with overtone.

Use, the peculiarities of rites, ceremonies and music associated with a particular ecclesiastical foundation. Before the Reformation the uses of Salisbury, York and Hereford were popular in the South, North and West of England respectively. The Sarum use, for instance, was used in St Paul's Cathedral at the time of Henry VIII.

A certain degree of uniformity now obtains throughout the Roman Catholic Church and throughout the Church of England so far as the rites and ceremonies are concerned, but in both cases a considerable variation in the music remains. In the Roman Catholic Church, plainsong, being official music, provides a small common factor in the musical use throughout that church, and a large amount of unsuitable music has been discarded from time to time as a result of Vatican control. No music is prescribed as official within the Church of England; any similarity between the musical use of one church and that of another is due to the temporary popularity of certain hymn books and psalters.

Ut, the first note or tonic of the scale in solmization.

V

Vagans, an old English name for a fifth part in a motet, so called because it might be of any compass, though commonly a second tenor.

Valentini, Pietro Francesco (d. Rome 1654), was an outstanding master of counterpoint. Amongst his canons (his greatest achievement) is one of the most remarkable subjects that have been invented, displaying an extremely large variety of possibilities of treatment.

Valve, the mechanism by which the length of the tube of a wind instrument is varied. The term is commonly used only in connection with brass instruments, but strictly speaking it should denote also the valves of woodwind instruments. The application of valves to the natural instruments of the brass variety may be considered as an invention of the early 19th century.

The valves now used are either piston or rotary. In each case the purpose of the valve is to divert the wind through an additional portion of tubing, thereby increasing the length of the whole tube and so lowering the pitch of the series of notes produced by varying the lip pressure. Three valves are commonly used, the first lowering the pitch a tone, the second a semitone and the third a tone and a half, in that order; by combining them two at a time or all together the pitch may be lowered by as much as three tones. A fourth valve, sometimes used, lowers the pitch a perfect fourth. (See illustration p. 300.)

Vamp, extemporise an accompaniment to a song or instrumental solo. The term dates from the early 18th century, at least, though commonly considered as modern slang. Though usually associated

THE VALVE

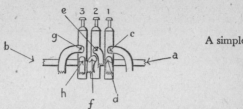

A simple system.

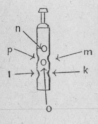

(a piston)

If no pistons are depressed, the wind entering at *a* passes straight through each valve to *b*.

If 1 is depressed, the wind passes through the extra tubing *c-d*. Similarly for 2 and 3; 2 adds *e-f* and 3 adds *g-h*.

l connects with *k*, *m* with *n* and *o* with *p*.

with performances of little artistic merit, vamping with skill demands much musical knowledge and understanding, and gives opportunity for a display of musicianship comparable with playing from a figured bass.

Vamp Horn, a form of megaphone used during the 18th and early 19th centuries in certain churches to assist in leading the singing or in announcing.

Variations, any extended composition in which the successive sections of the composition are each derived more or less directly from the theme. The writing of variations was one of the earliest means adopted for producing an extended composition, and has continued to attract the attention of composers until the present time.

In the stricter examples, either the melody, the bass or the harmony, as well as the form of the theme, is reproduced in each variation. In freer examples, each variation may present the theme in a different light, making little or no attempt to follow closely either the melodic or harmonic features of it.

Variations were a prominent feature of the compositions for the virginal by English composers such as Byrd and Bull. With them, either the harmony or the melody of the theme was retained prominently as the feature connecting the variations with the theme. During the 17th century variations on a ground bass became a particularly favourite form of composition. The chaconne and passacaglia both have variations on a ground as one of their distinctive features. Though the stricter forms of variations could give rise to some of the finest extended compositions of Bach, even Handel produced some trivial examples in which the melody and harmony are merely figured in the most obvious and mechanical manner. Haydn established a freer treatment of the variations, and paved the way for the consummation of the freest and most imaginative of Beethoven's essays. Mozart, hardly at his best in variation writing, made melodic ornamentation the basis of most of his sets of variations. Brahms excelled in the use of variation forms, and notable examples by later composers have added to the large-scale compositions in which the various principles of variations, strict and free, have been used.

Vaughan Williams, Ralph (b. Down Ampney 1872), still living.

Vautor, Thomas (f. 1616 – 1619), was an English musician. His published madrigals are included in *The English Madrigal School.*

Veiled Voice, an unclear quality of voice, not huskiness, said to be due to a temporary or permanent condition of the vocal chords. This veiled quality has been a distinctive feature of many outstanding voices.

Venetian Swell, the variety of shutters modelled on the laths of a Venetian blind and designed by Shudi in 1769 to replace the clumsy shutter previously used for the swell on the harpsichord. The pattern was soon adopted for the organ, and, with a number of refinements, has remained the pattern of organ swells until the present day.

Verdi, Giuseppe (b. Le Roncole 1813, d. Busseto 1901), was the son of an innkeeper. By the time he was ten, he showed such aptitude for music that his father, to his credit, sent him to the nearby town of Busseto, where he was employed by Barezzi, a grocer, a friend of Verdi's father, and a musical enthusiast. He also studied with Provesi, the local cathedral organist, and began to compose. In 1832 he was enabled to reach Milan, but failed to gain admission to the Conservatorium. After two years he returned to Busseto for a while, marrying Barezzi's daughter. He returned to Milan in 1839 with his wife and two children; in the same year his first opera, *Oberto*, was performed in the Scala theatre. This success was followed by the tragedy of the death of his wife and two children within a few months.

Verdi's next success was in 1824 with *Nebucco*. From that time his reputation as a composer of opera was established. His operas were produced regularly, and his fame spread. He accepted an invitation to London in 1847, and afterwards stayed in Paris. Three of his most popular operas, *Rigoletto*, *Il Trovatore* and *La Traviata*, were written in 1851. In 1859 he formally married Giuseppina Strepponi, a retired singer, who had been living with him for a number of years. For a year or so farming and politics were his main interests. In 1860 he was persuaded to stand for the first Italian parliament, was elected, and was a deputy for five years.

In 1869 Verdi was commissioned to write an opera to celebrate the opening of the Suez Canal, and for this he wrote *Aïda*, which was produced in Cairo two years later.

On the death of Rossini, Verdi proposed a Requiem in his honour, to be written by twelve leading composers, but the project collapsed. In 1873, on the death of the poet Manzoni, Verdi himself composed a Requiem, incorporating in it the *Libera me* which he had written for the Rossini Requiem. Two more operatic masterpieces were composed, *Otello* in 1886 and *Falstaff* in 1893, in each case to a first-class libretto written by Boito.

Almost all Verdi's youthful compositions are lost. His thirty operas form the great part of his writings. His small-scale compositions are negligible. In his last years he completed the *Quattro Pezzi Sacri*, which includes a *Stabat Mater* and a *Te Deum*.

He was buried in the oratory of the Home for Aged Musicians in Milan, which he had been responsible for founding in 1896, and was mourned as a national hero.

Vibrato (It.), the rapid slight variation in pitch of notes which passes unnoticed as an essential part of expression, particularly of string instruments, whose tone sounds dead without it.

Vicar Choral, another name for a 'lay clerk'.

Victoria, Thomás Luis de (b. Avila *c.* 1535, d. Madrid 1611), was the outstanding Spanish representative of the polyphonic school. He was probably ordained priest before 1565; at the end of that year the King granted him an allowance to enable him to study music in Rome, and the next year he was appointed as chaplain singer at the German College in Rome. He was appointed chaplain to the widowed Empress Maria in 1578, but does not appear to have returned to Spain till 1583, when he settled in Madrid.

Compared with that of Palestrina and Lassus, the quantity of Victoria's compositions is small, but their quality is consistently of the highest. He restricted himself entirely to the composition of sacred music. In his lifetime Victoria was able to have his works published in magnificent editions. His complete works were published under the editorship of Pedrell in 1896. Victoria is perhaps best known by the short motet, *Jesu Dulcis Memoria,* attributed to him, though its origin is not known. Of his masses, that based on his own motet *O quam gloriosum* is perhaps the best known. Probably the greatest of all his works is the setting of the Requiem Mass in tribute to the memory of the Empress Maria.

Vierne, Louis Victor Jules (b. Poitiers 1870, d. Paris 1937), achieved distinction as an organist and composer; he became organist of Notre Dame when he was twenty. He suffered from blindness throughout his life.

Vihuela, the Spanish equivalent to the lute, though of guitar shape. Three kinds of Vihuela were in use from the 13th to the 16th century, played with the plectrum, the bow and the hand respectively. The Vihuela was obsolete by the end of the 16th century.

Villanella (It.), a country girl. This name is properly reserved for certain unaccompanied vocal compositions similar to a madrigal.

Viol, the generic English name for bowed stringed instruments in the period following that of the medieval fiddle. The viol probably preceded the violin in design, as it certainly did in its repertory. The design of the early viol dates from the 15th century, and the mature viol remained in use alongside the violin until the 18th century. The viol had deeper ribs than the violin, and a flat back sloping off at the top; the inside was strengthened with crossbars and a broad centre piece on which the sound part rested. The sound holes were C-shaped, the shoulders curved upwards, the neck was broad and thin, and the finger board had movable frets. The number of strings varied, but was usually six. The viol was made in three main sizes, bass, tenor and treble. The bass viol was tuned:

like the lute. The tenor viol was tuned a fourth, and the treble viol an octave higher than the bass viol.

A double-bass viol, tuned an octave lower than the bass viol, was used in Germany and Italy. The modern double bass retains some of the characteristics of this instrument, in particular its shape and method of tuning. The viola bastarda and viola d'amore (respectively bass and tenor viols with sympathetic strings) are the more important representatives of the numerous lesser varieties of viol.

Viola, the oldest member of the violin family, similar to the violin, but larger, though smaller than the violoncello. The four strings are tuned:

that is, a fifth below those of the violin, so that the range of the viola is the same as that of the violin, but a fifth lower, though the higher notes are used less than the corresponding notes of the violin. Music for the viola is generally written with the alto clef, but the treble clef is used for the higher notes.

Violin, at first the name of a type of instrument rather than of a specific member of its family. The violin and the viol appeared in their distinct forms about the middle of the 16th century, the latter achieving popularity more quickly. The violin, brought to perfection by Stradivari by the end of the 17th century, superseded the viol in the 18th century: its position in music was assured when the quartet for strings became the prime medium for chamber music, and strings became the foundation of the orchestra.

The name violin was first applied to the instrument now known as the viola, and later became reserved for the smaller instrument. The violoncello appeared with the other members of the family and fills the normal role of bass. The double-bass, the largest member of the family, has not acquired the same final design as the others, and still appears with a number of variations. The design of the violin (and also that of the viola and violoncello) has not changed since the perfect model of Stradivari.

VIOLIN

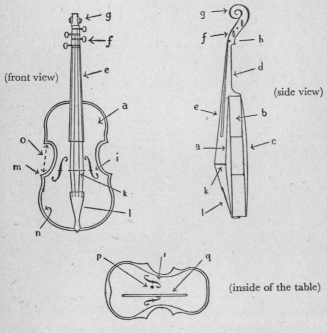

(front view)

(side view)

(inside of the table)

a table or belly	i sound hole
b ribs	k bridge
c back	l tail piece
d neck	m corners
e finger-board	n purfling
f peg	o bouts
g scroll	p sound post
h nut	q bass bar

The four strings of the violin are tuned:

The violin is normally played with a bow. Its compass is about three octaves, depending on the skill of the player; by the use of harmonics even higher notes may be obtained. When played pizzicato the effective compass is limited.

Violoncello, the third largest member in size of the strings of the orchestra. The four strings are tuned:

that is, an octave below those of the viola. The normal compass of the violoncello, about two and a half octaves, may more readily be extended upwards than that of the violin or viola, and pizzicato playing is more effective than on these other two. Music for the violoncello is generally written with the bass clef, but the tenor clef, or even the treble clef, may be used for the higher notes.

Viotti, Jean Baptiste (b. Fontanetto 1753, d. London 1824), was the finest exponent of violin-playing of his day. He was trained by Pugnani in the tradition of the Italian school founded by Corelli, and has been considered pre-eminently responsible for founding the modern school of violin-playing, which continues this dignified style.

Virdung, Sebastian (f. 1510), was the author of the oldest known treatise describing the precursors of modern musical instruments.

Virginal, a keyboard instrument, oblong in shape, in which the strings were set in vibration by jacks. The name was commonly used in England during the 16th and 17th centuries to include all quilled keyboard instruments, though towards the end of the 17th century it was often used in a sense excluding the harpsichord. Two explanations of the origin of the name have been offered — one that the virginal is so called because virgins commonly played on them, and the other that it was used as a successor to the psaltery and other non-keyboard stringed instruments to accompany the hymn *Angelus ad Virginem*.

Vitali, Giovanni Battista (b. Cremona *c.* 1644, d. Modena 1692), was a composer of a remarkable amount of dance music and a large number of sonatas. The sonatas are of interest in the early history of this type of instrumental composition.

Vitry, Philippe de (b. Champagne 1291, d. Paris 1361), was the author of the oldest treatise describing the new style in music which developed during the early 14th century, and which became known as 'ars nova'.

Vivace (It.), lively. Used as an indication of speed between 'allegro' and 'presto'.

Vivaldi, Antonio (b. probably Venice *c*. 1675, d. Vienna 1741), was a violinist and composer. His fame rests on his violin concertos, which were arranged by Bach for the clavier and organ. The merit of these concertos is in their form, the one aspect of composition over which Vivaldi was a master.

Vivo (It.), alive. Similar in sense to 'vivace'.

Voce (It.), voice.

Vogler, Georg Joseph, the Abbé (b. Würzburg 1749, d. Darmstadt 1814), was an organist, teacher, composer, and one of the most interesting personalities in the history of music. He attacked forcefully the musical teaching, the harmony and the organ construction of his day. He appears to have been most stimulating as a teacher, and to have gained in an astonishing manner the approbation and affection of his pupils.

Voice. The sounds of the human voice are produced in very much the same way as sounds are produced by man from a reed instrument. The voice has the same three essential components as reed instruments, namely, a wind supply, a reed, and a resonator. The wind supply comes from the lungs. The reed is formed by two elastic membranes in the larynx which are close together when vocal sounds are actually being produced. The resonator is the hollow part of the mouth, nose and neck.

Men's voices (with the exception of falsetto and castrato) are approximately an octave lower in pitch than women's voices. Broadly speaking, those voices with a higher range are the lighter, and those with a lower range the richer in quality. A developed human voice has a range of about two octaves. Men with a high, medium or low range are described as tenor, baritone or bass respectively, and women similarly soprano, mezzo-soprano or contralto.

Bass   Baritone   Tenor   Contralto   Mezzo-   Soprano
                                              Soprano

The division of voices into these six groups is somewhat arbitrary. The predominance of four-part vocal music for treble, alto, tenor and bass has resulted in singers with medium voices having to choose whether to join the higher or lower group, in neither of which are they quite comfortable; but training may well affect the natural lie of the voice by developing one extreme at the expense of the other, or by developing range at the expense of power or the reverse.

Boys' voices are similar in range to soprano. Men's falsetto voices fall between the women's voices and the natural voices of men, but are generally of more restricted range than natural voices.

Voix Céleste (Fr.), heavenly voice. This name is given to a soft gamba organ stop of 8-foot pitch on the manuals; the complete stop consists of two ranks, one of which is very slightly sharpened so giving a wavy effect. The voix céleste is usually on the Swell Organ. Commonly the two ranks are treated as separate stops, the voix céleste stop controlling the mistuned rank, the other rank being simply a gamba. The mistuned rank invariably extends downwards only an octave below middle C.

Volta (It.), time. *Prima volta*, first time. *Seconda volta*, second time.

Volte, an ancient French dance, described by Thoinot Arbeau, in triple time, containing many turns, and dubiously claimed by some French authorities as the ancestor of the waltz.

Volti (It.), turn. Used as a warning in the sense of turn over the page.

Volume, one of the attributes of a note. It depends on the amplitude of the vibrations causing the sound. The volume of a sound increases with the amplitude of the vibrations causing it.

Voluntary, any composition for the organ when played at a church service. The name has lost any precise meaning it may have had. It is used as a title for compositions of any form in a style suitable for church use.

Vox Humana (Lat.), human voice. This name is given to a soft reed organ stop of 8-foot pitch on the manuals, usually on the Choir Organ.

W

Wagner, Wilhelm Richard (b. Leipzig 1813, d. Venice 1883), was the son of the clerk to the city police court. Shortly after Wagner's birth his father died; a year later his mother married Ludwig Geyer, an actor and playwright, and the family moved to Dresden. Wagner received an education in classics. Any desires which he had towards music were incidental to his interest in poetry, but he became acquainted with Weber and liked his music. In 1827 the family returned to Leipzig, where the Gewandhaus concerts gave him the chance of hearing music (that of Beethoven in particular), and his interest in music increased. To the neglect of philosophy and aesthetics, for which he had been entered at the University, Wagner studied music more seriously; some of his youthful compositions, now forgotten, gained performance.

Wagner began his professional career as a musician in 1833, as chorus master at the Wursburg theatre. Nothing but small theatrical appointments followed, and he was constantly in financial difficulties. He left Germany in 1839 to try his fortunes in Paris; three more years brought little success. He gained performances of some of his compositions and became acquainted with the German folk tales which became the basis of the later operas, but the prospects of any great progress seemed hopeless. The score of *Rienzi* had been finished, and on its acceptance at Dresden he returned there in 1842. Wagner's first successes were with *Rienzi* and *The Flying Dutchman*. He was appointed Hofkapellmeister at Dresden in 1843, where seven years' service gave him considerable experience of church music at the Hofkirche. Meanwhile *Tannhäuser* was completed and *The Mastersingers* and *Lohengrin* were sketched, and he was evolving his theories of music-drama as an expression of philosophy through a combination of all the arts. He became involved in political disturbances, and in 1849 found it best to leave Germany, having achieved a measure of success in music.

During twelve years of exile Wagner lived first at Zürich; he was invited to and visited London in 1855 to conduct the London Philharmonic Orchestra. In 1859 he again went to Paris, leaving two years later with his finances hopelessly tangled. He returned to Germany in 1861. The next three years were particularly distressing financially, though he had become well established as a composer. He was struggling with his largest work, *The Ring*, which embodied his theories of music-drama; he published the poem alone as a literary work.

In 1869 King Ludwig II of Bavaria invited Wagner to work in Munich, granting him a stipend from the Privy Purse, and later commissioning him to complete the music for *The Ring*. Wagner moved to Triebschen in 1865, and in 1872 to Bayreuth which he chose as the site for a special theatre for *The Ring*. Ludwig's plans for such a theatre in Munich had not been realized.

The rest of Wagner's career is a record of the varying successes of his operas at the main musical centres. Though he made a number of concert tours, visited London again in 1877, and resided at Venice for a short while before his death, his interests centred in the foundation of the theatre at Bayreuth and the details of his plans for the stage and orchestra (the large orchestra demanded by his score was to be invisible, below the level of the stage).

Wagner's musical greatness rests on his music-dramas, *Rienzi*, *The Flying Dutchman*, *Tannhäuser*, *Lohengrin*, *Tristan and Isolde*, *The Mastersingers* and *Parsifal*, completed in that order, and *The Ring*, a cycle of four operas, *Rhinegold*, *The Valkyrie*, *Siegfried* and *The Twilight of the Gods*, written between the latter three of the other operas. The only other work commonly known is the *Siegfried Idyll*. His large output of purely literary work was concerned largely with opera and his plans for its reformation.

Waits, originally the night guards at city gates. They were provided with a reed instrument, known as a wait. By the 15th and 16th centuries, the waits were organized into bands supported by town councils, and often achieved a high degree of musical skill. Pieces of music supposed to be particularly associated with the waits of a certain town were also called waits. The waits, as the name of the official town musicians, survived into the 18th century.

Wakefield, Augusta Mary (b. Sedgwick 1853, d. Grange-over-Sands 1910), established the music festivals in Westmoreland which led to the present widespread popularity of competitive music festivals.

Waldteufel, Emil (b. Strasburg 1837, d. Paris 1915), achieved much success as a composer of waltzes.

Wallace, William Vincent (b. Waterford 1812, d. Château de Bagen 1865), was a successful composer of opera and pianoforte music. He is remembered by his opera *Maritana*.

Walther, Johann (b. Cola 1496, d. Torgau 1570), was the friend and musical collaborator of Luther.

Waltz, a dance achieving remarkable popularity in the 19th century, and giving rise to a larger repertory of music, both for dancing and for purely instrumental performance, than any other dance form. The origin of the dance is doubtful, though a German origin would appear probable from the derivation of the name from the German 'waltzen', to turn. French claims make the waltz a descendant of the volte. The modern waltz appeared about 1780 (having the ländler as its immediate ancestor or close relation) as a slow dance in triple time. It became popular first in Bohemia, Bavaria and Austria, and within a few years had reached England. The primitive form of the waltz, two sections each of 8 bars, may be seen in the compositions of Mozart and Beethoven. The combination of a number of waltzes with trios, introductions and codas was effectively made by Schubert, who may be credited with anticipating, or indicating the manner in which the waltz was to be treated later. Weber may be credited with leading the adoption of the waltz as a form for purely instrumental and vocal compositions not intended as an accompaniment for dancing.

In Vienna the waltz assumed a quicker speed and the form in which it is best known. An introduction, usually at a slow speed, leads to the main theme of the whole composition, which is followed by a number of separate waltzes ending with a recapitulation of the last sections as a coda. France and, even more so, England have failed to produce waltzes of the quality of those from Vienna, particularly those of the Strauss family with whom the waltz is so commonly and justifiably associated.

Ward, John (f. 1613 – 1629), was an English musician. His published madrigals are included in *The English Madrigal School*. Sacred music, music for viols and for the virginal by him is extant. He contributed to *The Teares or Lamentacions* compiled by Leighton.

Warlock, Peter, is the name under which Philip Heseltine composed, and by which he is commonly known.

Webbe, Samuel (b. 1740, d. London 1816), was one of the foremost writers of glees, and an enthusiastic writer of canons. He won many prizes from the Catch Club and was the first Librarian of the Glee Club. He published a collection of motets and another of masses in 1792. His son, *Samuel* (b. London *c.* 1770, d. Liverpool 1843), achieved distinction in the same sphere as his father.

Weber, Carl Maria Friedrich Ernst von (b. Eutin 1786, d. London 1826), was the most distinguished member of an Austrian musical family. The family left Eutin in 1787 and Weber's early years were spent travelling with the stage troupe, consisting mainly of members of the family, which his father directed. To begin with, Weber's musical ability failed to show itself, but later it developed rapidly. He studied under Michael Haydn, among others, to such purpose that in 1804 he was appointed Kapellmeister of the theatre of Breslau, a post he held for two years. The next seven years were spent in teaching, in concert tours and in composing. In 1813 he was appointed Kapellmeister to the theatre of Prague, a post he held for three years before being appointed Kapellmeister of the German Opera at Dresden, where he achieved considerable success. In 1824 his failing health interrupted his work. Two years later he travelled to London a very sick man, to direct a production of *Oberon*, and died some few weeks later.

Weber has been considered both the father of German opera and the most notable figure of the romantic movement in Germany. Three of his operas, *Der Freischütz, Euryanthe* and *Oberon*, are important, though not well known in England. His other operas and dramatic works, a large number of songs and some piano music are not commonly known. He wrote a negligible amount of chamber music. As a composer he is remembered mainly by his overtures and several isolated pieces.

Webern, Anton von (b. Vienna 1883, d. Mittersill 1945), was one of Schönberg's most important pupils. His compositions are mostly small in scale, delicate in texture, and highly concentrated. With Schönberg and Berg, Webern is one of the chief exponents of 'twelve note music'.

Weelkes, Thomas (d. London 1623), was an English musician. He was probably born between 1570 and 1580. He was sometime organist of the College at Winchester and later of Chichester Cathedral; he took the degree of B.Mus. at Oxford and styled himself gentleman of His Majesty's Chapel. He was a madrigal composer of high rank, and his published volumes of madrigals are included in *The English Madrigal School*. He wrote a number of services and anthems (unfortunately the former survive only in fragments), and contributed to *The Teares or Lamentacions* compiled by Leighton. Some instrumental music by him is also extant.

Wert, Giaches de (b. Antwerp *c.* 1536, d. Mantua 1596), was an important composer of madrigals. He is referred to by Morley as Jaques de Vert. His compositions enjoyed a wide popularity until the middle of the 17th century.

Wesley, Samuel (b. Bristol 1766, d. London 1837), and his son, *Samuel Sebastian* (b. 1810, d. Gloucester 1876), were both among the most eminent organists of their day, and Samuel Sebastian was a notable composer of English church music. To Samuel falls a great deal of the credit for spreading and encouraging a knowledge and appreciation of Bach. To Samuel Sebastian falls the credit for contributing works of a remarkably high standard to the repertory of church music at a time when the general level of English church music was at a particularly low ebb.

Whitbroke, William (f. early 16th century), was an English clergyman and a composer mainly of church music.

White, Robert (b. c. 1530, d. London 1574), was an English musician. He appears to have succeeded Tye at Ely. His importance as a composer has perhaps not yet been fully recognised. He is represented in *Tudor Church Music,* and some instrumental music by him is extant.

Whole Tone Scale, either of the two scales of six tones to the octave which may be taken from the chromatic scale.

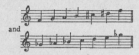

The notation is arbitrary. The two scales have no note in common, and in either scale the relation between every note and its neighbours is identical. The most characteristic feature of the scale is vagueness.

Whythorn, Thomas (b. 1528, d. after 1590), was an English musician. His publication of *Songes for three, fouer and five voices* of 1571 is of historical interest.

Widor, Charles Marie Jean Albert (b. Lyons 1845, d. 1937), was organist of St Sulpice, Paris, and taught at the Paris Conservatoire. Best known of his compositions are the notable contributions he made to the repertory of the organ.

Wilbye, John (b. 1574, d. Colchester 1638), was the son of a tanner of Diss and was probably born there. He became resident musician at Hengrave Hall in 1595 under Sir Thomas Kytson, and remained there till the death of Sir Thomas's widow in 1628. He spent his last ten years in retirement at the home of Lady Rivers, younger daughter of Sir Thomas, in Colchester.

Wilbye is generally considered as the finest of the English madrigal composers. His two large sets of madrigals are included in *The English Madrigal School.* He contributed to *The Triumphes of Oriana* and *The Teares or Lamentacions* compiled by Leighton.

Willaert, Adrian (b. Flanders c. 1480, d. Venice 1562), was a composer important for his church music and madrigals, and is considered the founder of the Venetian school.

Wilson, John (b. 1595, d. Westminster 1674), was one of the most prominent musicians of his time. He was a composer mainly of secular vocal music.

Wind Band, a band of wind instruments only. Though rarely treated as a medium for serious musical composition, the band of wind instruments, generally with percussion, has played an important part in social culture. Because of their obvious suitability for the purpose, wind bands have been generally used by armies. The full military band makes use of a great variety of wind instruments, but smaller bands often have only one kind of instrument, as the bagpipe, the fife, or the bugle. Others use brass instruments only, these being easier to learn than woodwind instruments.

Windchest (of an organ), the box running the length of the soundboard, which receives the wind from the bellows and supplies the wind to the pipes above. In the wind chest are the pallets which allow the wind to pass to individual pipes according to the keys and stops in use.

Wind Trunk (of an organ), the large pipe which carries the wind from the bellows to the wind chest.

Wind Way, the narrow slit between the lower lip and block of a flue organ pipe.

Wise, Michael (b. Wiltshire *c.* 1648, d. Salisbury 1687), became organist of Salisbury Cathedral in 1668. He held various appointments at the Royal Chapels, and enjoyed various privileges under James II. Much of his church music survives, mostly in manuscript.

Wolf, Hugo (b. Windischgraz 1860, d. Vienna 1903), was the son of a leather dealer who had a taste for music. His father, intending him for the family business, reluctantly entered him at the Vienna Conservatorium in 1875, Hugo having shown little interest in his school work, and much interest in music and literature. Wolf, little more successful at pleasing his teachers at the Conservatorium than those at school, was expelled after two years. For a short period he was second Kapellmeister at Salzburg. He was music critic of the Vienna Salonblatt for four years from 1886. With these appointments, teaching, and some little success with his compositions, Wolf struggled to make his living. He wrote spasmodically, periods of feverish work being followed by times in which he wrote nothing. In 1897 his brain gave way; he died paralysed and a raving lunatic.

Wolf's importance is entirely as a song-writer. Apart from an *Italian Serenade* for strings, his other compositions do not compare in perfection with his songs.

Wolf, the unpleasant sound of certain chords on a keyboard instrument tuned to any form of unequal temperament; also the unpleasant sound in certain bowed string instruments due to a defective vibration of the parts. The wolf on stringed instruments is found in some of the otherwise best instruments; its cause is not properly known and it is generally impossible to cure.

Wolf-Ferrari, Ermanno (b. Venice 1876, d. there 1948), was born of a German father, a distinguished painter, and an Italian mother. He acquired a considerable reputation in Germany and Italy as a composer of operas of the more lyrical type, the best known being *The Jewels of the Madonna.*

Wolstenholme, William (b. Blackburn 1865, d. London 1931), achieved distinction as an organist. He was born blind.

Wood, Charles (b. Armagh 1866, d. Cambridge 1926), achieved distinction as an organist, teacher and composer, and became Professor of Music in the University of Cambridge in 1924. He made many notable contributions to English church music.

Wood, Sir Henry Joseph (b. London 1869, d. London 1944), achieved outstanding success as the conductor of the Promenade Concerts at the Queen's Hall. The 'Proms' were managed for the first thirty-two seasons by Robert Newman, who may be considered their real founder. Wood conducted from the beginning of the series. He was knighted in 1911. The association between Sir Henry and Newman lasted until Newman's death in 1926, when it was feared that his death meant 'No more Proms'. From 1927 onwards the concerts were sponsored by the B.B.C., and they continued under Sir Henry's leadership at the Queen's Hall. In 1939 the special arrangements for broadcasting made the orchestra no longer available, but the concerts took place under the auspices of the Royal Philharmonic Society. The Queen's Hall was ruined in 1941. However, the concerts were continued at the Royal Albert Hall the following year. The B.B.C. resumed its control of them in 1942. With the assistance of Basil Cameron and later Sir Adrian Boult, Sir Henry remained in charge until his death.

Wood-wind, instruments of the flute, oboe and clarinet families when they form part of an orchestra or wind band.

Wrest-plank, the board in a pianoforte in which the wrest-pins are set. The wrest-plank is made of a number of layers of wood with the grain of each layer at right angles to those on either side, so ensuring a good grip on the wrest-pins.

Wrest-pins, the pins round which the wires of a pianoforte are twisted and by which the wires are tuned.

Wynken de Worde (f. late 15th and early 16th centuries), was the first English music printer.

THE WOODWIND

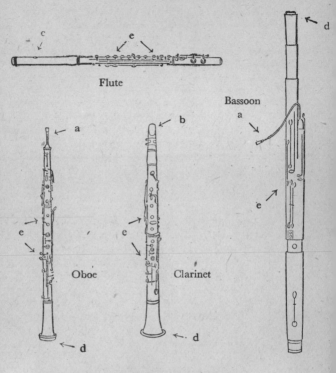

Flute

Bassoon

Oboe

Clarinet

a double reed   d bell

b single reed   e keys

c mouth hole   (not to scale)

X

Xylophone, an ancient and widespread instrument found particularly amongst the Poles, Russians and Tartars. It consists of flat pieces of wood or glass, tuned to a scale, which are struck with small hammers. Modern instruments incorporate a number of refinements, and the quality of the sounds produced differs a good deal from that of early instruments; their compass is usually

Y

Yodel, an English spelling of Jodel.

Yonge, *Nicholas* (b. Lewes, d. London 1619), compiled *Musica Transalpina*, the earliest collection of Italian madrigals with English words.

Youll, *Henry* (f. 1608), was an English musician. His published madrigals are included in the *English Madrigal School*. Nothing is known of the circumstances of his life.

Ysaye, *Eugene* (b. Liege 1858, d. Brussels 1931), became world-famous as a violinist, and achieved success as a conductor.

Z

Zacconi, *Ludovico* (b. Pesaro 1555, d. Venice 1627), was one of the most learned Italian theorists of his time. His *Prattica di musica* is one of the most important sources of information about 16th-century music available.

Zachau, *Friedrich Wilhelm* (b. Leipzig 1663, d. Halle 1712), is remembered as the teacher of Handel.

Zambra, an ancient dance of the Spanish Moors.

Zarlino, *Gioseffe* (b. Chioggia 1517, d. Venice 1590), was one of the most important musical theorists of the 16th century. Though Zarlino had a reputation as a composer, few of his compositions have survived. His fame rests on three treatises, *Institutioni Armoniche*, *Dimostrationi Armoniche* and *Sopplimenti Musicali*.

Zarzuela, a Spanish musical dramatic entertainment. The plot may be tragic, melodramatic or fantastic, but humour is an integral part of any zarzuela, which may often be a burlesque of a successful novel, opera or play. Zarzuelas generally last about an hour, two or three being given as an evening's performance.

Zither, a modern plucked string instrument. It is in many respects the national instrument of Bavaria, Styria and Tyrol. A great many varieties of zither exist; various tunings of the strings are adopted. The strings are in three groups; the melody strings are tuned:

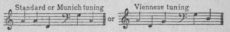

the harmony strings are tuned:

while the bass strings are tuned more or less in octave with the harmony strings, with the addition of some six strings descending lower by semitones. This peculiar arrangement allows most of the usual three-note accompanying chords to be played with the three middle fingers of the right hand. The melody strings are stopped by the left hand on frets arranged in semitones, and played by a plectrum attached to the thumb of the right hand. The modern zither should not be confused with the cither, to which, with many plucked string instruments, it is related.

APPENDIX

The following composers have died since June 1950:

Jaques-Dalcroze, Émile (b. Vienna 1862, d. Geneva 1950), came of Swiss parents. In 1892 he joined the staff of the Conservatory at Geneva. His songs and instrumental music have attracted some attention, particularly in Switzerland, but it is for his system of musical training known as Eurhythmics that he is best known.

Moeran, Ernest John (b. Osterley 1894, d. near Kenmare 1950), was of Irish descent. His childhood was spent in Norfolk where his father was a clergyman. He was educated at Uppingham and the Royal College of Music and later studied with John Ireland. From 1934 he lived in Kenmare.

The English countryside and the southern Irish coast were the inspiration of much of Moeran's music. Among his works are some lovely songs, several choral suites and instrumental chamber music, an exquisite violin concerto and a symphony.